The AMERICANIZATION
of the HOLOCAUST

The AMERICANIZATION of the HOLOCAUST

Edited by Hilene Flanzbaum

The Johns Hopkins University Press
Baltimore and London

Illustrations in chapter 6 are reprinted from *Maus: A Survivor's Tale* and *Maus II: A Survivor's Tale,* both by Art Spiegelman. Copyright 1973, 1980, 1981, 1982, 1983, 1985, 1986 and 1986, 1989, 1990, and 1991, respectively, by Art Spiegelman. Reprinted by permission of Pantheon Books, a division of Random House, Inc.

The Johns Hopkins University Press
2715 North Charles Street
Baltimore, Maryland 21218-4363
www.press.jhu.edu

Library of Congress Cataloging-in-Publication Data
will be found at the end of this book.
A catalog record for this book is available from the
British Library.

ISBN 0-8018-6021-0
ISBN 0-8018-6022-9 (pbk.)

CONTENTS

ACKNOWLEDGMENTS

This book grew out of a panel of the same name delivered at the 1996 Chicago Modern Language Association Convention. I owe a debt to the organizer and chair of that panel, Paula Geyh. I extend thanks to her and the other presenters, Jeanne Ewert, Andrew Weinstein, and Andrew Levy. For their lively and provocative follow-up discussion, I would also like to thank those who attended the session. I am grateful to my colleague, Marshall Gregory, for his diligent editing, and my student, Dana Sullivan Kilroy, for her research help. I also thank Walter Benn Michaels for his inspiration of this book. And to my husband, Geoffrey Sharpless, whose wisdom and skill allowed me to think with more depth and to write with more clarity, my most profound love and gratitude.

The AMERICANIZATION
of the HOLOCAUST

THE AMERICANIZATION
OF THE HOLOCAUST

In the past few years I have presented scholarship about the Americanization of the Holocaust and postwar American poetry in community centers, in college classrooms, and at literary conferences. While reaction to these presentations has of course differed, I have found a consistent objection to my assumption that Americans, including American Jews, said little about the Holocaust in the decade following World War II. This assumption, which I have gradually understood to hit a nerve, has never been the point of my work, only a supposition. Yet whether I am in a seminar room or a gymnasium, someone always finds my statement outrageous—if not blasphemous: "How can you say no one talked about the Holocaust in the 1950s?" Then the questioner usually supplies what he or she believes to be counterproof to my supposition: "We all saw Anne Frank. What about Anne Frank?"

As my alert questioners understand, *The Diary of Anne Frank* has long been the most important landmark in the Americanization of the Holocaust. This is true despite the current presumption by experts that it camouflages the event's full horror. First published in America in 1952 (in a heavily edited form), *The Diary of Anne Frank* has been the most widely read book about the Holocaust in America. In a survey conducted in 1996 at the University of Michigan, it was still named as the predominant source of Holocaust education: the text was required reading in high school for over half the students surveyed.[1] Even those who had not read the book knew Anne Frank's name and could connect it to the Holocaust, which is something they could not as consistently do with Adolf Eichmann, the Warsaw Ghetto, or Dachau. That the darker narratives of the Holocaust conveyed by these latter names have been obscured by Frank's "unfailingly optimistic" text is what troubles experts today.[2]

In the 1950s, Anne Frank's name-recognition and popularity were equally high. The *Diary* sold over five million copies in the first two decades it was in print; the stage play, first performed in 1955, won the Pulitzer Prize, the New York Critics Circle Award, and the Tony Award for best play; millions saw the movie when it premiered in 1959. Given this information, one can begin to see how my assertion that few people in the 1950s paid much attention to the Holocaust invites not only inquiry but objections.

The apparent inconsistency between my supposition and other people's objections tells us a great deal about the complicated event that current scholars call the Americanization of the Holocaust. On one level, the phrase simply groups the many ways that the Holocaust has been represented in American culture; on another, it is political and theoretical quicksand, providing all the pitfalls of postulating about history, nation, and ideology. In the first case, when we observe that the Anne Frank of the 1950s is not the Anne Frank of the 1990s, we just restate the commonplace notion that in forty years our understanding of history and culture has changed. Yet an inquiry into the specific historical and cultural changes that have attended the phenomenon of Anne Frank is neither simple nor commonplace. If the goals of the Anne Frank Foundation, when it first formed in the 1950s, could be "to use the name of Anne Frank as a symbol for hope and to further intergroup understanding in an atmosphere of freedom and hope," then it is clear that the Holocaust of the 1950s is not the Holocaust of the 1990s—or even the Holocaust of the 1980s, when the foundation publicized a much-altered statement of its goals as seeking "to educate on World War II, particularly the Holocaust, and to make known the current prejudice and discrimination affecting Jews today."[3] The difference between these two statements of the foundation's operating principles tells us as much about the changes in American culture—if not more—as it does about the Holocaust itself.

Certainly what Americans think and know and say about the Holocaust—and many other things—has shifted radically in the last forty years. In the case of what people think and know and say about the *Diary*, however, this is more than a theoretical observation; it is a material fact. The very text of the *Diary*, originally edited for material that Anne's father considered sexually suggestive or overly personal, has been only gradually returned to its original form. In 1986, 1989, and 1991, altered or restored versions appeared. In 1994, the "definitive" edition was finally published ("definitive," that is, until someone offers an even more definitive edition).[4]

Now widely available, *The Definitive Edition of the Diary of Anne Frank* shows clearly that previous generations, however much they thought they knew the truth, never got the whole story. In the 1990s, scholars routinely observe that *The Diary of Anne Frank*, whether in past editions of the text or in those versions produced for stage and screen, soft-pedaled the devastation of the Holocaust; they thus attribute the *Diary*'s popularity in America to its sugarcoating of gruesome subject matter. Both Lawrence Langer and Alvin Rosenfeld have written about the Americanization of the Holocaust in relation to Anne Frank, arguing, in Langer's words, that "there is little horror in the stage version; there is very little in the *Diary* itself. . . . They permit the imagination to cope with the idea of the Holocaust without forcing a confrontation with its grim details."[5]

Lawrence Graver argues similarly in *An Obsession with Anne Frank* (1995): he treats Meyer Levin's difficulties getting *The Diary* staged in an authentic form as evidence of the inadequacy of Holocaust awareness in the 1950s, which included the American Jewish community's reluctance to make too much of, or to acknowledge any special relationship to, the Holocaust. As Graver documents, the most troubling, as well as the most identifiably Jewish, parts of the *Diary*—Anne's nightmare, the Hannukah celebration, and the Gestapo hammering on the Franks' door—never appeared on stage or screen because the producers, who were themselves Jewish, felt compelled by their own sense of what would sell to "tone down" the play's Jewishness.[6] Anne's story, they decided, would have a greater appeal if it were told not as a story about Jewishness but as a story of universal appeal, about unfailing optimism and the strength of the human spirit as manifested in the face of terrible deprivations. Taken together, Langer, Rosenfeld, and Graver agree that as popular as the play and the movie were, neither rendered the actual horrors of the Holocaust or its correlation to deadly anti-Semitism. Past versions of Anne Frank failed to portray the Holocaust as scholars now, with the advantage of history, feel it ought to be portrayed.

The irony, of course, is that if the Anne Frank whom Americans met in the 1950s was not the "true" Anne Frank, neither is the Anne Frank they meet in the 1990s. Anne Frank's story continues to mutate. As recently as 1996, for instance, at least four new versions of Anne's story appeared: *Anne Frank and Me* premiered at the American Jewish Theater in December; *And Then They*

Came for Me: The World of Anne Frank toured the country in summer stock. *I Am Anne Frank,* a song cycle based on the diarist's life, opened at Alice Tully Hall in New York City; it was inspired not by the actual *Diary* but by another stage production based on Frank's life, *Yours, Anne,* which appeared in several national theaters and on public television in the fall of 1995. All of these versions of Anne Frank's diary are at least twice removed from witness; they grew out of responses to either reading a heavily edited version of the *Diary* (as the pre-1990 text was published) or seeing yet another adaptation of it (thrice removed, then, from either witness or primary testimony). When these adaptations are "treacly and manipulative, dreadful and banal" (as John Simon called *Yours, Anne* in *New York* magazine), they fuel the debate about the Americanization of the Holocaust.[7] The American tendency, in Alvin Rosenfeld's words, to "downplay or deny the dark and brutal sides of life and to place a preponderant emphasis on the saving power of individual moral conduct" is aptly illustrated by the creator of *Yours, Anne,* Enid Futterman, who observed, "Anne is not a victim, but a survivor. Because of her diary, she triumphed over her death at Bergen-Belsen."[8]

A discussion of the history and reception of *The Diary of Anne Frank,* then, leads directly to issues that have weighed heavily on Holocaust studies in the United States. First, its reception history suggests that the American perception of the Holocaust has been far from static; like all historical events, it has evolved in concert with larger social, cultural, and political movements. Second, and more troubling to some, our knowledge of the Holocaust in America has rarely been delivered by direct witness; it comes to us by way of representations, and representations of representations, through editors and publishers, producers and directors. Thus, the uniqueness of the Holocaust has seemed threatened: the event does not necessarily retain precedence over other historical events that Americans read about or see on television. Third, the American responsibility to remember bears a distinctive national character. Not only did the American Jewish community, the largest and wealthiest in the world, feel a moral imperative to remember and educate, it did so in the face of special challenges—in a society that has at times encouraged assimilation and one that is always, in the words of Graver, "governed by money, popular taste, media hype, democratic optimism and a susceptibility to easy consolation."[9]

For these reasons, the representation of the Holocaust in America takes place on an embattled stage, where a seemingly small gesture seems to take on cataclysmic resonance. With each important touchstone of Americanization—

whether it is the radio broadcast of Adolf Eichmann's trial for war crimes in 1961, commonly recounted as a formative moment of awareness; NBC's televising of the miniseries *Holocaust* in 1978 (to which Elie Wiesel, among others, responded with alarm, calling it "misleading, complacent, dangerous"); the opening of the United States Holocaust Memorial Museum in 1993; or the huge success of *Schindler's List* that same year—the discussion gets louder and more heated, rather than more muted and moderate as time passes.

In the 1990s, when interest in the Holocaust has ignited, the debate can be blistering. The construction of memorial structures stalls endlessly as communities and committees disagree about what constitutes proper remembrance: the United States Holocaust Memorial Museum took almost fifteen years to build while a presidential commission tried to balance claims of uniqueness with those of universality. A film like *Schindler's List* engenders such passionate partisanship and opposition, in mainstream newspapers and academic journals alike, that Indiana University Press has recently published a volume of essays containing only a few of the many contradictory responses to it.[10] Even the term *Americanization* is under fire. For some it automatically signals America at its worst: crassness, vulgarization, and selling out. Rosenfeld uses the term this way in his article "The Americanization of the Holocaust," in which he "wonders how any story of the crimes of the Nazi era can remain faithful to the specific features of those events and at the same time address contemporary American social and political agendas."[11] Michael Berenbaum, on the other hand, uses the term to defend the mission of the American Holocaust museum, which is "to tell the story of the Holocaust in such a way that it would resonate not only with the survivor in New York and his children in San Francisco, but with a black leader from Atlanta, a Midwestern farmer, or a Northeastern industrialist."[12] He thereby suggests that Americanization is a necessary, and noble, evolution of Holocaust remembrance.

Yet the high volume of debate is not reserved exclusively for such significant milestones as *Schindler's List* or the construction of the Holocaust museum. Because the stakes seem so high, issues of Americanization are hotly contested in circumstances that one might initially expect to be more flameproof. What does it mean, for instance, when Elie Wiesel receives the honor of throwing the ceremonial first pitch of the New York Mets' 1988 home season? Is it a tribute to Wiesel's suffering? Or does it naturalize the Holocaust in an absurd fashion? What does Daddy answer when his five-year-old son asks who that is throwing the ball, or why he is famous—that is, if Daddy even knows? What words from announcers should precede such an appearance? How, in the beginning of a baseball game, could they satisfactorily describe the Holocaust? And what should be said, to take another example, of *In Memory's Kitchen: A Legacy from the Women of Terezin,* a recently published pseudo-cookbook that collects the not-to-be-followed recipes provided by the prisoners of that concentration camp?[13] Is it a document that, with its grossly inaccurate ingredient amounts, glaring misspellings, and crucial omissions, touches and educates about the horrors of the Holocaust? Or is it a document whose publication posthumously humiliates these women who so painstakingly labored when starvation had robbed them of every clear thought?

Regardless, however, of who's arguing over what medium—movie, museum, or celebrity survivor—the conflicts among scholars and laypeople pile up: Is the Holocaust a unique event in history, or can it be compared with other genocides? What constitutes proper remembrance? Who has the right to tell the story? Can fiction or poetry or any artistic interpretation adequately—and morally—render the event? While scholars continue to try to answer these questions, the Americanization of the Holocaust has widened an already abundant field of exploration: How has the Holocaust been interpreted through an American ideological framework? Have artifacts of American culture approached the true horror of the event? What does it mean when representations of the Holocaust are created whole-cloth from other representations? Do Jewish Americans bear a larger burden of remembrance? What role should the Holocaust play in American Jewish life today and in the future?

Answers to these questions come from all disciplines and points of view. Theologians, philosophers, poets, novelists, political scientists, historians, and literary critics eagerly offer answers, or at least interpretations. In American academic communities, Holocaust research steadily grows. In 1990, about eighty books were published in the United States about the Holocaust; in 1995, over one hundred. A new field of study, the "Sociology of the Holocaust," now addresses "social problems, social control, social psychology, and deviance" as it relates to the Nazi genocide.[14] In 1995 and 1996, over one hundred dissertations focused on the Holocaust; entire scholarly journals are now devoted to its study (*Holocaust and Genocide Studies* from Oxford University Press and *History and Memory* from Indiana University Press). Publishers routinely underestimate the potential audience for books, sometimes dramatically so, as was the case with Knopf and Daniel Goldhagen's *Hitler's Willing Executioners,* which in 1997 attained tenth place on the *New York Times'* paperback bestseller list for nonfiction.

In popular culture as well the Holocaust has become deeply embedded in the American psyche. In the past several years Americans have seen the tremendous success of *Schindler's List.* Released with low commercial expectations in 1993, it earned $96 million by 1996 and won seven Oscars. In February 1997 the movie appeared on network television with the startling announcement that it would be uninterrupted by commercials—an incisive comment on the sacredness of the Holocaust in American culture (and all the more notable, perhaps, because the sponsor was Ford, a name that has for generations been linked to anti-Semitism). American viewers have also seen survivors telling their stories on cable television, and in 1995 they saw two survivors accepting Academy Awards merely for telling their stories on film. The Holocaust museum in Washington, D.C., boasts the largest attendance figures in history for a national museum: two million in its first year and five thousand a day (62 percent are not Jewish). In a recent issue of the *New York Times* (February 5, 1997) no fewer than four articles concerned the Holocaust, and one front-page article announced that our new secretary of state had just discovered that three of her grandparents had lost their lives in it—a topic I will explore further in a moment. On a local level, Americans now regularly commemorate the Holocaust in their churches and synagogues; "Literature of the Holocaust" courses are oversubscribed even in places like the University of Nebraska, where fewer than 1 percent of the students are Jewish; and Holocaust monuments and memorials have sprung up next to tennis courts and teeter-totters in neighborhood parks across the country.

Those who have wished and worked for wide Holocaust remembrance should feel that their prayers have been answered. Paradoxically, the extraordinary success of Holocaust remembrance in America has precipitated other problems. Most Americans seem so well acquainted with at least some version of the Holocaust that they freely invoke it in metaphor, and often with an inflammatory casualness. While most Americans generally accept public officials comparing atrocities in Serbia or Rwanda with the Holocaust, such easy metaphor-making is frequently distasteful to sectors of that same audience. When, for instance, O. J. Simpson's lawyer Johnnie Cochran accused the members of the Los Angeles Police Department of being Nazis and carrying out a Holocaust against black youths, Simpson's other lawyer, the Jewish Robert Shapiro, staged a televised interview with Barbara Walters to denounce Cochran and to say "that he was deeply offended" by the comparison. He added that they would never work together again.[15] Thus, even within a tragedy as seemingly removed from the Holocaust as the Simpson trial, strains of now-familiar battles about the politics of memory can be heard: Cochran and Shapiro's disagreement rehearses the familiar controversy over whether the Holocaust is an incomparable event. Was the genocide so great in magnitude that it cannot—should not, must not—be compared with other events? And what of the slippery slope that comparison produces and analogy leads to? When Americans use these terms freely, don't they rob from actual victims the language that they need to express their ordeal? Similarly, doesn't such common use of hyperbole, in Kathleen Jamieson's words, "exhaust the capacity of language to express outrage"?[16]

Yet even if you and I could agree that the answer to these last two questions is yes, the problem is not solved. Sooner or later we are bound to differ. Once we concede that some comparisons are appropriate, as in the case of the devastation in Serbia, for instance, how do you adjudicate the use of other comparisons that seem less appropriate? In short, if the Holocaust as metaphor is part of our common language, who can control who speaks it?

No one, of course. The only thing you can do is complain, and those complaints—often thunderous—have become a large part of Holocaust discussion in this country. Yet however irresponsible or invidious we may find Cochran's, or anyone else's, use of language, the true lesson of his example lies elsewhere. If the Holocaust, as image and symbol, seems to have sprung loose from its origins, it does not mean we should decry Americanization; rather, the pervasive presence of representations of the Holocaust in our culture demands responsible evaluation and interpretation. The many invocations of the Holocaust for many different purposes call for our sifting, sorting, analysis. Even Alvin Rosenfeld finds himself with little choice but to compare and critique; while he faults *Schindler's List* because it celebrates the rescuer rather than the victim, he clearly prefers it to Judy Chicago's Holocaust Project, which he finds "egregious."[17] Despite his obvious distaste for Americanization, Rosenfeld enters the fray because whether he likes it or not, the Holocaust has become an artifact of American culture. He certainly cannot control how or when or in what format the Holocaust will appear, but he can respond. In fact, he feels morally obligated to respond.

I want to return to that recent edition of the *New York Times* (February 5, 1997) wherein the first article about Madeleine Albright's family appeared, along with three other Holocaust-related articles ("Hidden Personal Histories of Survivors a Painful Nazi Era Legacy," "More on Albright's Past," "Victims Always Return"; Albright also captured the "Quote of the Day"). The disclosure about the death of Albright's grandparents and the religious conversion of her parents in order to escape Nazi persecution obviously held great personal importance for Albright, yet it also seemed to participate in a wide cultural drama for us all. The media attention to Albright's discovery and the *Times'* decision to run it as first-page news evince the tremendous currency of the Holocaust today. February 5, 1997, was not a quiet news day. The verdict of the Simpson civil trial came in; President Clinton had delivered the State of the Union address the night before. Alongside those stories ran the headline of an apparently equally important story: "Albright Grateful for Her Parents' Painful Choices." Perhaps the *Times* was compensating for not being able, because it is printed too early in the morning, to run the story a day earlier, as the *Washington Post* and *USA Today* had done; still, the ensuing discussion and three-day follow-up, letters to the editor, and columns on the Op-Ed page could have convinced someone who did not know better that the Holocaust was breaking news. Yet as unusually compelling as the Albright story was, it certainly is not unusual for the Holocaust to attract such high visibility. On February 4, 1997, a Holocaust-related story had also been the lead: the front-page headline on that day read "Three Nations Agree in Freezing Gold Looted by Nazis." In 1996 the *New York Times* published over five hundred Holocaust-related articles. Lest anyone object that the *New York Times* is not a fair indication of American attitudes since it serves a much greater Jewish contingent than other city papers, we should note that statistics from other major papers across the country do not tell a significantly different story. The *Washington Post,* for instance, published over three hundred Holocaust-related articles in 1996. For all intents and purposes, the Holocaust is a current event.

Certainly there have been peaks of interest before the last decade. As I mentioned earlier, Holocaust awareness in both 1961 and 1978 spiked upward. Yet in neither of those years did the Holocaust come close to attracting the amount of attention that it does today. The present level of interest forces the question, What has happened in the past decade to increase so dramatically

American interest in memorializing and observing the Holocaust? The answer to this question deserves a book-length study (and I am surprised, given the myriad publications on the Holocaust, that one has not yet appeared). For the purposes of this introduction, however, we will have to settle for a brief overview of some of the key issues.

In 1995, local religious groups all over the country commemorated the fiftieth anniversary of the liberation of Auschwitz. I visited my local synagogue in northwestern Indianapolis to hear Kurt Klein talk about liberating Gerda, the woman who would later become his wife. Their moving story, as most everyone now knows, was made into an Academy Award–winning documentary, *One Survivor Remembers,* which has appeared widely throughout the United States; Gerda Klein herself accepted the Oscar on national (and international) television. Although I had seen Kurt tell his story twice before— once on videotape at the Holocaust museum and once on the *Jerry Springer Show*—this time the account was especially poignant because he was obviously older and we cannot count on having his first-person presence forever. Elie Wiesel recently called survivors "the most endangered species in the world."[18]

One of the reasons for the increased attention to the Holocaust, then, rises from an inevitable awareness of the advancing age of survivors. This concern has motivated many to try to preserve survivors' primary testimony; Steven Spielberg, the most prominent in this category, has initiated and funded the Shoah Visual History Foundation. Certainly as survivors have aged, the discussion about the politics of memory and representation has become increasingly urgent. Yet Spielberg's life and example spotlight other reasons having little to do with representation that help explain why the Holocaust now occupies center stage.[19]

Forgetting for a moment Spielberg's enormous wealth and high profile, he is not unusual for his age group or moment in history—not in his attachment to the Holocaust. While some would credit *Schindler's List* with directing attention to the Holocaust—as it no doubt did—and starting a snowball effect, to do so is to miss the point of his example. This fervent Holocaust consciousness does not originate with Spielberg. Many of his generation, though they lack the resources to make movies or to fund foundations, have the same attachment to the Holocaust that he does—which arises from a complicated nexus of issues surrounding cultural and religious identity in America in the last several decades.

Born in 1947, Spielberg, like the great majority of baby-boomers, grew up in the 1950s in a culture that prized consensus and assimilation, and whose Jews were notably silent about the genocide in Europe. He was not, as he says, "a religious kid." What he knew about the Holocaust as a child cannot be certain; what is clear, however, is that very little in the popular culture of his day—he remembers Walt Disney, 1950s sci-fi, and Cecil B. De Mille movies as most influencing him—could have much enlightened him.

Everywhere Spielberg has said that his decision to make *Schindler's List* "was an outgrowth of his increasing Jewish awareness," a growing awareness common to his generation. Coming of age in the 1970s, Spielberg learned the lessons of an era devoted to diversity, to the elaboration of ethnicity and the exploration of one's heritage. It was no small moment when in the 1970s an episode of *Roots* surpassed the episode of Ricky Ricardo Jr.'s birth to become the most-watched television program in history. When second- and third-generation American Jews followed this attention to ancestry and investigated their roots, many of European descent found truncated lines. Grandparents who had come over before the war were often the only surviving sibling in families of six or eight; great-grandparents left in Poland, Germany, Russia, Hungary, had disappeared without a trace. These "deletions" drove the force of the Holocaust home with shocking lucidity.

Even those who had not lost ancestors, like Spielberg, renewed their sense of Jewish identity through the Holocaust. (I will shortly say more about the controversy surrounding this last statement.) For Spielberg, a longing for cultural connection sharpened after the birth of his son, the event he credits with beginning a ten-year process of self-reflection that culminated in his making *Schindler's List*. Again, his thoughts, if not his actions, are typical of baby-boomers, now accounting for one-third of the American population and exercising a dominant force in defining the values and agenda of American society. For the most part, boomers report that their need for social connection and commitment for themselves and for their children brings them back to their roots (Jewish or otherwise).[20] That those roots are replanted, not to mention pruned and shaped, by television programs and movies—making or watching them—says a great deal about how people acquire identities in our postmodern culture, as well as inviting some skepticism about the process. In any case, Spielberg reports that because he wanted to expose his kids to Jewish history, he decided to reimmerse himself in Judaism and, along the way, make a movie.

While most of us recognize *Schindler's List* as a positive contribution to the discussion of the Holocaust, along with the countless other contributions made by members of Spielberg's generation, the baby-boomers' rediscovery of Jewishness by way of the Nazi genocide has also fostered what Michael Goldberg in his book *Why Should Jews Survive?* calls the "Holocaust cult." Goldberg complains that "Holocaust veneration . . . has replaced God as the center of devotion," and that in order for Judaism to survive, it "must turn back to God."[21]

This undue devotion to the Holocaust has also been targeted by popular culture. A recent *Seinfeld* episode centered around the apparently comic notion that Jerry and his girlfriend were spotted by one of his enemies at the movie theater "making out during *Schindler's List.*" Although Jerry begs his enemy not to tell anyone, the secret gets out and Jerry is universally chided for what is commonly perceived as an impropriety bordering on barbarism. On another sitcom built around an American Jewish comic, Paul Reiser, a.k.a. Paul Buchman on NBC's *Mad about You,* wins an argument with his Gentile wife, Jamie, by comparing someone they know with Hitler, to which his wife responds, "You get me so mad—you know, if World War II hadn't happened, you wouldn't even know how to have a conversation." Popular culture has only recently stumbled upon the joke that Philip Roth made almost thirty years ago in his legendary *Portnoy's Complaint.* Here the rebel teenage son, Alexander Portnoy, spewing hatred for his parents and his Jewish heritage, angrily answers his sister's defense of his mother by screaming, "I suppose the Nazis make everything she says and does smart and brilliant too! I suppose the Nazis are an excuse for everything that happens in this house."[22]

These incidents may evince an insensitivity to Holocaust-related issues; at the same time I would argue that they also display Seinfeld's, Reiser's, and Roth's confidence about their place—the place of American Jews—in their culture. Their sense of safety makes it possible for them so openly to rebuke and expose their "own." In this important way too, they, like Spielberg, typify their generation. After being asked why the many Jewish American producers and directors before him had never made a movie about the Holocaust, Spielberg replied that "immigrant Jewish producers were having an identity struggle just wanting to become Americans." To make movies about the Holocaust would mean to draw attention to their ethnicity in a way that would impede assimilation. As this last quotation from Spielberg implies, that tension between being Jewish and being American has all but disappeared.

There can be little doubt that Jews in America have lost their outsider status: in fact, it would be negligent not to observe that in certain fields, including, but not exclusively, academia, journalism, and entertainment, they appear in disproportionate numbers. Moreover, Jews constitute less than 3 percent of the population but make up over one-quarter of *Forbes* magazine's annual compilation of the four hundred richest Americans.[23] Important byproducts emerge from the status and wealth of American Jews. First, of course, it has made remembering the Holocaust in America as prevalent as it is—for all its negative and positive applications. For instance, it became a crass joke in the American Jewish community in the 1960s that when a synagogue or a congregation needed money, all the rabbi had to do to get a bundle was to mention the Holocaust. This joke, however, which was meant to criticize the "Holocaust cult" as well as chasten American Jews for their impoverished spirituality, unfolds at a different angle when looking at the case of the Holocaust museum. When fund-raisers asked for donations from individuals to construct the museum, they received a good deal more than they expected—a staggering $168 million, no laughing matter at all.

Second, because that security is born out of genuine feelings of identification with and attachment to American culture, it gets harder and harder to render the Holocaust without incorporating American themes. And paradoxically, it is these themes that generate so much controversy. Spielberg, for instance, has often been condemned for making the hero of his Holocaust movie Gentile rather than Jewish; Harvey M. Meyerhoff (the first chairperson of the Holocaust museum's committee) was fired for trying to "universalize" the museum too much. Such censures are unreasonable. The very essence and hope of American Judaism is that it will coexist—and thrive—in a country that is overwhelmingly not-Jewish. Spielberg and Meyerhoff have achieved the kind of prosperity that would have been inconceivable had they not thoroughly imbibed the ideology of the dominant culture. They are in the position to bring the Holocaust to America's attention precisely because they have achieved so much; they have achieved so much because they are insiders; they are Americans. What they create must automatically bear the imprint of a multicultural but predominantly Gentile America. To expect otherwise is to expect the impossible.

As for the primacy of the Holocaust in establishing the identity of American Jews, many besides Michael Goldberg worry. Judaic scholars routinely express concern about the future of any religion that relies so heavily upon genocide as its defining moment. Because several of the contributors to this volume discuss this issue in detail, here I will only make the related remark that in an era in which the celebration of ethnicity has become almost mandatory, the Holocaust's cultlike status has been augmented by its use as a touchstone of victimization. As the earlier example of Johnnie Cochran's metaphor demonstrates, the Holocaust frequently enters discussions of ethnicity by becoming a measuring stick against which all oppression is measured.

In 1996, for instance, Joseph Crowley, an assemblyman from a largely Irish section of Queens, sponsored a bill that was passed by the state legislature and signed into law by the governor, mandating that the New York City school curriculum include a unit on the potato famine and the resultant mass starvation in nineteenth-century Ireland. When other politicians objected to making laws about what schools should and should not teach, Crowley cited as precedent a 1994 law that required schools to teach about human-rights violations, with particular attention to the inhumanity of genocide, slavery, and the Holocaust. On an interview on National Public Radio, Crowley further explained his rationale: Shouldn't Irish American students be given the opportunity to learn about their heritage? After all, African American students learned about slavery and Jewish American students got to talk about the Holocaust.[24] The question of what the potato famine, 150 years ago and three thousand miles away, has to do with children of Irish descent whose families have lived in the United States for five generations is open for inquiry; one might ask a similar question about slavery and African Americans and about Jews and the Holocaust. Yet Crowley and others seem to believe that learning about one's heritage automatically entails the glorification of suffering, as if without proving the persistence of persecution you cannot legitimate your claim to minority, or ethnic, status. Arthur Hertzberg claims "that the underlying message that Jews were getting from what came to be called the 'Holocaust industry' or 'Shoah business' was that Jewish identity involved suffering."[25] I would observe that this message has been heard across a wide spectrum of ethnic groups in America.

Certainly there are other less complicated and controversial reasons that account for our current interest in the Holocaust. Fifty years affords perspective and a necessary distance in both space and time from which the evaluation of horrendous and seemingly unfathomable events can be more calmly conducted. In the case of the Holocaust, especially, where for many years silence was deemed the only appropriate response by those who could not offer firsthand testimony, a general reluctance to speak was deepened by the desire to return to normality after the war. Furthermore, the tendency to understand the Holocaust as unique, which went hand in hand with special caretaking of its incomparability and unspeakability, has to a large extent broken down.

This is not because the Holocaust is not unique or incomparable or inde-scribable; it may be all three. Yet caretakers of commemoration have under-stood—crucially, I believe—that silence will lead to nothing but more silence. Finally what we realize is that there is no choice. If the Holocaust is to be re-membered at all, American historians, artists, writers, directors and produc-ers, sculptors, teachers, lawyers, and politicians must re-see and re-say it. It fol-lows that they can only do this as they see fit. "They will make mistakes," Michael Marrus writes of historians in *The Holocaust in History*, they will "choose inappropriate references, neglect certain vantage points, make clumsy generalizations, or fail to find words to describe what they know. Critics will demand they do better."[26] In other words, the representation of the Holocaust has entered the realm of common discourse. And accordingly it has become the responsible critic's job to evaluate, to analyze, to contextualize, and to make choices among the many renderings of the Holocaust we have in our na-tional culture. It is the point of this collection to do exactly that.

THE ESSAYS

The essays in this collection discuss the representation of the Holocaust in American culture in various fields and over a fifty-year period. Although a majority of them focus on the Holocaust as it is represented in contemporary American artifacts and discourses, the book also includes three historical es-says that provide necessary background for subsequent discussions.

In choosing these essays I had two primary goals. First, I sought to cover an assortment of media and genres, not limited to academic conversations or rarefied circles. The contributors to this book interpret the Holocaust as it has appeared in diverse American media and artifacts: movies, theater, architec-ture, advertising, survivor testimony, television, the discussion of race, and lit-erature and cultural theory. Second, I sought to provide an up-to-date barometer of Holocaust-related issues in America. Despite their focus on dif-ferent media, genres, and moments in history, these authors isolate and illu-minate prevailing areas of popular and scholarly engagement: the relation-ship of the Holocaust to American Jews as well as other ethnic groups, and most crucially African Americans; the perception of the Holocaust as it con-tinues to evolve over fifty years; the role of survivors' descendants in com-memorating the event; and the effect of Holocaust denial on the American perception of the event.

The collection opens with three essays that examine historical perceptions of the Holocaust in America. My own essay, "The Imaginary Jew and the American Poet," discusses the earliest period of reception, 1945–60. By comparing the work of Jewish American poet Karl Shapiro and Gentile American poet John Berryman, I argue that Shapiro's silence about the Holocaust in the decade immediately following the war opened the door for Berryman and other Gentile poets to take imaginary Jewishness as a metaphor for their marginalization from mainstream culture. Jeffrey Shandler's "Aliens in the Wasteland" reports that the Holocaust made early "guest" appearances on science fiction television of the 1960s. Programs like *The Twilight Zone* and the original *Star Trek,* Shandler argues, evoked the event without specifically naming it, in order to portray the Holocaust as an event with universal themes and applications. The third historical essay, Henry Greenspan's "Imagining Survivors," documents dramatic changes in America's treatment of survivors. Greenspan labels 1978 as a watershed year because it launched the national practice of celebrating a generic brand of "survivorship" that easily translated into a wider appreciation of and attention to Holocaust survivors.

James Young's essay, "America's Holocaust," extends his previously published work on Holocaust memorials. Here he discusses the meaning of the setbacks of the United States Holocaust Memorial Museum as well as the implications of its triumph. In "Inheriting the Holocaust" Andrew Furman looks at American Holocaust fiction, including the work of well-known writers like Saul Bellow and Philip Roth; he focuses, however, on Thane Rosenbaum's 1995 collection of short stories, *Elijah Visible,* in order to explore the burdens of memory and ritual for the second generation. Amy Hungerford's "Surviving Rego Park" also discusses the children of survivors. Looking at Art Spiegelman's *Maus* and Spielberg's *Schindler's List,* Hungerford explains how different Americans imagine themselves to be connected to the Holocaust today, and also suggests how representations of the Holocaust and common memorial practices advance a theory about language itself.

In "'Three Thousand Miles Away'" Joyce Antler reviews two recent productions of plays about the Americanization of the Holocaust—Arthur Miller's *Broken Glass* and Cynthia Ozick's *Blue Light*—and discusses how both repression and denial of the Holocaust have contributed to the American perception of the event as well as to the construction of Jewish American identity. In "The Cinematic Triangulation of Jewish American Identity" Sara Horowitz explores the relationship among Israel, the Holocaust, and Jews in American and Israeli films of the last thirty years. Horowitz discovers that the healthy and robust Israeli body is presented as an antidote for the Holocaust in several important American films, including *Exodus* and *QB VII*. Alan Steinweis, in "Reflections on the Holocaust from Nebraska," discusses how Holocaust awareness has influenced the treatment of American Jews and other minority groups in cities that are predominantly Gentile.

Two of the final essays engage in a conversation about how the ascendancy of the Holocaust in contemporary American culture has played out in an African American arena. Walter Benn Michaels's "'You Who Never Was There'" argues that cultural identities, whether African American or Jewish American, derived from imagined relationships with historical events are neither desirable nor inescapable. Laurence Thomas's "Suffering as a Moral Beacon" examines the reasons that African Americans and Jewish Americans have compared the Holocaust with American slavery in order to compete for the status of most-victimized.

Finally, in "Play Will Make You Free" Andrew Levy wonders just how far images of the Holocaust have sprung loose from their origins. Noticing that the advertising displays in Nike's Chicago store summon the architecture and iconography of Nazi Germany, he speculates about whether American corporations can deploy such symbology without invoking and evoking the Holocaust, anti-Semitism, and the totalitarian politics of that regime.

1   THE IMAGINARY JEW
AND THE AMERICAN POET

Hilene Flanzbaum

In 1945 John Berryman, a Catholic poet from rural Oklahoma, won the *Kenyon Review*'s annual contest for best short fiction. His eight-page story, "The Imaginary Jew,"[1] features a Southern boy in a New York City college who is brutally attacked after being mistaken for Jewish. In that same year Karl Shapiro, a third-generation American Jew, won the Pulitzer Prize for a collection of poetry called *V-Letter*.[2] In this volume of poems, written in the Pacific theater, where he was a soldier, Shapiro makes no mention of the Nazis, concentration camps, or anything related to the genocide of the Jews. Shapiro, who wrestled with questions of Jewish identity throughout his career, had nothing to say about events in Europe. Berryman, on the other hand, manifests in his story a ready identification with Hitler's victims. Taken together, these two postwar literary events provide an opportunity to explore a complex of issues involving the construction of Jewish American identity immediately following the Holocaust, the politics of the American poet's vocation in the 1940s and 1950s, and the nature of ethnicity itself—how it has been imagined and enacted in America in the second half of the twentieth century.

In *V-Letter* Shapiro steadfastly attaches himself to an idea of American unity, victory, and cultural vitality; in contrast, Berryman, like many poets of his generation, declares himself an exile from American culture and writes a story that features a Gentile character imagining himself the victim of anti-Semitism. At this level their positions obviously diverge—and indeed, as I will demonstrate, their views of the poet's social function and utility do differ greatly. Yet although they disagree about the poet's role, Berryman and Shapiro similarly deploy ethnicity, both relegating it to a world of invention and both understanding that it metaphorically signals opposition to a national identity. Thus, Shapiro's repudiation of actual Jewish identity is a way of asserting his commitment to national identity, while Berryman's embrace of an imaginary Jewish identity is a way of articulating his anti-Americanism.

Further, their discussion of ethnicity sheds light on the role of the American poet in the 1940s and 1950s. In *V-Letter* when Shapiro adopts various ethnic masks as a demonstration of the inclusive national spirit, his deferral of ethnicity corresponds to his insistence on maintaining the poet as a central figure in American culture. His subsequent critique of modern poetry aligns with this deferral. Berryman, stationed differently in the poetic debate, also deploys ethnicity as a metaphor for examining the poetic vocation. When he discovers Jewishness, however, he finds a handy trope for imagining the suffering and marginalization he feels in America. For both poets, then, the racial Jew no longer exists. For Shapiro, that Jew has been absorbed by America; for Berryman, the Jew has become a symbol for the alienated American poet—the symbol for himself.

Berryman is not the only imaginary Jew haunting the pages of modern American poetry. In fact, many appear at this time, but little critical attention or explication has followed them. In the years between 1945 and 1963, Randall Jarrell wrote and published at least seven poems about the death camps ("Protocols," which appeared in *Poetry* in 1945, is the first poem published in America about this topic); Berryman's projected Jewish identity continues into his masterpiece, *The Dream Songs* (1959–62); Robert Lowell finds his Jewish ancestor in *Life Studies* (1959); Charles Olson speaks from inside a concentration camp in *The Distances* (1951); and of course Sylvia Plath's Holocaust poems are widely known. While Plath's use of Holocaust imagery in *Ariel* (1960) has engendered much debate, there has been only the most fleeting mention of these other imaginary Jews, and until now no examination has been made of what their presence might signify either to American literature and culture or to Holocaust studies.[3]

Yet even this critical silence is instructive, for it suggests the many theoretical problems attending the artistic response to the Holocaust. If critics in the post-Holocaust world failed to notice Gentile poets claiming Jewish kinship, it may be because they respectfully observed the silence that the Holocaust seemed to demand, especially the Holocaust as represented by American

Gentiles. And in observing this silence, they were not alone. Even in the Jewish community, reaction to the Holocaust was slow in coming.

Critical silence mirrored the culture at large. As sociologist Charles Stember documented in the most exhaustive poll about attitudes toward American Jews in the 1950s, "Revelations about the death camps were not commensurate with the enormity of the horrors uncovered. In the 1950s, Americans responded more strongly to the plight of anti-Communist refugees than they had done to the death-camp survivors." This was not due to anti-Semitism; indeed, anti-Semitism showed its most radical decline in the years following the war. Stember attributes the lack of response to "a marked decline in the American public's awareness of Jews. . . . Both favorable and unfavorable attitudes towards Jews were declining."[4]

Despite the European genocide, then, Jews in America had lost most of their alien status. Like other Americans at the end of the war, Jews defined their problems in institutional rather than ethnic terms, and the principles of a monolithic national identity began to occupy a commanding place in the American scale of social values. For American Jews to identify with the Holocaust would have meant a substantial reversal; they would first have had to extract themselves from the well-blended composite of American identity into which they had seemingly melted.

This would not occur overnight. For over half a century Jews had struggled to efface their immigrant status and to adopt the ways of "real" Americans. Whether they remained religiously observant or not, most American Jews were eager to give up Old World customs and attitudes and happy to melt away their differences. Life in America was a "second birth: they approached the process of 'becoming American' with the same intensity and determination they applied to everyday life."[5] Identification with their European brethren would be hard to recultivate.

Some historians believe that these assimilative transformations were only superficial. Jews may have taken different names—80 percent of the fifty thousand Americans who changed their names in the late 1940s were Jewish—but many still defined themselves as Jewish.[6] Yet other historians maintain that assimilation was accomplished in spirit as well as affect. Lucy Dawidowicz reports that "in the thirties, even the secular options of Jewish identity began to disintegrate. Except for pockets of observant Jews, except for pockets of immigrant Yiddishists, except for pockets of Zionists, the mass of American Jews—immigrant and native born—looked upon Jewishness and Judaism as disabilities, liabilities and impediments to becoming full Americans."[7] Whatever one believes about the authenticity of assimilation, however, it seems clear that when American Jews said little about the Holocaust in the years immediately following the war, they manifested a reasonable perplexity over their connection to this catastrophic international event: Were they Americans who had won the war? Or were they Jews who had come close to complete annihilation? And indeed, what new territory would have to be negotiated in order to occupy both?[8]

While the consideration of these issues may account for some of the silence in the American Jewish community, Shapiro's *V-Letter* seems to display little confusion about his own affiliations. The expanded title of the volume, *V-Letter from the Pacific*, points to Shapiro's geographic and spiritual position:[9] for him, the war was in the Pacific, and he fought because America was attacked by the Japanese. This in itself is worth stressing. Our present-day conclusion that—for the large body of American Jews especially—the Holocaust was the central event of World War II results from an identification with ethnicity that simply did not exist in the mid-1940s. Shapiro's collection serves as a reminder that for most Americans, Jews and non-Jews alike, just as great a threat was felt from the Japanese as from Hitler.

Instead of manifesting any particular ethnic affiliation, Shapiro holds great stock in America, and his primary identification rests with the American soldier. Like the rest of the troops, Shapiro waits for his mail and misses his girlfriend; and like the ideal soldier, he has been thoroughly sold on the virtues of assimilation.

In the preface to *V-Letter* Shapiro writes, "I have not written these poems in accord with any doctrine or system of thought or even a theory of composition. I have nothing to offer in the way of beliefs or challenges or prosody. I try to write freely, one day as a Christian, the next as a Jew, the next as a soldier who sees the gigantic slapstick of modern war" (vi). While critics have debated the success of Shapiro's experiments in dramatic personae, just as they debate the authenticity of Jewish assimilation in general, his assertion that he is one day Jewish and one day Christian shows his strong compulsion to digest and incorporate difference. In this volume the "synagogue dispirits the deep street" because it is a site of civil conflict: "The stone survival that laments itself, / Our old entelechy of stubborn God, / Our calendar that marks a separate race" (30). The public library, however, is exalted as the great American instrument of absorption: "These teachings break through wide-flung doors, / The Talmud, Naso, and the Rights of Man" (26). Similarly, Shapiro celebrates Thomas Jefferson as "the most serious of all our poets" (19) and Ben Franklin as "the star of Reason" (21).

When the poems do take up Jewish topics or themes, they reveal, at the very least, ambivalence. In the poem "Jew" Shapiro begins, "The name is immortal but only the name, for the rest / Is a nose that can change in the weathers of time or persist / Or die out in confusion or model itself on the best" (27). Indeed, as far as Shapiro is concerned, it is the Jewish insistence on an outmoded tribalism that has caused such great problems. The poem concludes, "Our name is impaled in the heart of the world on a hill / Where we suffer to die by the hands of ourselves, and to kill" (27). Nor does Shapiro sympathize with any benighted Jewish figures. In a poem entitled "Shylock," he interprets the character in a strikingly elementary and unsympathetic manner: "Nothing will repair / This open breach of nature, cruel and wracked" (28).

As this critique of Shylock suggests, the poet eagerly divests himself of any appearance of ethnic loyalty. In *V-Letter* Shapiro emerges as the perfect product of the nationalist spirit of the 1940s, when World War II melted Americans into the cauldron more completely than any previous event, producing a brotherhood of Americans from all backgrounds. Assimilation became a necessary adaptation if Americans were to unite to win this war, and thus "all reinforced the idea that what united Americans was a great deal more important than what divided them. All implied that the differences between classes, races and ethnic groups would be submerged in fighting the war."[10]

Certainly Shapiro willingly buries his ethnic identity. Of all the dramatic masks he wears in the volume—Indian, Communist, or Robinson Crusoe—he returns several times to a Christian persona, invoking Jesus as a universal symbol of innocence and consolation. In "Christmas Eve: Australia" the speaker says,

> I smoke and read my bible and chew gum,
> > Thinking of Christ and Christmas last year,
> > And what quizzical soldiers standing near
> > Ask of the war and Christmases to come,
> > And sick of causes and the tremendous blame
> > Curse lightly and pronounce your serious name. (9)

Perhaps his most positive poem concerns the "Christmas Tree," which he praises for its sweetness, joy, and loveliness, finally effusing, "I think the history of praise / Is central in this present-flowering green" (20–21).

But as is true of Shapiro's other fleeting ethnic identities, even this ecstatic Christianity is easily shed. For Shapiro has written poems about being Jewish and Christian, Native American and African American, wounded and healthy; and it is indeed part of his point that as the composite American—and most important, as the ideal American soldier—he can be any of these things. Shapiro's role as an American soldier subsumes all other roles; in fact, soldiering offers his only consistent identity. Thus, it would be wrong to suggest that Shapiro has lost a sense of himself; rather, he roots his identity in the experience of an American soldier and the victory that America represents, which means the erasure of any scarring ethnic marks. He expresses the national sentiment that an American can be anything as long as he is patriotic. In fact, reviewers became so involved with Shapiro's "Americanness" that David Daiches protests, "Whether Shapiro is trying to take his place in a National contest beside Miss America of 1944 or the Typical American poet of 1950" is not the point. Daiches concedes, however, that the volume is "an object lesson in contemporary American war poetry."[11]

Not only is *V-Letter* an object lesson in American war poetry; Shapiro also intends to be the exemplary American. In his desire to be typical, Shapiro must give up not only his ethnic identification but also any identification he may feel with the intellectual community. He writes in the poem "Sunday: New Guinea," a pastoral fantasy of a Sunday at home, and also of an America buoyantly aware of itself as a nation joined by news, radio, brotherhood—and not torn apart by civil, racial, or intellectual conflicts:

> I long for our disheveled Sundays home,
> Breakfast, the comics, news of latest crimes,
> Talk without reference, and palindromes,
> Sleep and the Philharmonic and the ponderous Times
>
> . . . .
>
> I long for lounging in the afternoons
> Of clean intelligent warmth, my brother's mind. (13)

Although slightly more literary than the average man's, Shapiro's desires are still markedly pedestrian and middle class: he wants breakfast, the comics, enough sleep, and the Sunday paper. Such luxuries, denied him as a soldier, contribute to his version of an ideal nation, as does the brotherhood he also envisions. His geographical displacement in *V-Letter* leaves him with the strong desire to reconcile the alien aspects of his experience and to create a poetic vision both local and grounded. For Shapiro, poetry heals and unites;

it has a social function, it makes community, and it is central to the well-being of America. For all these reasons Shapiro's views contrasted with the dominant literary sensibility of Modernism: that America must be escaped and American culture transcended. Estranged from this part of the ethos of the intellectual community, then, Shapiro began to define himself as a poet for the middlebrow American. Before and after he wore a soldier's uniform, Shapiro remained antagonistic to the goals of high Modernism and suspicious about the inaccessibility of Modernist poetry. He wanted a wide audience because he sought a public voice and a public persona. To this end he could no more claim devotion to Jewishness than he could tolerate the withdrawal of the poet from American life. Thus, he contested the conventions of modern poetry that soon dominated the canon. In a bitterly ironic essay entitled "A Poet Dissects the Modern Poets," published in the *New York Times Sunday Magazine* in 1945, Shapiro took aim at Eliot, Auden, and many other unnamed American poets whom he called "anti-middle class, anti-lyrical, difficult to comprehend and [having] no place in the contemporary world."[12]

In another document of disaffection, "Essay on Rime," published in the July 1945 issue of *Poetry,* Shapiro wonders

> How and when and why
> Did we conceive our horror for emotion
> Our fear of beauty? Whence the isolation
> And proud withdrawal of the intellectual
> Into the cool control-room of the brain?
> At what point in the history of art
> Has such a cleavage between the audience
> And poet existed?[13]

He appears to be talking straightforwardly to Eliot, whose "Tradition and the Individual Talent" echoes throughout this poem and who is largely responsible for the poetic climate Shapiro abhors.

This cleavage between audience and poet, the sine qua non of the modern poet's existence, signified for Shapiro the American poet's forsaking of national responsibility. He complained in "A Poet Dissects the Modern Poets" that several of our most important poets could not even determine their own nationality: he described Eliot as "American-English" and Auden as "English-American." This disorientation about citizenship prefigures the modern poet's preoccupation, most notably Eliot's and Pound's, with peopling an international literary community. For the middle generation of poets, however, most of whom did not leave America, a link to internationalism was partially—and perhaps ironically—established in the metaphor of Jewish ethnicity.[14]

I say ironically because "middle generation" refers to poets who came of age in the decades succeeding Eliot, and thus their self-configuration as Jewish, and alien, grew out of the poetic lessons they learned at the knees of Eliot and Pound—poets we today routinely associate with anti-Semitism. The plight of the canonical American poet that has him finding himself in close company with the Jew—marginalized, forgotten, and victimized—results from a careful adherence to the high Modernist prescriptions Pound and Eliot held so dear.

Although poets frequently find themselves at odds with mainstream culture, at no time in American literary history did they feel more embattled and more on the brink of extinction than in the years following World War II. The reasons for the poet's increased alienation from mainstream America during this period have long been the subject of critical attention. The difficulty and obscurity of high Modernist texts, their unintelligibility to a general reader, and the high Modernist's studied avoidance of popular culture provoked a backlash of antipathy toward poetry. Further, in the wake of the war, popular culture boomed as it never had before and provided a more intense competition for the reader's attention.

The poet's estrangement from this growing mass of consumer culture is evidenced in a continuous and lively stream of complaint that poured out of literary journals. Between 1945 and 1960 the poet raises his jeremiad to a high art form. Indeed, it seems a part of the American poet's—as well as the critic's—job to bemoan his diminished status and to foretell imminent catastrophe for the man of letters. Jarrell's "Obscurity of the Poet," Allen Tate's "To Whom Is the Poet Responsible," and Delmore Schwartz's "The Isolation of the Poet" are a few of the more well-known examples of this genre. In these essays the writers brandish their increasing alienation from the American audience.

In their despondency we hear the first soft murmurings of Jewish kinship. A brief recapitulation of some of the highlights of these essays will prove the point. Schwartz writes, "In the unpredictable and fearful future that awaits civilization, the poet must be prepared to be alienated and indestructible. He must dedicate himself to poetry, although no one seems likely to read what he writes; and he must be indestructible as a poet until he is destroyed as a human being. He does feel that he is a stranger, an alien, an outsider; he finds himself without a father or mother, or he is separated from them by the opposition between his values as an artist and their values as respectable members of modern society."[15] Tate writes about a new nation, where the only citizens are poets and the only responsibilities "poetic": "To whom is the poet responsible? The poet has a great responsibility to his own. He is responsible to his conscience. In the French sense of the word. . . . He is responsible for the virtue proper to him as a poet."[16] Jarrell is bitter and ironic: "The poet is a condemned man for whom the state will not even buy breakfast—and as someone said, 'If you're going to hang me, you mustn't be able to intimidate me into sparing your feelings during the execution.'"[17]

Jarrell's words, as well as Tate's and Schwartz's, underscore what many take for granted about this poetic period: this middle generation of twentieth-century American poets, however prolific and accomplished they were, configured themselves as outsiders, even antagonists to the public. Abandoned by a national audience, the poet's sense of alienation had come to signal his superiority to a debased American culture. In the face of the hostile, crass, and ignorant public they see, American poets somewhat melodramatically predict their ultimate exile or extinction.

This version of the American poet, as opposed to Shapiro's, announces that the poet has been forsaken by culture and country, but that he has a personal and national responsibility—despite this desertion of his nation and his fellow citizens—to carry through. He writes for the wiser nation of the future: he appeals to a transcendent sense of justice and responsibility, believing—or perhaps only hoping—that history will redeem his suffering and canonize his words.

That poets are seldom appreciated in their time or nation corresponds to the plight of Jews, long held to be chosen but nationless. The American poet's desire, at this time, to become an international figure partially results from the mediocrity he sees at the heart of American life and the greater cultivation he sees in Europe. Jarrell's friendship with Hannah Arendt bears witness to this: as he wrote to her in 1951, "I am now firmly convinced of the superiority of European education and culture."[18] How incongruous that Jarrell and Arendt should agree on the advanced state of European culture, considering what had just transpired there—which included, of course, Arendt's very real persecution. Yet the belief that the bulk of Americans could not appreciate good poetry was endemic at this time and gave rise to a sensibility that eschewed public esteem and national prominence. Popularity and public access were viewed increasingly as signs of mediocrity, while ambiguity and difficulty came to be the signs associated with high culture and the canon of Modernism.

These developments pushed the study of poetry into an academic enclave and pushed Shapiro further from the spirit that informed the American poetic canon. For inasmuch as it was possible, Shapiro enjoyed fame and success as a public poet. His poems appeared almost weekly in the *New Yorker;* he was profiled for *Scholastic* magazine ("Soldier Poet!") and the *Saturday Review;* he wrote frequently on the meaning of poetry in American life. Shapiro, a poet of clear political and national allegiances, found no sympathy for the *poète maudit,* this figure of alienation that was being cultivated in other poetic corners. His very insistence on a poetry that sprung from the heart of the American experience, written in a more accessible style, made him a popular figure in the late 1940s. Thus, in 1945 Shapiro's Pulitzer Prize came as no surprise, since he had become a middlebrow favorite, a model citizen and a spokesman against the obscurities of Modernist poetry. A Jew who labeled himself an American soldier and who produced a victorious vision of America undivided at a time of great external threat held great appeal to a notoriously conservative awards committee.

But when in the following year Robert Lowell won the Pulitzer for *Lord Weary's Castle,* it ushered in a new era, not only of Pulitzers but of American poetry. Critics noted that the tenor of American poetry had changed permanently, and for the better. Lowell's text—replete with irony, allusiveness, and metaphysical wit, containing at least seven types of ambiguity and a foreword by Allen Tate—made him the leading poet of his generation, but it also reinforced the notion of a very difficult and obscure poetry that targeted a critical or academic audience while distancing many general readers. Here Shapiro's literary reputation began its steep decline.

Lord Weary's Castle boils over with references to elitism and exile, though Lowell did not connect these images to Jewishness until he wrote *Life Studies* (1959). John Berryman, Lowell's friend and poetic ally, laid the groundwork for an entire generation of American poets when he explored the metaphor of Jewishness in his story "The Imaginary Jew." In this incipient statement of alienation, the protagonist, a Gentile Southern boy, has never particularly noticed Jews. Soon after he enters college in 1933, he learns that Rosenblum and

Hertz, two of his best friends, are in fact Jewish. "This discovery," he says, "was the beginning of my instruction in social life proper—construing social life as that from which political life issues like a somatic dream" (532).

From there the character notices that he has a "special sympathy and liking for Jews—which became his fate, so that [he] trembled when he heard one abused in talk" (532). The story picks up years later at the brink of American involvement in World War II, when the character stumbles across clusters of men in a New York City park arguing about Roosevelt's foreign policy. The character, who supports American entrance into the war and who defends FDR, is suspected by them of being Jewish. An Irishman begins to heckle him: "You talk like a Jew. . . . You probably are a Jew. You look like a Jew." The character protests loudly, "I'm not Jewish and I don't look Jewish." The Irishman replies definitively, "You look like a Jew. You talk like a Jew. You *are* a Jew." The character continues to protest, growing more and more excited as the crowd becomes more and more threatening: "Prove it, prove that you're not a Jew," the mob demands. "Recite the Apostle's Creed" (538).

In his agitation the character cannot remember it. He has papers in his wallet that may prove he is of Irish descent, but he grows rebellious and will not furnish them. Still insisting that he is not Jewish, he cries, "You have no evidence that I am." At this moment the Irishman "leaned forward from the rail, 'Are you cut?'" he asked. Rather than show what one must guess would be ultimate proof that he is not Jewish, the character flees. In the days that follow he realizes that he had been victimized, not "altogether unjustly." His persecutors were right—he was a Jew: "The imaginary Jew I was was as real as the imaginary Jew hunted down, on other nights and days, in a real Jew. Each murderer strikes the mirror (the lash of the torturer falls on the mirror), and cuts the real image, and the real and the imaginary blood flow down together" (539).

This story has been little examined by either scholars of literature or scholars of Jewish studies; it deserves much closer attention than it has received. It is, first, remarkable that Berryman understood so much about the persecution before many Americans had processed the true horror of what had transpired in Europe. He understood the importance of "papers" to prove or disprove Jewish identity, and the importance of circumcision—as is evident in the Irishman's final demand that the character, if not Jewish, show his "uncut" penis. But more significantly, the story deserves attention because it meditates on the meaning of ethnicity, and especially the condition of Jewish ethnicity, in America in 1945.

While the story unquestionably deals with collective guilt and responsibility, another salient theme emerges: Berryman asks, Who is really a Jew? Those who look Jewish? Those who talk like Jews? Those who support Roosevelt's foreign policies? From the beginning of the story the character has maintained that "he is spectacularly unable to identify Jews as Jews,—by name, cast of feature, accent or environment,—and this has been true, not only of course before the college incident, but during my whole life since" (532). Here Berryman disputes not only the category of a Jew defined by racial criteria but also the Jew defined by cultural criteria. Indeed, the characteristics associated with cultural Jewishness—language, appearance, behavior—are invisible to him. Having never seen a Jew or even been given the necessary "cultural capital" to spot one, he is ill equipped to deal with his social milieu at college. As he reports after learning that Jews were excluded from certain houses, "What I took to be an idiotic state was deeply established, familiar and acceptable to everyone else" (532).

Berryman implies that ethnic distinctions can be made only in a context where such signs have already been laden with meaning. And even so, such "meanings" are derived incorrectly—for since he looks like a Jew, appearance after all means nothing, or, quite paradoxically, everything. In either case, there is certainly no true designation of Jewishness. Is an uncircumcised penis finally the only mark of difference, the only "real" evidence? The character's unwillingness to provide the actual proof that he is not Jewish suggests Berryman's point: that there is finally no physical mark of ethnicity. Rather, it is a state of mind, or—to analogize it once more to the life of the poet in the middle generation—a club one voluntarily joins.

Berryman's final assertion that he is just as Jewish as anyone else relativizes any claims of ethnicity. Indeed, he feels Jewish, and that is enough; conversely, if you think I am Jewish, then for all intents and purposes, I am. His declaration that Jewishness is a state of mind—either something one mysteriously feels, or something just as mysteriously perceived by one's audience—has dramatic implications for American poets in the 1940s. Such a declaration opens the door to metaphorical Jewishness, for Berryman and other American poets.

That Berryman is able to claim the category of Jewishness for himself spotlights the void in the cultural American landscape that the assimilated Jew has left. In other words, it is precisely Shapiro's claims to being American that have made becoming Jewish an option for Gentile poets. Shapiro's assertion that he is not marginal and no one's victim corresponds to his lack of Jewish ethnicity; at the same time, his position thrusts Jewishness into the world of metaphor. As the final phrase of Berryman's story indicates—"the real and the imaginary blood flow down together"—conventional notions of blood ties in ethnic determination must be suspended (or at least they will be temporarily). The enlightened person of the post-Holocaust world understood that genealogical claims to Jewishness reeked of anti-Semitism. The Nazi's extermination of the Jews had made such categorizations repugnant. For what reason, ultimately, had the Jew been murdered? For what biological or even cultural imperatives had Jews been singled out? In the Germany of the late 1930s, Jewishness could certainly not be defined by attendance at synagogue, geographical assembly, cultural markers, self-definition, or physical characteristics. Finally, the Nazis defined Jewishness as some concoction of blood— a designation that had no power anywhere but in the anti-Semite's imagination. The Nazis believed in these distinctions as if they were in fact based in some verifiable reality. But the enlightened understood that singling out Jews on the basis of some unassailable genealogy was morally reprehensible and epistemologically suspect. When we take the enlightened position, that Jews are just like everybody else and perfectly assimilable, then it follows that Jewish ethnicity has no clear referent.[19] Indeed, as the many scholarly works devoted to defining Jewish identity attest, what it means to be Jewish, when one is not religiously observant and racial criteria are known to be bogus, becomes more and more difficult to specify.

In the post-Holocaust world, where the most recognizable feature of Jewish identity became victimhood, John Berryman has no problem slipping into the role. Berryman's work is replete with imagery of victimization, but while his imaginary blackness has been examined, his metaphorical Jewishness stands yet to be explored.[20] We should note, first, that Berryman's early identification with the Holocaust marks the American poet's disaffection from mainstream culture, and second, that Shapiro's interest in being a central player in postwar America precludes any identification with Jewish ethnicity. Shapiro is not a victim of anti-Semitism; he has not been persecuted for his "blood"; he is not "Jewish."

To this end, in 1945 Shapiro does not claim any special relationship with the victims of the Holocaust. I base this statement not only on V-Letter but also on a 1946 poem in the Partisan Review called "The Conscientious Objector." In this poem Shapiro offers absolution to those who did not fight, writing, "Yet you who saved neither yourselves nor us / Are equally with those who shed the blood / The heroes of our cause."[21]

There is ample reason to believe that Shapiro had Robert Lowell in mind when he wrote this poem.[22] First, Shapiro must have known that Lowell, the most famous conscientious objector of his generation, had gone to prison for thirteen months in 1943; second, Shapiro's invocation of the *Mayflower* in the opening lines of the poem recalls Lowell's lineage as well as his famous poem "The Quaker Graveyard in Nantucket," published the previous year in the *Partisan Review*. Lowell did not have a poem in this issue of the *Partisan Review*, but Shapiro's poem, which appears after a poem written by Jarrell and before one written by Berryman, seems to stand as a placemarker for Lowell himself. The very placement as well as the subject of this poem suggests Lowell and invites further scrutiny.

Whereas Shapiro embraced his role as an American soldier in World War II, Lowell had made headlines when he refused to fight. In a letter to President Roosevelt, Lowell accused Americans of perpetrating the same barbarism and violence as the Japanese and the Germans. In taking such an unpopular stance, Lowell of course reproduced a central dynamic in the careers of American poets at this time: he dissented from the common opinion; he held a view that his fellow citizens would punish but his conscience would reward. Certainly his unimpeachable pedigree made such dissent possible. Yet even the staunchest America-Firsters changed their minds when the Japanese bombed Pearl Harbor. Not so Lowell.

Thus, in ending his poem with the lines "Your conscience is / What we come back to in the armistice," Shapiro makes a statement worthy of our attention. First, of course, he continues to protest "the folly of war," as he had done in *V-Letter* (vi). Second, in praising the C.O. he still takes into no special account the genocide of the European Jews. And third, unwittingly or not, Shapiro acknowledges Lowell's supremacy—both professional and cultural. Lowell had an untarnished and rising literary reputation. He was also of a quintessentially American lineage; he was highbrow and Anglo-Saxon, with a legendary social conscience and a manner that bespoke gentility.

"The Conscientious Objector" evidences Shapiro's struggle to inhabit Lowell's America, even though Lowell, ironically, had already abandoned it. Always a harsh critic of America, Lowell found nothing in World War II to make him feel more patriotic. It would not be long before Lowell himself declared

Jewish kinship; not only did he find his Jewish ancestor (Mordecai Myers in *Life Studies*), but in a letter to Ezra Pound he said he found Pound's views on the Jews inexplicable and asked "for some clarification on this race thing." After all, didn't Pound know "he was part-Jewish"?[23]

Given Lowell's lineage, such a redefinition of his identity is remarkable, yet within this discussion of poetic vocation it seems quite understandable. For Lowell too—perhaps watching his friends do it so ably—has learned how to deploy ethnicity. When he showcases his distant ancestor Mordecai Myers in the prose section of *Life Studies,* he does so because he understands that Jewish ethnicity provides an alternative to a repugnant and blameworthy national identity. In finding the exotic ancestor in a family steeped in blue-blood genealogy, Lowell redeems himself as a marginal figure and clarifies his position as poet. As a primary document of confessional poetry, *Life Studies* casts the American poet as "representative victim."[24] Thus, it should be no surprise that Lowell finds himself feeling at least partly Jewish. Indeed, in such a context even Pound himself may be "a bit of a Jew."[25]

But by the time Plath wrote those words in "Daddy" (1960) and Lowell published *Life Studies,* the free-floating signifier of Jewishness was about to take root. In 1958 Shapiro published a collection called *Poems of a Jew,* and in the preface to this volume he admonished himself for his past indifference to the Holocaust: "The German Jew grew up more German than the Kaiser himself, the French Jew had to be reminded by the Dreyfus Affair that he was still not French enough, and so on. The hideous blood purge of the Jews by Germany in the twentieth century revived throughout the world the spiritual image of the Jew."[26] Shapiro, who has also believed himself to be more American, perhaps, than Lowell himself, now remembers and identifies with his Jewishness and, most important, feels the freedom to claim it as his primary identification. The tide has indeed turned: in a few years Plath's Holocaust poems will meet a storm of protest from those offended by a Gentile appropriating the Holocaust for her own use. In the 1960s, American Jews would begin to claim the Holocaust as their own; like Karl Shapiro, who needed to be reminded of his Jewish spirituality by the "hideous bloodpurge," many Jewish Americans would interpret the European tragedy as a clarion call for a commitment to ethnic, rather than national, identity.

2 ALIENS IN THE WASTELAND

American Encounters with the Holocaust
on 1960s Science Fiction Television

Jeffrey Shandler

More than a half-century since it took place in Europe, the Holocaust is very present in American discourse. Accounts of the mass murder of civilians in Bosnia, Rwanda, and Chechnya often recall the Holocaust; as historian Peter Novick notes, "It is invoked as reference point in everything from AIDS to abortion."[1] Indeed, the Holocaust serves as a model for understanding events in America's own past, including the historical persecution of Native Americans and the enslavement of African Americans. But how did the Holocaust—which neither happened in America nor directly involved the great majority of Americans—attain such powerful stature as a moral paradigm in this nation's public culture? To begin to answer this question, examining how the Holocaust has been represented—in literature, art, music, broadcasting, museums, monuments, public ceremonies—is at least as important as considering the events of the Holocaust themselves.

Indeed, in America (unlike Israel or most of Europe) representations have always facilitated most people's primary encounter with the Holocaust. The media have figured prominently in this ongoing phenomenon since the spring of 1945, when newspaper articles, radio broadcasts, and theatrical newsreels reported the conditions of Nazi concentration camps that had just been liberated by Allied forces. Discussions of Holocaust media usually focus on major popular works—for example, the extensive attention paid to the 1993 film *Schindler's List*, or, a generation earlier, the stage (1955) and film (1959) versions of *The Diary of Anne Frank.*

When the discussion turns to televised presentations of the Holocaust, the *Holocaust* miniseries, first aired on NBC in April 1978, usually figures as the quintessential example. As important as this telecast is—like *The Diary of Anne Frank* and *Schindler's List,* it has had a significant impact on Holocaust memory culture both in the United States and abroad—it is also worth turning attention to works of less renown. This is especially important when considering what distinguishes television's presentations of the Holocaust. Indeed, the subject's increasingly frequent, almost routine presence on American television in recent decades—in news broadcasts, dramas, documentaries, public-affairs programming, even advertising—is key to understanding this medium's particular impact on Holocaust memory culture in this country. Moreover, the distinctive character of television—an inherently dramatic, recombinant medium; viewed primarily in intimate, domestic settings; providing large audiences with an endless, multichannel flow—has played a strategic role in establishing the Holocaust as one of the most powerful moral paradigms in contemporary American discourse.[2]

American television first dealt with the Holocaust in the early postwar years, as the broadcasting industry began building a national audience for the medium. By the end of the 1950s, its formative decade, the television industry had presented several dozen broadcasts that dealt in some way with the subject. These include original dramas for prime-time "playhouses," programs for ecumenical religion series, documentaries on the history of World War II and the Third Reich, and even several installments of the popular entertainment series *This Is Your Life.*[3] It was in the ensuing decade, however, that television helped establish the Holocaust as a familiar, almost routine, part of American public culture.

The 1960s witnessed the consolidation of television as a fixture in American culture, rising to a preeminent status among the nation's mass media. A novelty in 1950, the television set was a presence in over 90 percent of American homes a decade later, and the average American spent several hours a day watching television. At the same time, the 1960s are often characterized as a period of American television history that offered routinized programming, which lacked the innovative excitement of the medium's early years. At its worst, critics claimed, television had devolved into a "vast wasteland,"[4] to quote the famous words of former FCC chairman Newton Minow.

During the 1960s, episodic series became the mainstay of prime-time television entertainment in America. Most of these series offered what were, in effect, individual dramas of a particular genre (e.g., police cases, tales of espionage, or westerns), usually linked by the presence of continuing roles (doctors or reporters) and locations (courthouses or schools). While they were rooted in consistent characters, plots, and settings, these series afforded opportunities for guest performers in occasional roles and, similarly, the "guest" appearance of special topics. These "guest" topics introduced variety into the episodic series' routine. In particular, this strategy enabled producers to address topical, controversial issues that were not otherwise portrayed in primetime entertainment. Moreover, producers of these series hoped to attract viewers to dramas offering "provocative involvement with relevant themes"[5] and thereby counteract negative assessments of television as mere frivolous, hackneyed entertainment.

The Holocaust has figured as one such provocative "guest" topic on episodic television series beginning in the 1960s. Most of these are dramas about attorneys *(The Defenders),* private detectives *(Sam Benedict),* and law enforcement officers *(Dragnet, The FBI).*[6] Through stories of individual criminal cases involving Holocaust survivors, former Nazis, or neo-Nazis, these episodes explore the larger challenge of coming to terms with the injustices of the Holocaust in the early postwar era. These episodes feature recurring plots (such as the capture of a Nazi war criminal) and imagery (swastikas or numbers tattooed on the forearms of former concentration camp inmates), which evince the consolidation of the Holocaust as a readily recognized historical concept in American public culture at this time. Moreover, the larger issues addressed in these "guest" appearances by the Holocaust demonstrate its emergence as a moral paradigm in American discourse. In these dramas the Holocaust sometimes serves, for instance, as a test case in the limits of social justice, or as a study on the nature of evil.

Other genres of episodic series—especially science fiction—presented more inventive "guest" appearances by the Holocaust. Indeed, science fiction's conventions of traveling through outer space and forward or backward in time, of fabricating whole new worlds and defying the laws of nature, offer an unrivaled expanse in which to engage imaginatively with all manner of topical "guest" issues. The great flexibility and selectivity that producers exercise in science fiction programs reveal much about the significance they attach to the various contemporary subjects being explored in supernatural guise. At the same time, these qualities of the genre also engender its limitations for examining a specific issue in an invented, analogous setting.

The Holocaust first made a "guest" appearance on *The Twilight Zone* during that program's third season. This program, which aired on CBS from 1959 to 1965, does not typify episodic series; there are no recurrent characters or situations linking the installments. Rather, the episodes share a larger common theme: the exploration of what series creator Rod Serling called "another dimension, a dimension not only of sight and sound, but of mind, a journey into a wondrous land whose boundaries are that of imagination . . . the Twilight Zone."[7] During his heyday as a television playwright, Serling wrote several television scripts that dealt with the Holocaust. In addition to two *Twilight Zone* episodes, there is his 1960 script for *Playhouse 90*, entitled "In the Presence of Mine Enemies," which is set in the Warsaw Ghetto, and "Hate Syndrome," a 1966 drama about neo-Nazism and Jewish self-hatred, for the syndicated religion series *Insight*.

Serling's first *Twilight Zone* episode to deal with this subject, entitled "Death's Head Revisited," aired on November 10, 1961.[8] This broadcast took place a few months after the war crimes trial of Adolf Eichmann, held in Jerusalem, had been shown on television in the United States and around the world. Like most episodes of *The Twilight Zone*, "Death's Head Revisited" uses supernatural situations and events (realized through a variety of visual and audial special-effects techniques) to explore social and ethical issues of general relevance to American audiences (in this case, issues raised by the Eichmann trial) in otherworldly "morality plays."[9]

This half-hour drama begins with the arrival of a man, who identifies himself as Mr. Schmidt, at an inn in a small town in Germany. The innkeeper seems to recognize him and tells Schmidt that he reminds her of someone who had been there during the war; he responds that he spent the war at the Russian front. Schmidt asks the innkeeper about there having been a concentration camp nearby, and he presses her to utter its name: Dachau.

At this point Serling (who narrates off-camera) explains that Schmidt's real name is Lutze, and that seventeen years earlier he had been a captain in the SS. Now Lutze plans a nostalgic visit to the former concentration camp, his "old haunts. . . . What he does not know, of course," Serling continues, "is that a place like Dachau cannot exist only in Bavaria. . . . By its very nature, it must be one of the populated areas of the Twilight Zone."

The scene changes to the grounds of the former concentration camp. Lutze arrives and walks around the courtyard. As he looks at various landmarks—former gallows, barracks, and offices—ghostly images of camp inmates, dressed in striped uniforms, fade into view and then disappear. Recalling his past, embodied in an apparition of himself wearing his SS uniform, Lutze surveys all that he sees with satisfaction. Suddenly a man in a striped prisoner's uniform appears, standing in front of one of the camp buildings. Addressing Lutze as Captain, the former prisoner says, "We've been waiting for you."

Lutze, frightened, turns to run for the gate. The image cuts to a shot of the gate swinging shut and its lock bolting by itself. Lutze turns around; the man in the uniform is standing closer to him. Lutze recognizes the man as Alfred Becker, a former inmate. Lutze tells Becker to stop addressing him as Captain, as he is no longer a soldier. "The uniform you wore cannot be stripped off, it was part of you," Becker responds. "A tattoo, Captain"—Becker displays a number on his arm "a skull and crossbones burned into your soul." Lutze tells Becker that "that's all in the past"; during the war he simply "functioned as I was told." There is an eerie moaning; Becker tells Lutze that it is the sound of his victims, outraged by Lutze's dismissal of his wartime activities: "Ten million human beings were tortured to death in camps like this. . . . And you come back to your scenes of horror and you wonder that the misery that you planted has lived after you!?"

A nightmarish sequence follows, in which Lutze finds himself surrounded by a group of stern-faced men in prisoner's uniforms. Becker announces that the inmates of Dachau will try Lutze for "crimes against humanity." As his trial begins, Lutze loses consciousness. When he reawakens, Becker informs Lutze that the trial is over; he has been found guilty, and a sentence has been handed down: "From this day on you shall be rendered insane."

Lutze runs for the gate to the camp; it won't open. Becker appears suddenly at his side, saying, "At this gate you shot down hundreds of people with machine guns. Do you feel it now, Captain? Do you feel the bullets smashing into your body?" The sound of machine-gun fire is heard; Lutze writhes in pain and staggers across the courtyard. Becker continues to lead Lutze from one part of the camp to another, describing the suffering of the Nazi's victims at each site. Lutze screams, reels from place to place, and eventually falls to the ground as though having a violent seizure. Becker stands over the tormented man and concludes, "Captain Lutze, . . . this is not revenge, this is justice. But this is only the beginning. . . . Your final judgment—will come from God."

The epilogue to "Death's Head Revisited" fades up on a shot of policemen, a taxi driver, and a doctor standing over Lutze, who has been heavily sedated. They wonder what could have turned him into a "raving maniac" in the two hours since the driver left him at the gate. The doctor surveys the camp grounds and asks, "Dachau. . . . Why do we keep it standing?" As the camera pans around the camp, Serling replies off-camera:

> All the Dachaus must remain standing—the Dachaus, the Belsens, the Buchenwalds, the Auschwitzes. . . . They must remain standing because they are a monument to a moment in time when some men decided to turn the Earth into a graveyard. Into it they shoveled all of their reason, their logic, their knowledge—but worst of all, their conscience. And the moment we forget this, . . . then we become the gravediggers. Something to dwell on and to remember—not only in the Twilight Zone, but wherever men walk God's Earth.

"Death's Head Revisited" implicitly retries Eichmann in the otherworldly court of the Twilight Zone. In so doing, Serling's script abstracts and simplifies the Eichmann trial, offering viewers a more satisfying, if much less complex, drama than did the four months of proceedings televised from Jerusalem. The fictitious Captain Lutze metonymizes Nazism, as Eichmann did in his war crimes trial. (Serling's script hints at this parallel through the occasional detail, such as Lutze's changing of his name and seeking refuge in South America after the war.) Unlike the Eichmann trial, however, "Death's Head Revisited" presents the origins of Nazism as a supernatural, absolute evil, stripped of any ties to history. The *Twilight Zone* drama further reduces the trial to a contest between two individuals: Lutze versus Becker. Significantly, the script never explains why Becker had been interned in Dachau; his name might signify either a German or a Jew. Becker and his silent, anonymous fellow inmates try and condemn Lutze on generalized "crimes against humanity." In contrast, Eichmann was charged by the Israeli government with crimes against the Jewish people as well as against humanity, and his trial was staged, in part, as an effort to demonstrate the singular nature of Nazi persecution of European Jewry and the central role that anti-Semitism played in Nazi ideology.

The spectacle of Eichmann on trial had proved frustrating and unsatisfying to many viewers. His ordinary appearance and undemonstrative demeanor doubtless played an important role in the widespread acceptance of Hannah Arendt's summing up of the Eichmann case as a lesson in the "banality of evil."[10] In contrast, "Death's Head Revisited" portrays its Nazi war criminal as a histrionically depraved sadist who clearly delights in the torment of his victims. Serling's drama offers viewers an imaginary trial of its villain that delivers swift, unambiguous, and demonstrative justice, thereby satisfying impulses that television's protracted presentation of the actual Eichmann trial left unfulfilled for many. Thanks to both the technical capabilities of television's special effects and the liberating possibilities of the science fiction genre, "Death's Head Revisited" was able to offer viewers the rewarding spectacle of the victims of Nazism rising from the dead to bring their persecutor to justice. In contrast to Eichmann's much-debated fate—at the time of this *Twilight Zone* telecast the international press was full of suggestions as to how the Israeli court might appropriately punish him[11]—Lutze's sentence provides viewers with the fulfillment of seeing the depraved tormentor become the victim of his own tortures.

In other "guest" appearances on American television in the 1960s the Holocaust is invoked as a means of addressing contemporary events and issues that are less directly connected to the Nazi persecution of European Jewry. "Patterns of Force," an episode of the original *Star Trek* series (shown on NBC from 1966 to 1969), also demonstrates how the Holocaust iconography of American television can play a critical role in the dramatic realization of the Holocaust as a moral paradigm. "Patterns of Force," which first aired on February 16, 1968, is a typical installment of *Star Trek*. It offers an encounter between the inhabitants of a fictitious planet and the crew of the starship *Enterprise*—who are mandated by the interplanetary Federation to patrol the galaxy, in order to gather scientific information and promote security. Although set in the twenty-third century, these tales of space travel, like the otherworldly morality plays of *The Twilight Zone,* resonate with social issues that concern contemporary American audiences. In this episode the *Enterprise,* under the command of Captain Kirk, visits two neighboring planets: Ekos, reputed to be inhabited by "a primitive, warlike people in a state of anarchy," and Zeon, which "has a relatively high technology and [whose] people are peaceful."[12] The *Enterprise*'s crew is looking for John Gill, a former acquaintance from Earth. A prominent historian who was once Kirk's mentor, Gill was sent to Ekos by the Federation years earlier as a "cultural adviser," but he hasn't been heard from for years.

Kirk and the *Enterprise*'s science officer, Mr. Spock, arrive on Ekos, where they discover, to their astonishment, that the planet has been transformed into a replica of Nazi Germany in the 1930s. Ekosians, wearing jackboots and swastika-adorned uniforms, have taken on the role of Nazi aggressors, while Zeons are the victims of the Ekosians' hatred and persecution. On a public "viewing screen" (i.e., a large outdoor television) Kirk and Spock watch a news report announcing that "today the *Führer* has ordered our glorious capital to be made Zeon-free." (The voice-over on the news report accompanies vintage black-and-white footage from the Nazi era, including images of Wehrmacht troops marching in formation, intercut with original shots, also in black and white, that feature characters who later appear in the episode.) The news broadcast ends with a salute to the "*Führer*"—whom Kirk recognizes as none other than John Gill.

Kirk and Spock resolve to find Gill and learn how he came to be the leader of this replication of the Third Reich. They disguise themselves as Nazis, only to be discovered and arrested. In prison they meet Isak, a Zeon captive whom they had seen being beaten in the street earlier, who is a member of an underground resistance movement. Spock asks Isak why the Nazi Ekosians hate Zeons. Isak replies, "Because with no one to hate there would be nothing to hold them together. So the party has built us into a threat, a disease to be wiped out."

Spock and Kirk escape from prison with Isak. He introduces them to members of the Zeon resistance movement, who are headquartered in an underground sewer. Eventually Spock and Kirk infiltrate Nazi headquarters and find Gill, who has been drugged into compliance by Melakon, the Nazi Ekosians' second in command. Roused from his drug-induced stupor, Gill explains that he "interfered" with the Ekosian culture because the planet was "fragmented, divided." He decided to take a "lesson from Earth history" and replicate the Third Reich because it was the "most efficient state Earth ever knew." At first the plan worked, Gill explains, until Melakon took over and initiated a campaign of racial hatred against the Zeons. With Kirk's help, Gill broadcasts an announcement denouncing Melakon and canceling the assault on the Zeons. Melakon is assassinated by Isak, but not before the Ekosian fatally shoots Gill. As he dies, Gill tells Kirk, "I was wrong. The noninterference direction is the only way. We must stop the slaughter. . . . Even historians fail to learn from history. They repeat the same mistakes. Let the killing end." Then, with Ekosians and Zeons reconciled, Kirk pronounces the planet to be "in good hands" before returning with Spock to the *Enterprise*.

As in the Holocaust's other "guest" appearances on television, "Patterns of Force" evokes the Nazi era with the appearance of swastikas, SS and Gestapo uniforms, and Nazi salutes, as well as vintage black-and-white footage from the Nazi era. In addition, the dialogue is sprinkled with idioms associated with the Third Reich: "*Führer*," "Final Solution," "racial purity," and so on.

But rather than signaling to viewers a drama set during the Nazi period or against the background of a postwar neo-Nazi movement, these elements are signs of a fictitious totalitarian culture; indeed, they figure as an integral part of its realization.

Moreover, the ease with which viewers recognize these Nazi terms and symbols signals the potential for universal adoption of the principles of the regime that they represent. Not only were Ekosians thus able to become Nazis in a matter of a few years; both Zeons (who are physically indistinguishable from Ekosians) and Earthlings such as Kirk can "pass" for Ekosian Nazis. (When Kirk first dons his Gestapo disguise, Spock comments dryly that he "should make a very convincing Nazi"; by implication, anyone—even the series' protagonist—can easily become a Nazi.) In this science fiction replication, Nazism is presented as a discrete and externally induced phenomenon—imported to this part of the universe by the "alien" John Gill. On its own, Nazism—its ideology, vocabulary, gestures, and wardrobe—instigates genocidal strife between Zeon and Ekos, who otherwise have no apparent history of hostile relations.

Indeed, "Patterns of Force" uses Spock to dramatize the ordeal of being stigmatized as "other," rather than doing so through the conflict between Ekos and Zeon. The son of a human mother and Vulcan father, Spock has greenish skin, pointed ears, and prominently slanted eyebrows. The consequences of Spock's "alien" manner and appearance are a running feature of the series. Thus, when Spock disguises himself as an SS officer in "Patterns of Force," Kirk comments that the helmet he wears "covers a multitude of sins." Later, while trying to enter Nazi Party headquarters in search of Gill, they are stopped by a suspicious Ekosian superior officer. He orders Spock to remove his helmet while Ekosian soldiers surround him, their weapons drawn. As Spock complies with the order, the camera closes in on his face, and ominous background music swells to a suspenseful climax as the scene ends.

Spock plays a focal role in a later scene that directly evokes Nazi racial policies. When he, Kirk, and the resistance fighters infiltrate Nazi Party headquarters in search of Gill, Kirk creates a momentary diversion by pretending to be a Zeon officer who has discovered an "alien" spy (Spock) masquerading as a Nazi. Kirk turns Spock over to Melakon, who, as an expert on the "genetics of racial purity," analyzes the specimen: "Note the sinister eyes and the malformed ears—definitely an inferior race. Note the low forehead, denoting stupidity—the dull look of a trapped animal." Melakon orders Spock executed: "I want the body saved for the cultural museum. He'll make an interesting display." (Spock is, of course, rescued before any harm befalls him.)

Viewers of *Star Trek* have variously understood Spock's archetypal "otherness" as analogous to that of African Americans and Asians, among other cultural groups.[13] Here, however, the connections between Spock's alien identity and Jewishness seem deliberate. Race science figured prominently in the ideology of Nazi anti-Semitism, and the Third Reich had planned to exhibit Jewish culture after the war in a "Central Museum of the Defunct Jewish Race." Spock's unmasking in the earlier scene resonates with stories of Jews living under Nazi occupation who attempted to pass as non-Jews, only to be "betrayed" by physical differences—notably circumcision—that can be concealed but not easily undone. (Knowing that actor Leonard Nimoy, who plays Spock, is a Jew might further reinforce this association for some viewers.) Other references in the script also suggest that the creators of "Patterns of Force" modeled the conflict between Ekosians and Zeons on the Nazi persecution of Jews in particular. Zeons have names similar to those of biblical heroes (besides Isak, there are Abrom and Dovid), while the name Zeon is perhaps a deliberate play on Zion.

Indeed, the image of Zeons rising up to defeat their enemies may have recalled a more recent Zionist triumph for some of the first viewers of "Patterns of Force," which was aired on February 16, 1968, less than a year after the Six-Day War between Israel and its neighbors. However, the drama resonates even more powerfully with the United States' military involvement in Vietnam and the burgeoning American antiwar movement. Throughout the 1960s American television audiences had been watching another drama of "advisers" who had originally been sent to observe a foreign conflict—which in this case was presented on nightly news reports. By 1968 these advisers had actively intervened in the internal operations of the struggle and escalated the violence between North and South Vietnam, which compelled increasing numbers of Americans to protest. Gill's final words in "Patterns of Force" ("Let the killing end") seem less meaningful with regard to the immediate dramatic situation (he has already called off the attack on Zeon) than they are as a tragic figure's final words of wisdom, addressed to the drama's audience.

Indeed, this and several other episodes of *Star Trek* are, according to Alasdair Spark, part of an extensive effort to "represent a mythic reworking" in science fiction—"the best available medium—of the American experience in Vietnam."[14] John Hellmann argues, in his study of "American myth and the legacy of Vietnam," that such science fiction "reworkings" of the United

States' experiences in Vietnam offered "a vision of Americans' opportunity, in the midst of a fallen mythic landscape, to take control of their destiny by taking control of their national consciousness, and thus self-consciously work out the implications of the Vietnam experience for their larger journey through history."[15]

Yet in "Patterns of Force" Gill concludes that "even historians fail to learn from history"—a striking departure from the notion, embodied in George Santayana's often-quoted phrase, that "those who cannot remember the past are condemned to repeat it."[16] Gill's words are not simply more pessimistic; they subvert Santayana's faith in the social value of documenting and studying history. Indeed history, as embodied by Gill, is a threat to *Star Trek*'s utopian vision of future interplanetary social harmony. The notion of "history repeating itself"—enacted here by vintage footage, costumes, gestures, and rhetoric—is understood as dangerous not because of a failure to learn from past mistakes but because of a failure to escape history's destructive power. Far from offering edification, history in "Patterns of Force" provides the blueprint for genocide. All that prevents Nazi Ekosians from destroying Zeons are the universalist forces of good, embodied by the multinational crew of the *Enterprise* and the edenic ideals of the Federation. This episode of *Star Trek* is a cautionary tale, warning that another Holocaust is the potential consequence of misguided efforts to make a progressivist application of the "lessons" of history. The Holocaust is thus conceptualized as a kind of sociopolitical Flying Dutchman, careening through space and time; as the title "Patterns of Force" implies, it is a powerful paradigm with the potential for repeated reenactments.

The Holocaust's "guest" appearances on American television in the 1960s demonstrate how broadcasters sought ways of accommodating the desire to address serious, controversial issues while delivering a reliable, consistent product of broadest possible appeal. By presenting it as a paradigmatic moral issue of universal significance, American broadcasters helped to situate the Holocaust in the nation's canon of contemporary social concerns. Along with race relations, poverty, the nuclear arms race, government corruption, environmental issues, and so forth, the Holocaust began to be understood as a concern for all Americans.

In the ensuing decades the Holocaust has continued to turn up as a "guest" on many more of American television's episodic series. In addition to more broadcasts in series about crime (including episodes of *Cannon, Columbo, Quincy, M.E., Kojak, L.A. Law, Bodies of Evidence,* and *Law and Order*) there have been installments of the newspaper series *Lou Grant,* even the situation comedy *All in the Family* and the children's adventure series *The Adventures of Superboy,* that deal with the Holocaust.[17] This growing roster of appearances has helped turn the Holocaust into what one critic termed a "household" word in the United States, a subject with which many Americans now feel they are on familiar and intimate terms.[18] The Holocaust seems attainable, comprehensible, and therefore applicable to other situations.

Television thus epitomizes America's singular embrace of the Holocaust. Even though—and yet also because—it is an event remote from most Americans' experience or environment, it is widely available through an expanding inventory of mediations as a paradigm that has attracted repeated encounters. Remarkably, the passage of time has not made the Holocaust less available to Americans; instead, it has only developed a deeper and more varied set of symbolic associations. This poses a challenge both to historical understandings of the Holocaust as rooted in a particular constellation of social, political, economic, and ideological contexts, and to philosophical approaches to the subject that place the Holocaust on an ontological plateau of its own. American television's presentations of this subject may not represent well the historian's Holocaust or the philosopher's, but they do offer distinctive insights into how this extraordinary chapter of history has become a moral fixture in the daily lives of millions of Americans.

3 IMAGINING SURVIVORS

Testimony and the Rise of Holocaust Consciousness

Henry Greenspan

1978

In his book *Preserving Memory,* Edward Linenthal reflected that 1978 was "a crucial year in the organization of Holocaust consciousness" in the United States.[1] He recalled the public reaction to the Nazi march in Skokie, Illinois; Jimmy Carter's establishment of a presidential commission on the Holocaust that would eventually oversee the creation of the United States Holocaust Memorial Museum; and the airing of NBC's miniseries *Holocaust,* watched by an estimated 120 million people over four evenings that April. The television drama especially was a watershed event and began a trend that has continued. "From 1962 until 1978, Hollywood made almost no films directly related to the Holocaust," historian David Wyman observed. Since *Holocaust,* he noted, there has been a steady stream.[2] Raul Hilberg, reflecting on the transformation, also pointed to the significance of 1978. Along with all the other developments, he described the surge in academic study of the Holocaust that began at that time:

> Here, in the United States, something happened. We can almost pinpoint when. It was roughly 1978. Naturally such developments don't really have a precise date on which they begin. And yet, here was a television play that the author, Gerald Green, could not have sold to any network five or ten years earlier. Here was a nationalization of the Holocaust by Executive Order establishing a President's Commission. . . . Here, we see the multiplication of books about the Holocaust, of courses about the Holocaust, of curricula about the Holocaust, of conferences about the Holocaust.[3]

Here too was the emergence of Holocaust survivors in American public awareness. Through their participation in the newly forming commemorative activities and institutions—and particularly in their increasingly celebrated role as witnesses—survivors also began to be heard in the late 1970s, often for the first time.[4] In Joan Ringelheim's 1992 survey of survivor testimony collections in the United States, for example, virtually every project—thirty-seven of forty-three—had been founded since 1977. The great majority of these were established by the mid-1980s, less than a decade after, as Hilberg put it, "something happened."[5]

While I was not initially aware of being part of a more general trend, my own formal interviewing of survivors also began in 1978. This was for a study on form, context, and motive in survivors' retelling of Holocaust memory—issues that continue to guide much of my work.[6] What I did not anticipate when I began, however, was the centrality of listeners, and our history as listeners, in survivors' own reflections. Again and again survivors asked, Why was it that Americans (and not only Jewish Americans) were suddenly so interested in their testimony? What had changed after thirty years? And even with all the films and books and oral history projects, how well do listeners actually hear what survivors are trying to convey? Given the expectations and presumptions that listeners clearly bring, how well *can* they hear? The last two questions continue to emerge in my interviews with survivors—even more often today than twenty years ago.

These are the key questions, originally survivors' own questions, that organize what follows. First, I discuss some of the ways survivors and their recounting have been received and imagined during the years since liberation, with particular attention to the changes that arose in the late 1970s. Inevitably this means painting with broad strokes, trying to elucidate major trends and tendencies—what I call "discourses"—rather than attending to the variety of manifestations and exceptions those trends always embrace. Second, I focus on the discrepancy between these discourses about survivors and what survivors seem actually to have to tell us—particularly as that discrepancy has developed since the late 1970s. The gap ought not to be surprising. Changing ways of receiving survivors reflect less and less the Holocaust than fears and wishes emerging from our own historical circumstances. Indeed, the ways we have imagined survivors can be quite powerful indicators of wider cultural trends, trends that are not always for the better.

Even under the most promising circumstances, however, listening to survivors presents unique challenges. And it will help set a context for what follows to describe first a much more deliberate effort to imagine survivors and survival: the effort within my own classroom.

TO BE AND NOT TO BE

A Language Course

While listening to survivors' reflections, nothing is more common than to think we follow when we do not. If we have a particular stake in what we are hearing—and we virtually always do—we are not apt to doubt whatever confirms our expectations. But even aside from needs or motives, we can only hear the words we hear. Primo Levi argued that retelling the destruction required a new language—even a new *kind* of language.[7] But the language survivors use is, in actuality, the same as our own. Their references, however, are to memories we do not share, and even their silences, however abrupt and consuming, do not betray their source.

In my undergraduate seminar at the University of Michigan, "On Listening to Holocaust Survivors," I try to convey the challenges we face. As one of the first exercises I cite this passage from Elie Wiesel: "Hamlet was just romantic and the question he asked himself was too simplistic. The problem is not: to be or not to be. But rather: to be and not to be."[8] I then ask, "In the context of a survivor's experience, what does it mean 'to be and not to be'? Indeed, what can it possibly mean for anyone 'to be *and* not to be'?"

My students are not shy. The more existential among them—and there are many—rise quickly to the challenge. "It means Wiesel's spirit died, and now he just lives on in body." That is almost always the first and most popular interpretation. I respond, "*Did* his spirit die? Could he, for example, have written *Night* without it?" (I could have also wondered—and later do—what makes them so sure that his body did *not* die?)

We go on. Someone says, "It means he has two lives: the one before the Holocaust, and the one after. His life is split in two." "OK," I ask, "in which one is he being? In which one is he not being?" The class itself splits in two: "He's not in his life from before because it was destroyed." But then: "He's not in his new life because he has lost everything." Confusion rises. I stir it up: "So, in effect, he's not anywhere?" "Yeah, it means he's half-dead," someone volunteers, with a level of enthusiasm that is itself half-dead. "So he's just sort of bummed out, good days and bad days?" Someone may then say this: "It's like he's two places at once. He's still in the camps. And he's also not."

"Two places at once." This has more promise, especially when we juxtapose other voices that my students have started to hear. "I live within a twofold being," says Charlotte Delbo in the extraordinary pages that Lawrence Langer especially has brought to our attention.[9] A man whose video interview we've watched says, "Each one of us lives on two levels, the normal, the so-called normal, and the not." In her memoir *Saving the Fragments* Isabella Leitner writes, "It is hard enough to live in one world; we are destined to live forever in two." Elsewhere she reflects, "We have these double lives. I talk to you and I am not only here."[10]

"Two places at once." I suggest to my class that there is no image more re-curring in survivors' reflections than this radical, unresolvable doubleness. "It's a paradox," someone volunteers, perhaps the theorist of "half-dead" re-born as a dialectician. Another discussion evolves along the following lines: A paradox is when two apparently contradictory things make sense at some higher, synthetic level. But here there is no higher level. It never makes sense to be and not be at the same time. We cannot resolve this contradiction through any logical operation, and so the idea of "paradox" is misleading. But perhaps we can still accept the contradiction *as* a contradiction. That is, we can simply grab one side, and grab the other side, and hold on.

From there, many things become possible. Returning to Delbo, we may note that while the two worlds she describes encircle each other, pull against each other, negate and sometimes disfigure each other, they also have strangely nothing to do with each other. "Thirst," Delbo wrote, evokes either normal thirst or the sensory memory of *that* thirst. Both cannot be real and true at once, even though both remain, at the same time, real and true.[11]

And further, at the core of that world—returning as a nightmare, flash-back, terror, taste, or smell—we do indeed find "not to be"; we find death it-self. My students read from Jean Amery: "Torture blots out the contradiction of death and allows us to experience it personally." And "whoever was tor-tured stays tortured."[12] Wiesel wrote, "Death is something other, something more, than the simple absence of life. . . . Death may invade a creature even though life has not yet departed."[13] In her recurring nightmare Delbo is in-vaded again and again: "The pain is so unbearable, so exactly the pain I suf-fered there, that I feel it again physically, I feel it through my whole body. . . . I feel death seizing me, I feel myself die."[14]

The problem is "to be and not to be." As a number of interpreters have suggested, the word *survival* itself becomes problematic.[15] Here, at least, it is not a living beyond and after but an ongoing life and an ongoing death, a liv-ing after and a dying after, in some kind of permanent irresolution.

If my students have a hard time getting to this point, they are not alone. Even among those who have spent years attempting to understand the dualities inherent in surviving, the debates continue: Is it "death in life" or "life in death" that should be the primary focus? Trauma or resilience? Injury or strength? Those who focus on resilience tend to dismiss those who focus on injury. The latter group, equally certain of their data, are dismissive in turn. Meanwhile, what the literature may most reveal—and here I speak especially about the psychological literature—is less about survivors than about our own uncertainty, as well as our capacity to improvise. Recurrently, in the best work one sees constructs invoked that have little grounding in *any* theory but are required *descriptively* nonetheless. Thus, we read of "integration" despite persisting "psychological black holes";[16] of shattered "basic trust" alongside "islands of surprisingly good functioning"; of "encapsulated" normal adjustment together with "encapsulated" disorganizing terror.[17] Thirty years ago psychiatrist Henry Krystal, himself a survivor, observed, "It is not rare in the 'survivor syndrome' to see people fully sane during the day, but psychotic every night."[18]

"The problem is: to be and not to be." Despite all the efforts that have developed to make psychological sense of survivors' experience, the truth is that we are still struggling. Existing concepts simply do not well enough explain how the obvious strengths, creativity, and engagement so many survivors demonstrate really *can* coexist with a severity of injury that is also indisputable.[19] Perhaps reflecting survivors' own struggle, psychological writing about survivors is also a literature of unresolved contradictions.

In the culture at large, the response to survivors has been less subtle. Speaking broadly, rather than even engaging the contradictions and dualities that constitute surviving, the tendency has been to take one side or the other and make it the whole. Thus, responding to the deaths survivors know—and which to us they represent—survivors are depicted as archetypal victims, guilty, ghostly, silent, and estranged. Focusing on ongoing life—the fact of survival itself—the same survivors are celebrated as heroic witnesses, tellers of tales, redeemers of the human spirit and of hope. As I shall elaborate, each of these poles has generated its own discourse—rhetorics that are now invoked almost automatically in public references to survivors.

It was the dominance of these rhetorics—what I have called "celebratory" and "psychiatric" discourse—that became characteristic of public response to survivors in the late 1970s and that continues today. Earlier, however, survivors were greeted in a very different way. In order to grasp the transformation, those first years should also be revisited.

Another Kind of Exile

The general lack of American interest in the Holocaust and in survivors during the first decades after the war is now well known. What is perhaps less known, however, is that this was not simply an absence, a vacuum of responsiveness, but an active process of suppression and stigmatization. Perhaps also less known is the response of survivors themselves to the silencing they experienced.

Before survivors became "the survivors" they were known by other names. For many years in this country they were "the refugees," the "greeners" (greenhorns), or simply "the ones who were there." Associated with the horrifying newsreels of the liberated camps—even though many had survived in hiding or under false identity and had never been in a camp—they evoked a shifting combination of pity, fear, revulsion, and guilt.[20] In general, they were isolated and avoided. Elie Wiesel summarized:

> As they reentered the world, they found themselves in another kind of exile, another kind of prison. People welcomed them with tears and sobs, then turned away. I don't mean parents or close friends; I speak of officialdom, of the man in the street. I speak of all kinds of men and women who treated them as one would sick and needy relatives. Or else as specimens to be observed and to be kept apart from the rest of society by invisible barbed wire. They were disturbing misfits who deserved charity, but nothing else.[21]

During these years, then, to be singled out as a Holocaust survivor meant to be singled out indeed: a "sick and needy relative," "a specimen to be observed." Manny Petchek, a survivor of Auschwitz and other camps, recalled the way he was singled out and known:

> People would meet me and say, "OHHHHH! Did you know that he was in a concentration camp?!" That's all it was left to! Nobody asked about it. Nobody asked, "How was it there?" Just: "He was in a concentration camp." It was pity, and that was that. "This is my nephew,"

my uncle would introduce me, "you know, *he* was in a concentration camp."[22]

"That's all it was left to," one must assume, because in these years that said it all.

Clearly, nothing in these attitudes would have encouraged survivors' recounting or the kind of public occasions for "bearing witness" that were to evolve later. While there was a flurry of testimony in the months immediately after the war—and again during the period of the Eichmann trial in 1961—the receptivity of listeners was short-lived.[23] In fact, many survivors recall being directly silenced, even when—in spite of all—they did try to talk about it. Manny continued:

> I personally would have felt much better if I could have talked about it. I didn't feel that I couldn't. Nobody cared. I mean, people, everybody was talking they didn't want to hear about it. They didn't want to listen. No, they said, "We heard about it." Or, "We don't want to hear about it because we saw the newsreels." . . . We felt very uncomfortable suppressing it all the time. And dreaming about it. And having nightmares about it. It may sound silly, but I heard this expression when I first came to this country: "When you laugh, everybody laughs with you. When you cry, you cry by yourself." And that's exactly what we did.

Strangely enough, quite a number of survivors recall this particular song lyric about laughing together and crying alone. It must have epitomized the spirit of adjustment, putting the past behind one, moving on—the spirit, in short, of the times.

A "Conspiracy of Silence"?

Typically these years of silencing are discussed in terms of a "conspiracy of silence": the notion that, just as others were not yet ready to hear, survivors themselves were not yet ready to speak. It is difficult to generalize. Unquestionably most survivors were hesitant. Recounting meant finding words for horrors for which there are no words. It meant confronting listeners' misunderstanding, resistance, and, sometimes, outright rejection. It meant remembering, and sometimes reexperiencing, terror or humiliation or a torment that survivors like Delbo describe as death itself. For all of these reasons, recounting could be agony. But equally agonizing was the prospect of not recounting. Primo Levi insisted that "the need to tell our story . . . was an immediate and violent impulse," a "primary need" like "the need to eat or to drink."[24] And we have heard Manny affirm that he would have wanted to talk about it—that he himself *could* have talked about it.

Like the duality of survival itself, an ongoing life together with an ongoing death, it may be most accurate to understand survivors' wish to speak and their wish to remain silent simply *as* a contradiction. That is, it is neither the case that survivors "wanted to talk about it" nor that "they didn't want to talk about it." In most instances survivors wanted both, both at once, without integration or synthesis. Wiesel said of his memories, "It is as impossible to speak of them as not to speak of them."[25] Survivors' retelling takes form within these twin impossibilities, as their lives take form within other contradictions, equally unresolved.

What is perhaps most interesting is that even survivors who first recall not having wanted to "talk about it" often come to suggest, in a later interview, that this was actually not the case. Such, for example, was true of Paula Marcus, a survivor of Birkenau and Ravensbruck. Initially Paula remembered not having been willing or able to speak of her experiences: "I hid it even from myself, for many years." She was thus surprised when, in our third interview, she reviewed diary entries she had written during the first days after liberation, literally within forty-eight hours of having survived a death march. Then fifteen years old, Paula wrote in 1945 about the extraordinary care with which she and a few other Auschwitz survivors were received in a former prisoner-of-war camp in which they happened to be liberated:

> The men look at us with astonishment. We are still in our dirty camp clothes, so it is not surprising that they are shocked by our appearance. . . . We don't understand each other's languages, but we do understand their kindness and compassion. Soon we are able to take warm showers and sink into bed. How good it feels!
>
> The room fills with inquiring Frenchmen, Yugoslavs, British, and others of many nationalities. They are soldiers, former prisoners-of-war, who had not seen anyone like us before. They are interested in our fate. . . .
>
> Even at this moment, the crematorium remains our nightmare. We are telling everybody about it, whether we want to or not. Our stories are only about the crematorium, whether we want to or not. Because ei-

ther in my dreams or when I am awake, I can only see the flames in front of me. And the vision never fades.

Too much talk is tiring. The visitors are courteous. They would like to stay longer, but the doctor makes them leave.[26]

Paula's entry suggests recounting as the compelling impulse, the "primary need," that Levi described. Amidst the compassion and interest of her listeners, she and the other survivors retell memories of the crematoria "whether we want to or not." The survivors become tired; otherwise, the men would listen longer.[27]

Despite the nightmare that continued to consume her, Paula recalled this time at liberation as one of the most confirming in her life. She was surrounded by a warmth and solidarity that were scarcely conceivable after the terror and degradation she had just escaped; and she responded with hope. A day after she wrote the entry above, she noted, "We talk about the past and the future. And the future and the past. Now good will come. . . . I think we could get back very fast to a regular life—a normal, human way of life—as we were used to years before." Buoyed by others' care, she apparently found it possible in 1945 not only to know both an ongoing death and an ongoing life but also to retell both.

Two years later, now far from the group she had known at liberation, Paula expressed an entirely different mood in her diary. She had become isolated and frustrated, unable to share her memories or her distress with anyone. Indeed, this was a period in which Paula's diary itself became more and more important as an alternative, private context of recounting. "God, what's wrong with me?" she wrote. "I'm choked with my own cry. I'd like to cry but I can't. Today I came home all angered, for no reason." In a related entry she suggested more about why she might have choked her cry and why she was so angry. "It's hard to be smart," she noted. "But it's harder yet, with a smart head, to live as though ignorant."

Three years later, in 1950, Paula felt even more isolated. She now expressed much greater conflict about how she had and had not followed her "smart head" and why she lived "as though ignorant." By this time she had arrived in the United States and had discovered the mood, and even the song lyric, that Manny also remembered. Twenty years old, writing on the fifth anniversary of her liberation, Paula confided to her diary:

Five years is like half a century when you live your life with bitterness

and reminiscing. . . . Is this anger? Is this conscience? Is this self-awareness or self-criticism? . . .

Five years. It's not long to write it down. And it's easy to pronounce
it. But when I remember, I am carried back even more clearly than any-
time before. But why?

I don't know what I am. I don't know when I'm doing right or
wrong. Am I right when I'm thinking? And for what I am thinking?
Many times, I think I was just born for trouble. To be a burden and sorrow to everybody, because I cannot laugh. They say, "If you laugh,
everybody laughs with you. And if you cry, you cry alone." Yes my diary,
here I am—in America! . . .

But nobody's right and nobody's wrong. Only the truth is right. But
that is so rare. Now I'm pushing the years back. For me, that's like
putting the clock back a few minutes. Time elapses. But the impossible
does not fade from my eyes.

As remains characteristic of her, Paula now questions herself as much as she
questions outwardly. She only knows that "the truth is right," and, exactly as
she had written at liberation, the truth was an "impossible" that would not
fade from her eyes.

Looking back at these entries more than thirty years later, Paula expressed
mixed feelings. "It scares me to think how angry I was," she noted, "how desperate and how frustrated." But she was also still attached to the young
woman she had been and relieved to discover that she had not succumbed to
silence without a struggle. "Now I look back. It's frightening. But I am able to
realize that I still had feelings. I wasn't dead altogether. There was still a soul
deep down that wanted to come to the surface." This was also the context in
which Paula first spoke about the silencing *imposed* on survivors. If this was a
"conspiracy of silence," Paula made it clear that she joined late and without
enthusiasm. She recalled:

I had to really suppress it. To me, *I* was right. But the other side would
say, "Keep it to yourself because you will be locked up." Because everybody lived, "This is to forget!" You know, "Hush up your bad dreams!"

We were ashamed. We were made to feel ashamed. So I covered up.
"I'm fine, Joe! *That's* not me! How are *you?*" Because we were trying to
find a place in the community. We had to survive again, in a new country. We tried to get along, you know, "I'm an American too."

Manny likewise recalled the effort to adapt to circumstances and to "survive again":

> So what are we going to do? Ask for sympathy? "Come on! I'm a survivor from the Holocaust! Have some sympathy!"?
>
> *No!* We had to adapt ourselves to the mainstream. To make a new life. To fend for ourselves. . . . Here it's different. It's individual! *Everybody* is for themselves! You have to survive![28]

Continuing Isolation

Early on, then, many survivors learned to be "survivors" in a more typically American sense. At the same time, when they did "adapt to the mainstream," as so many successfully did, most discovered that they were still isolated. In Wiesel's phrase, "the invisible barbed wire" remained. And what he and other survivors recall can only be described as a continuing need, on the part of others, to view them as "sick and needy relatives," objects for observation or for pity. Thus, Manny notes that he remained the "nephew from the concentration camps" even after years of being well established in the States. However contradictory, to be an appropriate representative of the horror could be as much a demand on survivors as to be "an American too." Thus, Jack Goldman recalled:

> I was always uncomfortable when people would expect me to be the emaciated, depressed survivor every minute of my day. "Oh, you look so well," they would say, surprised that a year after liberation I no longer weighed eighty pounds, as I did when the Americans rescued me. And having a dull job and loving music, I used to whistle or hum a tune, without even knowing what I was humming or what the tune was, and people would say, "How can you whistle after all you've gone through?" Such questions seemed so ridiculous to me.[29]

Notwithstanding the song lyric, then, when survivors laughed or hummed a tune, the "whole world" did *not* laugh with them—perhaps because if that much fellowship was granted, the potential fellowship of fate might also have to be granted. Either way, it is no wonder that Manny concludes, "I was, as they say, 'part of the mainstream.' But I was not *in* the mainstream. Because I was very much alone. Very much."

Romancing Survival

Looking back from the perspective of the present, it is easy enough to be indignant about the silencing and stigmatization that survivors faced during the first years. Their exclusion from the common life, even while being enjoined to adapt to it, was simple and direct. The general refusal to listen to their recounting was blunt and undisguised. Yet perhaps there is also a sense in which these responses, exactly because they were so direct, can also be recalled with a certain nostalgia. Certainly they do reflect a genuine dread and revulsion in the face of the Holocaust, which are exactly the appropriate responses. And few could have imagined during these early years that those who survived that destruction would eventually be greeted as celebrants of life, redeemers of the human spirit, voices of heroic affirmation.

That, however, is precisely what happened. In an interview from the late 1970s, Sally Grubman, a survivor of Auschwitz and Ravensbruck, described the transformation:

> There is a tremendous interest in the Holocaust that we didn't see when we came. . . . I see an awakening of consciousness, but also some confusion about the reality. American Jewish teachers invite me into their classrooms to speak, but they do not want me to make the Holocaust a sad experience. They want me to turn us into heroes and create a heroic experience for the survivors. There is this book they use, *The Holocaust: A History of Courage and Resistance*, but the Holocaust was never a history of courage and resistance. It was a destruction by fire of innocent people, and it's not right to make it something it never was.
>
> We are not heroes. We survived by some fluke that we do not ourselves understand. And people have said, "Sally, tell the children about the joy of survival." And I can see that they don't understand it at all. If you're in a canoe and your life is in danger for a few minutes and you survive you can talk about the joy of survival. We went through fire and ashes and whole families were destroyed. And we are left. How can we talk about the joy of survival?[30]

In the first years after liberation, the Holocaust evoked terror, guilt, and a continuing unwillingness to believe. And, so soon afterward, making it "something it never was" was far less an option. The destruction and its implications could only be denied more directly, and the direct silencing and exclusion of survivors reflected that denial. Only much later, beginning in the 1970s, did a "tremendous interest" in surviving the Holocaust develop. Strange as it seems, once treated as the most alien of men and women, survivors were greeted more and more often as the most representative.

Unquestionably many factors contributed to the upsurge of interest in survivors and in the Holocaust more generally in these years. The passage of time itself, the evolving self-confidence and self-consciousness of the American Jewish community, the changing political climate in Israel, and the general American self-questioning after Vietnam have all been implicated.[31] In my own work I have argued that it is essential also to consider the much wider preoccupation with public and private disaster, destruction and victimization, surviving and survivalism, that became pervasive in America in the 1970s.[32]

These issues are extraordinarily complex, and I can only be schematic here. Suffice it to say, then, that beginning in the mid-1970s, images of "survival" and "survivors" emerged everywhere in American popular culture, manifest in all sorts of seemingly disparate contexts. As Christopher Lasch was the first to describe, everyday persistence and coping as much as actual life-and-death struggle were suddenly portrayed in survival terms. Applied so broadly, the rhetoric of extremity served both to express a persistent sense of crisis and, by overstatement, to dilute it. But whether invoked with irony or with dead seriousness, being "a survivor"—more specifically, being known as "a survivor"—became a kind of fashion.[33]

Thus, while a wave of docudramas depicted life after mass disaster—natural and nuclear, environmental and genocidal—the new people-magazines headlined as "survivors" almost everyone whose careers had staying power: Lauren Bacall, David Brinkley, or B. B. King. As victims of genuine terror became the center of public interest and everyday discussion—rape survivors, domestic violence survivors, survivors of childhood incest and abuse—there was an explosion of "How to Survive" guides covering every life contingency from the loss of a love, to falling in love, to getting a job, to "surviving" the job once you got it. While paramilitary "survivalist" groups formed to prepare for civilization's end, virtually every civilian sphere—from work life to family life, fiscal health to physical health—was framed in the new language of surviving and survival. A 1979 *New Yorker* drawing by Warren Miller perfectly captured the cachet that being "a survivor" had suddenly acquired. Depicting the archetypal two men stranded on a desert island, its caption had one exclaiming to the other, "That's what we are, all right—survivors! People will say, 'Hey, those two are real survivors! Talk about survivors—look at those two!' Yes, sirree, no doubt about it, when it comes to survivors, we really. . . ."[34]

Holocaust survivors are "real survivors." And I am suggesting that the "tremendous interest" in Holocaust survivors that Sally Grubman described may be more helpfully understood in the context of these cultural trends than simply in terms of some new readiness, on survivors' part or ours, "to talk about it." In addition, the irony of the desert island cartoon highlights a paradox at the very heart of the new survival rhetoric. On one side, it is clear that "surviving"—as an ideal or a fashion—represents a *constriction* of hope and horizon. In Lasch's phrase, it reflects "an age of diminishing expectations": an age of downsizing, insecurity, cynicism, and distrust. Being "a survivor," in other words, is what you hope for when the spheres of cultural, interpersonal, and political life seem consistently to discourage hoping for much else. At the same time, like the two guys on the island, it is possible to make a virtue out of such necessity. Survival can be hyped and romanced. One can search, in its extremity, for lessons and legacies, affirmation and inspiration, new models of salvation or simply of success.[35]

So, in essence, we began to do with Holocaust survivors. As survival eclipsed adjustment as a primary virtue in American culture at large, our response to these survivors also underwent a transformation. Out of "the ashes" or "the darkness" or "defeat," we began to look for heroes and victories and "the joy of survival."

Divided Discourse

The new rhetoric of survival as triumph and redemption has not meant, as is sometimes assumed, that we have not continued to view Holocaust survivors exclusively as victims. Indeed, reinforced by an increasingly popularized mental health discourse about survivors, and about traumatic victimization more generally, representations of survivors as guilty, despairing, shattered, or dead have become more fixed than ever.[36] The old language of "sick and needy" has become more clinical but no less persistent. "All of these people walk around like human wrecks, like ghosts," exclaimed a discussant at a psychiatric conference on survivors' trauma, perhaps forgetting for the moment that the conference was itself organized and run by survivors—hardly a job for wandering spirits.[37] Likewise, in later years only the naive would ask a whistling

Jack Goldman how he could "do that, after all he had been through." More likely, the significance of his behavior would be assumed: perhaps as his way of "coping" or "denying" or—in the most likely phrase—as Jack Goldman's way of "surviving."

Thus, two quite distinct ways of imagining survivors have evolved since the late 1970s: a ceremonial rhetoric in which we honor survivors as celebrants and heroes, together with a psychiatric rhetoric in which the same survivors are ghosts and wrecks. Between the two, both the ongoing life and the ongoing death that survivors know *are* represented. The problem, as I have suggested, is that each of these ways of representing survivors has evolved into a separate and self-sufficient discourse. And, indeed, so self-sufficient have these discourses become that they are increasingly detached not only from each other but also from remembering the Holocaust itself.

On one side, then, survivors are now everywhere invited to "bear witness." The interest in testimony that Sally Grubman noted continues to accelerate, and its collection and distribution—in the greatest possible quantity, through the most contemporary possible means—have become a modern crusade. The accompanying rhetoric, however, remains traditional, even folk. We honor the "tales" and "stories" survivors retell, the "legacies" they bestow, their courage and heroism in speaking at all. Indeed, so much do we celebrate the *act* of testimony—congratulating survivors for giving it and, perhaps, ourselves for getting it—that the specific content of that testimony is left as mostly background. That is, survivors' speech tends to be esteemed in the abstract—as the idea of testimony rather than the reality. At times it seems specifically to be acclaimed instead of being listened to.

Meanwhile, another rhetoric is also heard. There is seemingly knowledgeable talk of posttraumatic stress, survivor guilt and shame, nightmares and depressions. Here too the perspective remains abstract. Just as the particulars of testimony become background when we celebrate witnessing itself, so the specific personal and historical content of survivors' pain becomes secondary when memory is reduced to symptoms. As *consequences* of the Holocaust— psychological by-products—symptoms need only be noted and counted. Even when survivors themselves speak of their guilt or their depression, as they often enough do, this is more likely to be taken as diagnostic confirmation than as an invitation to further discussion. In this way the psychiatric discourse on symptoms, like the celebratory discourse on testimony, remains self-sufficient and uninterrupted.

At times the oscillation between these two rhetorics can be particularly striking. Several such instances occurred during the American television coverage of the first World Gathering of Jewish Holocaust Survivors, held in Jerusalem in 1981. The reporters' comments are worth reviewing because of how clearly they demonstrate that even well-informed listeners, guided by the best intentions, can by compelled by ceremonial and psychiatric discourse.

For example, after the lead-in photographs of corpses, crematoria, and terrified victims with which all the programs began, one of the commentators made the following introductory remarks to the first broadcast of the series:

> In the opening sequence we showed you a glimpse—even a glimpse is enough—of the savagery of the Holocaust. We didn't do this to shock you, although it is shocking. We did it so that you can better understand the triumph of the human spirit. One cannot understand what it means to have been a survivor unless you know *what* they have survived.
>
> These heroic people who are gathered here today have not come to resurrect the nightmares of the past. They have not come to mourn. They have come to celebrate life. To bear witness. And to pass it on to their children and their children's children. This is more valuable than all the material assets they could pass on. *This* is their true legacy.[38]

From the start, one might wonder how it is possible to "bear witness" without mourning and without resurrecting "the nightmares of the past." In fact, the scenes from the Gathering that immediately followed—survivors grouped around message boards and holding up signs in search of those they had lost—seemed to have everything to do with mourning and resurrection.[39] But these remarks alone already suggest greater involvement with the idea of "heroic people" gathered to "bear witness" than with the content that witnessing is about. Of that—represented by the opening photographs— "even a glimpse is enough." And what we are really aiming to understand, in any case, is something else: "the triumph of the human spirit."

Still, as notable as this celebration of survivors as heroic witnesses, themselves engaged in "celebrating life," was the appearance further on in the broadcasts of a quite different way of discussing survivors and their legacies. The shift was particularly apparent as the commentators turned to those whom they called "the bearers of the legacy," the children of survivors. For what had earlier been applauded as a sacred transmission was now portrayed as the passing on of psychic burdens and universal affliction. And within this rhetoric the nightmarish past not only was resurrected but had gained virtual possession of the intergenerational future. Thus one reporter introduced her interviews with children of survivors:

> Throughout the world there are tens of thousands of young people who have never met. And yet they dream the same nightmares, share the same fears, and have to deal with the same emotional problems. Although they live separated by continents, they shared an experience which has marked them for life.[40]

If this change of discourse was not clear enough, the questions that the reporter then asked the three children of survivors who were interviewed—an Israeli, an American, and an Australian—left no doubt about the transformation. They proceeded:

> Do you have any particular nightmares?
> Do you think there is a problem between survivors and their children in an inability to communicate?

And, finally, a question that seemed to finish off the previously invaluable legacy once and for all:

> Do you feel that you'll ever get rid of the legacy of the Holocaust?

For their own part, the children of survivors who were interviewed had no difficulty coming up with exemplary nightmares, family tensions, and related problems. But they also appeared discomfited by the direction of the questions and seemed to be pushing to speak about something else. For all, this involved more essential ways that the Holocaust had entered into their awareness. Thus, the Israeli said that "the Holocaust is part of me, as everything is part of me. As my hands are part of me. As my eyes are part of me." Referring to the nightmare she had remembered, the American was quick to add, "More than that—those are only things that happened a few times in my life, more than that, it's something that goes with me through my everyday life." Likewise, the Australian agreed that she would never "get rid of the legacy of the Holocaust." However, she continued, "Nor do I want to. It's part of my history. It's part of, it goes back to the whole Jewish history." At least in the segments of the interviews that were broadcast, these comments were never followed up with further questions or discussion. They were left as simple assertions, perhaps as protests, which did little to modify the primary theme that nightmares, fears, and emotional problems were now what "the legacy" was about.

Even so, the matter was not left within psychiatric discourse either. Toward the end of the broadcasts, while discussing the fact that there would never be another such gathering of survivors, the commentators again raised the theme of redemptive rebirth through the passing of the legacy. One commentator had this to say in final summary: "It is true that this is, this was, a one-time event, a moment in history. But I do not think it will disappear. There was a legacy that was passed on, there were seeds that were sown, there will be flowers that will blossom forth from this, through the second generation, through the children of survivors, and through all of us who have observed this week."[41] It was left up to us, the viewing audience, to determine what sort of flowers these might be and how to understand their rootedness in a legacy presented alternately as priceless and pathogenic. Meanwhile, we might also wonder how much more, excluded by the language of both veneration and diagnosis, remains unheard, perhaps unspoken.

A Division of Labor

There should be no misunderstanding: survivors should be honored and their testimony cherished. Likewise, whatever the struggles of survivors or their children in the aftermath, these ought to be understood in the most serious way. The problem with the celebratory and psychiatric discourses discussed here is that testimony and the realities of survivors' and their children's lives are *not* seriously engaged. Rather, as I have emphasized, in place of entering into actual testimony, celebratory discourse fixes on the idea of "bearing witness." As typically invoked, the psychiatric discourse functions similarly: charting "emotional problems" substitutes for entering into the impact of the destruction for anyone in particular. That is why, I think, the children of survivors who were interviewed protest. Their knowledge of the Holocaust is not a checklist of symptoms, they each insist, but something complexly lived: "part of me," part of "my everyday life," "part of my history." And that is also why, I think, their protests are ignored. To pursue them would require the kind of developing dialogue that discourses like these preclude.

In the end, then, the split between celebratory and psychiatric discourse overlays a more profound division: a "division of labor" within the process of recounting itself. On their side, survivors' "job" is to talk about the Holocaust, to be witnesses or testifiers or passers-on of legacies. Our "job," by contrast, is to talk about survivors, either as heroic people who have such a task to fulfill or as haunted victims of the destruction. Whichever rhetoric we invoke, two discrete and disconnected monologues are now created between survivors and ourselves. Survivors provide witnessing and testimony about the Holocaust; we provide observations—or testimonials—about survivors.

Legacies and Last Words

In recent years the rhetoric of intergenerational transmission—of "true legacies" passed on "to children and to children's children"—has become particularly salient in discourse about survivors. Indeed, references to survivors having, leaving, or bestowing legacies have become iconic. Whether speaking of a legacy of trauma, of testimony, of Hitler, of Schindler, of night, or of dawn, there is probably no word used more often in connection with survivors than *legacy*. Companion references to survivors as "storytellers," "tellers of tales," or—more postmodernistically—"weavers of narrative tapestries" are almost as ubiquitous. Both "legacies" and "stories" evoke primal images of a people's narrative tradition and its transmission. They suggest meaningful continuity in historical time and coherent recounting of historical times. Enticed by such language, it is easy to miss the irony that the coherence of stories and the continuity of legacies are precisely what remembering the Holocaust undoes.[42]

To speak of legacies is also to evoke the idea of endings—of final messages delivered, last words uttered. The commentary on the 1981 Jerusalem gathering was thus typical in declaring it a "one-time event, a moment in history" that would never happen again. Other gatherings of survivors likewise tend to be described as unique and never to be repeated, invoking the image not only of testimony but specifically of *final* testimony, of testament. And, indeed, the notion that the survivors are all dying was repeated almost as often twenty years ago, in the 1970s, as it is (with more statistical justification) today, partly reflecting—and perhaps partly reflected in—all the legacy talk.[43] Thus, it seems that at the same historical moment that survivors' words were suddenly in demand, they were in demand as "last words": what you pass on to children, what you leave before you leave.

It is this orientation to "last words" that is at the heart of the two discourses that have developed since the late 1970s. On the one side, there are survivors' "last words" as they are invited to tell their story, leave their legacy, and—by implication—disappear. On the other side, there are our own "last

words" as we eulogize the heroes and pity the victims—that is, as we put ourselves in the role of those who will survive the survivors and bid them farewell
("there were seeds that were sown, there will be flowers that will blossom
forth"). Neither survivors' final testimony nor our final testimonial brooks
interruption or elucidation. They lead, once again, to discourses that are one-
way, self-sufficient, and closed.

Now survivors, in fact, *do* have legacies, and there is a great deal that they,
like all parents, do pass on to their children. But—exactly the converse of our
usual expectations—these legacies are rooted not in the Holocaust nor in
having survived the Holocaust but in what can be salvaged and recreated *in
spite of* the Holocaust. Listen to Paula Marcus as she struggles to define her
own legacy within and against the prevailing rhetoric, including its imagery
of one-way transmission and imminent demise:

> But, you know, my wish is always, as I'm getting older—I mean, I'm not
> dying yet! I hope I'm not dying yet!—but what did I achieve in my own
> little circle? In my own family? What was I able to leave for them? What
> is the word I want to use? The word they always use? "Legacy." What is
> my "legacy"? I don't know.
>
> Do they look at me as a quote-unquote "survivor"? Do they have
> compassion because now they understand what happened? And so they
> understand me instead of I understanding *them?* You know, it's a both-
> ering thought!

For Paula, being a "quote-unquote 'survivor'" is here what contributes *least*
to her sense of "legacy." She is concerned with particular relationships between a mother and each of her children, and she is against whatever one-way
presumptions go with "quote-unquotes."

Paula then reflected further about what legacies, her own and others', may
actually entail:

> But, on the other hand, every parent, every person who leaves a legacy
> in this life, it's a very little minor thing. I'm thinking of my own parents,
> especially my father, because unfortunately my mother I remember
> only vaguely. . . .
>
> When I go to the synagogue, which I don't do that often, but I always
> hear my father's voice. And I always recall, at certain prayers, how much
> joy he got out of singing that particular one. He wasn't extremely reli-
> gious. He was just good-hearted, believing, so pure within his world.

. . . And he enjoyed singing *En K'elohenu*. And he excelled! You know, his voice just—!! And every time I sing that, I feel that this is why I enjoy it—because my father enjoyed it. . . .

So, actually, what is a legacy? It's a very, it's one little thing if you are going to make it a legacy. I can't. Whatever I work on, it's up to you what you take out of it. How you translate it for yourself. And for that you have to be fortunate. To be able to enjoy these little things that are given.

Contrary to what her listeners might expect, the legacies Paula describes do not emerge from the destruction, from triumphing over the destruction, or from suffering after the destruction. They are simply the normal things of life—a father's voice, a favorite hymn, a remembered pleasure—the stuff of survivors' legacies as they are of all of ours, even if survivors also carry knowledge of such legacies' terrible fragility.

AN EPILOGUE: *SCHINDLER'S LIST* AT CHASE MANHATTAN

In early March 1996 the *New York Times* published a weeklong series of articles entitled "The Downsizing of America" that focused on the massive layoffs at the largest American companies since the late 1970s. Describing "the most acute job insecurity since the Depression," particularly among middle-class Americans, the series drew heavily on a rhetoric of war, killing, and survival to make its point. "On the Battlefields of Business, Millions of Casualties," read the headline of the opening article: "The tally of jobs eliminated in the 1990's—123,000 at AT&T, 18,800 at Delta Airlines, 16,800 at Eastman Kodak—has the eerie feel of battlefield casualty counts."[44] Subheadlines focused attention on "The Stunned Survivors" and "Survivors' Cynicism," while the articles described a "Darwinian struggle" of "colleague against colleague," a rising confusion among "deracinated workers," and the "insidious effects" of "survivor's syndrome," "survivor guilt," and "post-traumatic stress syndrome" among those who still clung to jobs.[45]

In fact, the articles described a number of different kinds of "survivors." Some were savvy gamesmen such as the man who confided, "I know what needs to be done to survive. Just be quick on your feet. I've laid the groundwork in terms of networking. . . . I know the right people." Others found that it was exactly their "networks" that had to be "downsized." One employee "began to think of himself and his colleagues as the 'walking dead.'" He became suspicious that his best friend at work was politicking against him and ended their regular lunches. "The friend did not protest. Apparently he had drawn similar conclusions." Still others accepted the chaos, such as a young man who reflected, "I can't imagine any corporate entity owes anyone a career." He had been a freelance musician and was used to not knowing "if the gig will be there tomorrow." Perhaps most typical were the "cynical survivors" who, as was constantly repeated, "downsized their expectations." One man had been actively involved in programs for workplace improvement. Now it's "pay me, don't play me"; now "it's just a 9-to-5 job for me."[46]

The *Times* series garnered a lot of attention. And certainly the stories it retells are as good snapshots as any of the wider context of "surviving" in America today. In Lasch's "age of diminishing expectations" and "minimal selves," these "survivors" had learned to live with less of almost everything: commitment, solidarity, integrity, control, continuity, trust, and, of course, job security, wages, and benefits.[47] And here there are no compensatory celebrations of life or spiritual triumph or the other honoraria that we seem to bestow on survivors of the infinitely worse.[48]

With that in mind, the corporate "survivor" most immediately relevant to the present discussion was a woman who kept a quite extraordinary diary. She still has her job and allowed the *Times* to publish excerpts from the diary only on condition of anonymity:

Entry: "A huge cloud of uncertainty hangs over each employee. Officially, we still haven't been told a thing about the acquisition. . . . The sleepless nights begin."

Entry: "Every day I have lunch with my friend G. . . . He will probably have to relocate out of state. . . . We will probably not see each other again."

Entry: "The company has been sold . . . which will result in the loss of thousands of jobs. . . ."

Entry: "My boss left last month. There's no one left to report to."

Entry: "I ran into B today. He wasn't offered a job and is devastated. . . . Any sense of joy I had at being on 'Schindler's list' of employees who've got jobs with our new parent corporation has been wiped out."[49]

Strange as the juxtaposition may seem, the metaphor to "Schindler's list" is naturally made—appropriately, in my view, for it does capture a simple truth about survivorhood better than much in more public discourse. That truth is that to be a survivor means most essentially what it means most literally: not to triumph, but simply to still be around after most of one's fellows have been lost or discarded.

The juxtaposition also captures a truth about the times. For certainly there is a bit of ironic brilliance about life in the 1990s, particularly middle-class life, expressed by the metaphor and by the escalating helplessness and isolation that led up to it. More general analyses of such helplessness and isolation in contemporary America are not hard to find—the perceived erosions of coherence, connection, civility, public trust, public life, society itself—choose your observer and choose your terms. The *New York Times* editors chose Michael Sandel and featured this passage from his *Democracy's Discontent* in their series:

> Two concerns lie at the heart of democracy's discontent. One is the fear that, individually and collectively, we are losing control of the forces that govern our lives. The other is the sense that, from family to neighborhood to nation, the moral fabric of community is unraveling around us. These two fears—for the loss of self-government and the erosion of community—together define the anxiety of the age.[50]

That anxiety, according to Sandel, flourished in the 1970s and 1980s and continues unabated today. Within the same period, Americans "discovered" trauma, victimization, Holocaust survivors, and survivors of all sorts of other horrors and crimes. That preoccupation also continues today. Perhaps we are reassuring ourselves that things could be so much worse. Perhaps, beneath an outward placidity, we fear that things might actually become so.

4   AMERICA'S HOLOCAUST

Memory and the Politics of Identity

James E. Young

The further the events of World War II recede into time, the more prominent its memorials become. As the period of Holocaust is shaped in the survivors' diaries and memoirs, in their children's films and novels, public memory of this time is being molded in a proliferating number of memorial images and spaces. Depending on where these memorials are constructed and by whom, these sites remember the past according to a variety of national myths, ideals, and political needs. Some recall war dead, others resistance, and still others mass murder. All reflect both the past experiences and current lives of their communities, as well as the state's memory of itself. At a more specific level, these memorials also reflect the temper of the memory-artists' time, their place in aesthetic discourse, their media and materials.

Memory is never shaped in a vacuum; the motives of memory are never pure. Both the reasons given for Holocaust memorials and museums, as well as the kinds of memory they generate, are as various as the sites themselves. Some are built in response to traditional Jewish injunctions to remember, others according to a government's need to explain a nation's past to itself. While the aim of some memorials is to educate the next generation and to inculcate in it a sense of shared experience and destiny, other memorials are conceived as expiations of guilt or as self-aggrandizement. Still others are intended to attract tourists. In addition to traditional Jewish memorial iconography, every state has its own institutional forms of remembrance. As a result, Holocaust memorials inevitably mix national and Jewish figures, political and religious imagery.

By themselves, monuments are of little value, mere stones in the landscape. But as part of a nation's rites or the objects of a people's national pilgrimage, they are imbued with national soul and memory. For traditionally the state-sponsored memory of a national past aims to affirm the righteousness of a nation's birth, even its divine election. The matrix of a nation's monuments emplots the story of ennobling events, of triumphs over barbarism, and recalls the martyrdom of those who gave their lives in the struggle for national existence—who, in the martyrological refrain, died so that a nation might live. In assuming the idealized forms and meanings assigned this era by the state, memorials tend to concretize particular historical interpretations. They suggest themselves as indigenous, even geological outcroppings in a national landscape; in time, such idealized memory grows as natural to the eye as the landscape in which it stands.

In the pages that follow I neither survey the hundreds of public Holocaust memorials in America nor offer a strictly aesthetic critique of the handful I examine. As I have suggested elsewhere, neither a purely formal nor a historicist approach accommodates the many other dimensions at play in public monuments.[1] Rather than merely identifying the movements and forms on which public memory is borne, or asking whether or not these memorials reflect past history accurately or fashionably, I pursue what Peter Burger has called a "functional analysis of art," adapted here to examine the social effects of public memorial spaces.[2] This is to suggest that the "art of public memory" encompasses not just these memorials' and museums' aesthetic contours, or their places in contemporary architectural discourse. It also includes the activity that brought them into being, the constant give and take between memorials and viewers, and, finally, the responses of viewers to their own world in light of a memorialized past. By reinvesting these memorials with the memory of their own origins, I hope to highlight the process of public art over its often static result, the ever-changing life of the monument over its seemingly frozen face in the landscape.

THE FIRST AMERICAN MEMORIALS

The first public Holocaust commemoration in America took place not after the war at all but at the very height of the killing, on December 2, 1942—as a mass protest. On this day, according to the Jewish Telegraphic Agency, some five hundred thousand Jewish workers in New York City stopped work for ten minutes, both to mourn those already killed and to protest the ongoing massacre. In a gesture of sympathy, several radio stations observed a two-minute silence before broadcasting memorial services at 4:30 that afternoon.[3] Similar commemorations followed the next spring, culminating in several mass public memorial ceremonies, including a pageant held at Madison Square Garden in March 1943, called "We Will Never Die" and dedicated to the two million Jews who perished at the hands of the Germans that year.[4] Other public memorials included mass rallies called by the Jewish Labor Committee to mourn the destruction of the Warsaw Ghetto. The largest single Holocaust memorial event during the war took place on April 19, 1944, the first anniversary of the Warsaw Ghetto Uprising. On the steps of New York City Hall, over thirty thousand Jews gathered to hear Mayor Fiorello LaGuardia and prominent Jewish leaders honor the memory of fighters and martyrs who had died in the uprising one year before.

At another massive public ceremony in October 1947, the next mayor of New York, William O'Dwyer, dedicated a site in Riverside Park between Eighty-third and Eighty-fourth Streets and marked it with a plaque reading, "This is the site for the American memorial to the Heroes of the Warsaw Ghetto Battle, April–May 1943 and to the six million Jews of Europe martyred in the cause of human liberty." The plaque, with its characteristically American emphasis on being "martyred in the cause of human liberty," remains to this day, but the memorial was never built. As is often the case, the subsequent story surrounding the unbuilt memorial can be more instructive than the finished memorial could ever have been.

In 1964, when a group of Jewish American survivors of the Warsaw Ghetto Uprising submitted a design for a Holocaust memorial at this site to New York City's Arts Commission, they were turned down for three reasons. First, according to the arts commissioner, Eleanor Platt, the proposed design by Nathan Rapoport was simply too big and not aesthetically tasteful. It would, in her words, set a regrettable precedent. Second, such a monument might inspire other "special groups" to be similarly represented on public land— another regrettable precedent. And finally, according to parks commissioner Newbold Morris, the city had to ensure that "monuments in the parks . . . be limited to events of American history."[5] That is, he suggested, the Holocaust was not an American experience.

For the Jewish survivors of the Holocaust who had immigrated to America after World War II, and who regarded themselves as typical "new Americans," such an answer challenged their very conception of what it meant to be American in the first place. For the first time a distinction had been drawn between "events of American history" and those of "Americans' history." Did

American history begin and end within the nation's geographical borders? Or did it, as most of the survivors believed, begin in the experiences abroad that drove these immigrants to America's shores? With the recent dedication of the United States Holocaust Memorial Museum in Washington, D.C., it could be said that America has recognized the survivors' experiences as part of a national experience—and has in this way made the Holocaust part of American history. American memory might now also be said to include the memories of all Americans.

At the same time, such a museum necessarily raises other difficult questions: What role does the Holocaust play in American thought and culture, in American religious and political life, in relations between Jewish Americans and other ethnic groups? To what extent will it necessarily be universalized in a society defined by pluralist and egalitarian ideals? To what extent has it become a defining preoccupation for Jewish Americans, a locus of memory and identity? The answers to these questions are complicated and ever-changing.

As the shape that Holocaust memory takes in Europe and Israel is constrained by political, aesthetic, and religious coordinates, the shape of that memory in America is no less guided by both American ideals and experiences of this time. Unlike European memorials, however, often anchored in the very sites of destruction, American memorials are necessarily removed from the "topography of terror." Where European memorials located in situ often suggest themselves rhetorically as the extension of events they would commemorate, those in America must gesture abstractly to a past removed in both time and space. If memorials in Germany and Poland composed of camp ruins invite visitors to mistake the memorials for the events they represent, those in America inevitably call attention to the great distance between the memorials and the destruction. The meaning in American memorials is not always as "self-evident" as that suggested at the camps, places of deportation, or destroyed synagogues. In this sense, American memorials seem to be anchored not so much in history as in the ideals that generated them in the first place.

In America the motives for memory of the Holocaust are as mixed as the population at large, the reasons variously lofty and cynical, practical and aesthetic. Some communities build memorials to remember lost brethren, others to remember themselves. Some build memorials as community centers, others as tourist attractions. Some survivors remember strictly according to religious tradition, while others recall the political roots of their resistance. Veterans' organizations sponsor memorials to recall their role as camp liberators. Congressmen support local monuments to secure votes among their

Jewish constituency. Even the United States Holocaust Memorial Museum in Washington was proposed by then-president Jimmy Carter to placate Jewish supporters angered by his sale of F-15 fighter planes to Saudi Arabia. All such memorial decisions are made in political time, contingent on political realities.[6]

AMERICA'S NATIONAL MEMORIAL TO THE HOLOCAUST

Of all the Holocaust memorials in America, none can begin to match in scope or ambition the national memorial and museum complex that opened in April 1993 in the heart of the nation's capital. Situated adjacent to the National Mall and within view of the Washington Monument to the right and the Jefferson Memorial across the Tidal Basin to the left, the United States Holocaust Memorial Museum is a neighbor to the National Museum of American History and the Smithsonian Institute. It enshrines, by dint of its placement, not just the history of the Holocaust but American democratic and egalitarian ideals as they counterpoint the Holocaust. That is, by remembering the crimes of another people in another land, it encourages Americans to recall their nation's own idealized reason for being.

"What is the role of [this] museum in a country, such as the United States, far from the site of the Holocaust?" Charles Maier has asked. "Is it to rally the people who suffered or to instruct non-Jews? Is it supposed to serve as a reminder that 'it can happen here'? Or is it a statement that some special consideration is deserved? Under what circumstances can a private sorrow serve simultaneously as a public grief?"[7] Before such a museum could be built on the Mall in Washington, explicitly American reasons would have to be found for it.

The official American justification for a national memorial in the nation's capital was provided by President Carter in his address to the first Days of Remembrance commemoration in the Capitol Rotunda, April 24, 1979:

Although the Holocaust took place in Europe, the event is of fundamental significance to Americans for three reasons. First, it was American troops who liberated many of the death camps, and who helped to expose the horrible truth of what had been done there. Also, the United States became a homeland for many of those who were able to survive. Secondly, however, we must share the responsibility for not being willing to acknowledge forty years ago that this horrible event was occurring. Finally, because we are humane people, concerned with the human rights of all peoples, we feel compelled to study the systematic destruction of the Jews so that we may seek to learn how to prevent such enormities from occurring in the future.[8]

Not only would this museum depict the lives of "new Americans," but it would also reinforce America's self-idealization as haven for the world's oppressed. It would serve as a universal warning against the bigotry and antidemocratic forces underpinning such a catastrophe and call attention to the potential in all other totalitarian systems for such slaughter.

As a national landmark, the national Holocaust museum would necessarily plot the Holocaust according to the nation's own ideals, its pluralist tenets. In the words of the U.S. Holocaust Memorial Council, therefore, the Holocaust began "before a shot was fired, with persecution of Jews, dissenters, blacks, Gypsies, and the handicapped. The Holocaust gathered force as the Nazis excluded groups of people from the human family, denying them freedom to work, to study, to travel, to practice a religion, claim a theory, or teach a value. This Museum will illustrate that the loss of life itself was but the last stage in the loss of all rights."[9] In being defined as the ultimate violation of America's Bill of Rights and as the persecution of plural groups, the Holocaust encompasses all the reasons immigrants—past, present, and future— have for seeking refuge in America.

When cultural critics protested that such a museum, though necessary, would be a blight on the Mall, the memorial council countered, "This Museum belongs at the center of American life because as a democratic civilization America is the enemy of racism and its ultimate expression, genocide. An event of universal significance, the Holocaust has special importance for Americans: in act and word the Nazis denied the deepest tenets of the American people."[10] That is, the Holocaust memorial defines what it means to be American by graphically illustrating what it means not to be American. As a reminder of "the furies beyond our shores," in one columnist's words, the museum would define American existence in the great distance between "here" and "there."[11]

This would be the beginning of what the museum's project director, Michael Berenbaum, has termed the "Americanization of the Holocaust." In Berenbaum's words, the museum's story of the Holocaust would have to be

told in such a way that it would resonate not only with the survivor in New York and his children in Houston or San Francisco, but with a black leader from Atlanta, a Midwestern farmer, or a Northeastern industrialist. Millions of Americans make pilgrimages to Washington; the Holocaust Museum must take them back in time, transport them to another continent, and inform their current reality. The Americanization of the Holocaust is an honorable task provided that the story told is faithful to the historical event.[12]

Of course, as Berenbaum also makes clear, the story itself depends entirely on who is telling it—and to whom.

As it turns out, putting the memorial museum on the Mall has not only Americanized the Holocaust but has also set a new national standard for suffering. After seeing the Holocaust formally monumentalized on the Mall, visitors may begin to view it less as an actual historical event and more as an ideal of catastrophe against which all other past and future destructions might be measured—or pitted. Moreover, the museum has issued an implicit challenge to two other long-suffering American ethnic groups, African Americans and Native Americans, who have responded by proposing their own national institutions for the Mall and nearby. Indeed, when informed that the National African American Museum would be located in an existing building of the Smithsonian Institute, Illinois representative Gus Savage responded angrily that since "Jews and Indians had their own place on the Mall," so should African Americans.[13] Given the Mall's own dark past as the former site of holding pens for newly arrived African slaves, the National African American Museum will be placed in an especially difficult position: not only will it be asked to share an authentic site of African American suffering with other groups, but it will also be faced with the unenviable task of teaching Americans that the topographical center of their national shrine is also the site of America's greatest, ineradicable shame.

THE ARCHITECTURE OF AMERICAN HOLOCAUST MEMORY

Beyond the museum's place in the heart of America's monumental civic culture, the next layers of meaning were negotiated in the building's design itself, both its architectural form and the exhibition narrative it houses. Chosen from a large field of competitors, James Ingo Freed, a principal in I. M. Pei's New York architectural firm, began by articulating the fundamental problems facing him on all fronts. He would have to begin, he said, by bridging the two landmark buildings on either side of the memorial's 1.7-acre lot: the gray limestone and neoclassical lines of the hulking Bureau of Engraving to the south, and the ornate red-brick Victorian Auditors Building to the north. From here his aim would be to "take the conditional [i.e., situational] circumstances of [the museum's] location and weave them together with its content."[14] This is in some ways the double-edged dilemma facing any architect and monument builder: How will design and materials used for the way they speak to the environment now speak to the museum's content? Specifically, in the case of a Holocaust memorial, how will the brick and limestone chosen for its neighborhood architectural resonance generate meaning in Holocaust memory?

At the same time, Freed wanted to use this space to challenge—or at least to critique—Washington's monumental facade. How to challenge the Mall's monumentality from a monumental structure on the Mall? How to do this while remaining answerable to the capital's Fine Arts Commission, whose first principle is to regulate and keep a relatively uniform appearance on the Mall? How to make a building that would disturb consciousness on the one hand while conforming to a highly regulated and uniform architectural set of guidelines on the other?

For the self-conscious architect, every structure is also a metaphor, created to serve one physical purpose but also to stand figuratively for an idea, a time, an event, a people. In Freed's eyes, for example, "The metaphor of the guard tower was the watching, the overview, the distancing of the persecutors from the prisoners" (63). How, then, would his building figure the memory it was designed to house? The essential problem of design for a plural nation was resolved by Freed in a relatively simple yet profound formulation. It is important, as he put it, that "memory be sufficiently ambiguous and open ended *so that others can inhabit the space, can imbue the forms with their own memory*" (64, my emphasis). Like other memorial designers before and after him, Freed has insisted on keeping forms open-ended, abstract enough to accommodate all rememberers, especially those who come after his generation. "We wanted an evocation of the incomplete," he wrote. "Irresolution, imbalances are built in. For instance, the screen in the front portal is not there to force a reading, but to make evident the need for interpretation" (64).

"It is my view," Freed wrote, "that the Holocaust defines a radical, but hopefully not a final, break with the optimistic conception of continuous social and political improvement underlying the material culture of the West."[15] This view led, in turn, to a fundamental architectural dilemma: how to represent the Holocaust as an irreparable breach in the Western mind without violating the strictly enforced architectural harmony of the nation's capital? Freed's answer was an exterior that conformed to the Fine Arts Commission's strict guidelines and an interior that metaphorically removes visitors from the capital. "When you walked out of Washington," Freed wrote, "I wanted to separate you from the city formally and spatially; but before you stepped into the Hall of Witness, I also felt that you had to go through an acoustical change, a disturbance like a drumbeat. Something to tell you that you are coming to this place, to make you pay attention" (65).

When visitors now enter, they find themselves in a great "raw steel structure, without cover or enclosing planes, except that the walls have panels of glass. These panels are the Walls of Nations, where every nation that suffered deaths is identified by a panel of glass" (Freed, 70). Visitors proceed diagonally through the Hall of Witness, the path lighted by a diagonally cut skylight high above. Elevators at the end of this path take visitors to the fourth floor, where the historical exhibit begins. But to enter the exhibit, visitors must cross a bridge made of glass blocks, what Freed describes as "a dangerous path" (70).

After finishing the exhibition walkthrough, the visitors' last stop at the detached Hall of Witness, like their first, also resonates brokenness, an irresolution of form and meaning. In this great open skylit gallery, absence reigns, and an architectural emptiness recalls the void left behind by a people's mass murder. Where structure and form figuratively reflect senses of brokenness and irreparability, the steel trusses and brick more literally recall the materials out of which the Nazis built their own houses of destruction. The roof and its skylight are thus both skewed and fragmented, even as they are bound with steel trusses, representing lines inside that are deliberately twisted, without reassuring angle or form.

The discontinuity and fragmentation preserved in the museum's interior architectural space cannot, however, be similarly conveyed in the exhibition narrative itself. Like all narrative, that created in the exhibition necessarily depends on the continuous sequence of its telling, the integrative coherence of history's emplotment. Though housed in a structure reverberating brokenness and the impossibility of repair, the exhibition itself exists solely on the strength of its internal logic, the linear sequence by which events of the Holocaust are ordered in their telling.

When the museum opened in 1993, this telling began with the visitors' own immediate, personal leap of identity.[16] Though now discontinued, the interactive personal identity cards initially issued to visitors by the museum are worth recalling. Here visitors could choose to type their age, gender, and profession into a computer, after which they would be issued the identity card of someone like themselves who was caught up in the Holocaust. At three stages of the exhibit, visitors could have their "personal identity" cards updated, so that with every passing year in exhibit-time, the personal history of what might be called a visitor's "phantom-guide" would be revealed further. At the end of the permanent exhibition, visitors would insert their cards into a television monitor and meet the companion face to face through oral history—or, if the phantom-companion had died, the memory of the deceased would be conveyed by surviving family and friends.

On the one hand, this device allowed individuals a chance to personalize history, to know it "as if it happened to us," in the Passover refrain. For a moment, at least, the victims were rehumanized, invigorated with the very life force of the visitors themselves. But at another level the device may have perpetrated a small but significant deception. By inviting visitors to remember their museum experience as if it were a victim's Holocaust experience, the personal identity card asked us to confuse one for the other. While the "experiential mode" has come into increasing favor in museums, it is also a mode that encourages a certain critical blindness on the part of visitors. Imagining oneself as a past victim may not be the same as imagining oneself, or another person, as a potential victim, the kind of leap necessary to prevent other "holocausts." All of which obscures our contemporary actual reality of the Holocaust, which is not the event itself but *memory* of the event, the great distance between then and now, between there and here. This distance, not the Holocaust itself, is our preeminent reality now, no less than the Holocaust was the victims' preeminent reality then.

In addition, a further twist was detected by Jonathan Rosen: "The irony is that many Jews during the Holocaust scrambled to acquire false papers in order to survive the war—the papers of non-Jews. There is a reverse principle at work here, as if everyone were expected to enter the museum an American and leave, in some fashion, a Jew."[17] If this is true, then precisely the opposite effect of a unifying experience has been achieved: Americans enter whole, only to exit in their constituent parts.

With or without the identity cards, however, the visitors' experience begins appropriately with America's first direct Holocaust experience—that is, through the eyes of the American GIs who liberated Buchenwald and Dachau. In this opening section we view footage of the camps at their liberation filmed by the army, images that convey both the shock of the Americans and the gratitude and relief of the survivors upon being liberated, many of them about to become new Americans. With a little chronological slippage, in fact, it could be said that as potential Americans, many of the victims in these films were already American somehow. Indeed, many became American solely on the strength of their experiences as Holocaust victims: for them, the Holocaust was the beginning of their becoming American, making the Holocaust an essential part of their American identities.

And then, unlike European Holocaust museums, which begin and end with the destruction of Europe's Jews, and unlike museums in Israel, which often show the prewar European diaspora as already half-dead, the United States Holocaust Memorial Museum reflects an essential exilic bias, showing the great vibrancy and richness of Jewish life lost in the Holocaust. The tragedy in this context is not just how European Jewry was destroyed, or the gruesome remains at the end, but the richly complex life lost—the thousand years of civilization extirpated, unregenerated, unrepaired. The Holocaust is defined here not as mere killing, but as an immeasurable loss.

Because the American experience of Nazi Germany in the 1930s was necessarily mediated by newsreels, newspapers, and radio broadcasts, the media experience itself is recreated in the next section of the museum. Visitors enter a typical American living room in 1939, complete with a radio broadcasting news reports, newspapers and magazines discussing the times. This was the American experience, in all of its limited and necessarily mediated ways.

To reach the next section, on ghettoization, visitors traverse a narrow bridge like the ones that once linked the outside world to the ghettos. Then they walk on authentic cobblestones from the Warsaw Ghetto and view other artifacts, such as a sewing machine, a baby carriage, a policeman's bicycle, and other items showing the range of life in the ghetto, each artifact a metonymic reminder of the actual life once animating it. Though this museum also shows images of Jewish life before and after the Holocaust (e.g., a moving temporary exhibition that depicts the full and textured life of a young Jewish boy before the war), it also features many of the artifacts of destruction (such as victims' shoes and photographs of mounds of hair) brought from various concentration camps around Europe.

I fear, however, that if visitors come to know an entire people only by their scattered belongings, memory of life itself is lost. Nowhere among this debris do we find traces of what bound these people together into a civilization, a nation, a culture. Visitors who are moved to memory mainly by the heaps of scattered artifacts they view in Holocaust museums may miss the interconnectedness of lives that made these victims a people. The lives and the relationships between them are lost to the memory of ruins alone—and will be lost to subsequent generations who seek memory only in the rubble of the past. Indeed, by overly relying on such artifacts for their memorial presentations, any Holocaust museum in America, Europe, or Israel risks perpetuating the very images by which the killers themselves would have memorialized their Jewish victims.

After the ghetto experience in this museum narrative comes mass murder, beginning with the *Einsatzgruppen,* the mobile killing units of the SS responsible for murdering some 1.5 million Jews in the Soviet Union. Film images of these killings are simultaneously presented and hidden: a four-foot-high tin wall will keep young children from looking into the abyss, visible only to their elder siblings and parents. Or, for those survivors who, in Berenbaum's words, "don't need to see or feel what they can never forget," or who grow claustrophobic, or who just cannot bear the horrible images, there will be a detour, an escape ramp away from the crowds and horror.[18]

A section on concentration camps follows, replete with half an actual barrack imported from Birkenau. Again, according to Berenbaum, this and other artifacts are used to refute the lies of Holocaust negationists. Once inside the barracks, visitors view a scale model of the gas chambers designed after a similar model on view at Auschwitz. Canisters of Zyklon-B, long deactivated, attend this section along with contracts of the construction companies that built the gas-chamber and crematorium complexes, guaranteeing a longevity of twenty-five years. "Issues of corporate behavior—with all their ethical ramifications—must be confronted squarely in this tower," Berenbaum writes.

After the death exhibits, visitors find both respite and some sense of vindication in sections on resistance and "the courage to care." Here the stories of ghetto fighters and partisans are told alongside those of other heroes, such as Raoul Wallenberg (who saved one hundred thousand Jews in Budapest) and the French village of Chambon (where Jewish children were hidden and protected).

Finally, like the museum narratives in Israel, where lives were rebuilt after the Holocaust, this exhibit also ends with the "return to life." For this is the story of an ideal shared by America and Israel: both see themselves as lands of refuge and freedom. What follows is then a story of immigration, the long journey from "Old World" D.P. camps, ravaged towns, and anti-Semitism to the "New Worlds" of Jewish statehood and American egalitarianism. It is the story of America's absorption of both immigrants and their memories, the gradual integration of Holocaust memory into American civic culture. At the end the museum suggests itself as the ultimate triumph of America's absorption of immigrants, the integration of immigrant memory into the topographical heart of American memory.

In his introduction to the museum walkthrough, Berenbaum addresses the reciprocal exchange between a monument and its surroundings that takes place upon exiting the museum. It is not only a matter of the memorial's meaning being shaped by its context—the Holocaust Americanized in this case—but also of the surroundings being re-viewed in light of the Holocaust memorial. "When people leave the U.S. Holocaust Memorial Museum," Berenbaum writes, "the monuments to democracy that surround it—to Lincoln and Jefferson and Washington—will take on a new meaning." Such American icons of democracy will either be affirmed for the ways their ideals prevented similar events in America or, in the eyes of Native Americans, African Americans, and Japanese Americans, reviewed skeptically for the ways such ideals might have prevented, but did not, the persecution of these groups on American soil. Every visitor will bring a different experience to the museum, as well as a different kind of memory out of it.

AGAINST A CULTURE OF COMPETING CATASTROPHES

By all accounts, the United States Holocaust Memorial Museum has been a resounding success. By the time it opened, over 150,000 people had donated some $200 million to its construction. These funds were used not just to build its enormous edifice but also to collect some ten thousand artifacts from around the world, including an authentic Treblinka boxcar, a Danish fishing boat used in the rescue of that country's Jews, an actual barrack from Birkenau, and two thousand pairs of children's shoes from Auschwitz. The projected holdings of the archives and library of one hundred thousand volumes make it the largest Holocaust repository and study center in America. To the amazement of its curators and the consternation of its maintenance staff, more than two million people visited the museum in its first year, nearly three times what had been anticipated.

Here I would like to raise an issue—though not one that argues against the United States Holocaust Memorial Museum, which continues to serve important national and historical roles. But rather, just as I would warn against the tendency in visitors to make the remnants of destruction they find in this (or any) museum the center of Holocaust memory, I would also caution against making Holocaust memory itself the center of Jewish American identity. While it is clear that the museum does not mean to encourage either tendency, I do fear that for too many Jewish and non-Jewish American visitors to the museum, the icons and debris of destruction have begun to displace the thousand years of European Jewish life that was lost, even as the place of the Holocaust in Jewish history and memory is being magnified to the near exclusion of all else.

In America the traditional impulse to anchor memory in historical crisis is further complicated—and exacerbated—by a number of additional factors unique to the contemporary Jewish American experience. For in America's culture of assimilation, where explicitly religious differences are tolerated and deemphasized, it is almost always the memory of extreme experience that serves to distinguish the identity of minority groups from the majority population. Indeed, one of the central *topoi* of American New World identity, beginning with the progenitors of America's "majority population"—the Pilgrims—is the memory of Old World oppression.

With the rise of a newfound ethnic pride among African Americans, Jewish Americans, and Native Americans during the 1960s, the power of a vicariously remembered past to bind otherwise alienated groups grew increasingly attractive. As African Americans recalled their enslavement and Native Americans their genocide, Jewish Americans began to recall the Holocaust as the crux of their common heritage. But even as the memory of mass suffering was binding together the members of these communities, it also set the stage for an implicit competition between the various cults of victimization. Two-dimensional identities constructed solely around the memory of past suffering began to clash as groups asserted the primacy of their tragic past over that of others. America was becoming a culture of competing catastrophes.

One of the results of this competition has been a narrowing of each group's experience, a dividing of these groups' histories from one another. Instead of learning about the Holocaust through the larger study of Jewish history, many Jews and non-Jews in America now learn the whole of Jewish history through the lens of the Holocaust. Likewise, all many Americans know about African Americans is their degraded condition as slaves, or about Native American history its grisly end. In each case, entire centuries of rich life and culture are reduced to the detritus of destroyed civilizations.

Today the Holocaust continues to occupy a central place in both Jewish and non-Jewish consciousness. In a plural and diverse society, it has also entered a universal realm, becoming a standard and currency by which many disparate groups measure their pasts, even as they come to know a part of Jewish history. Over time, however, Holocaust memorials and museums in America will also be asked to invite many different, occasionally competing, groups of Americans into their spaces. In the most ideal of American visions, however, the memory of competing catastrophes will not continue to divide Americans from one another but may lead each community to recall its past in light of another group's historical memory. In this way each group might also come to know more about their compatriots' experiences in light of their own remembered past.

I would like to conclude with a disturbing little vision I had during the dedication of the United States Holocaust Memorial Museum in 1993. Along with millions of other Americans, I watched as Elie Wiesel mounted the stage amid fluttering American flags on the podium and began his dedication speech. And like many others, I was surprised but pleased when he interrupted his speech, turned to face President Clinton, and said in so many words, "Mr. President, I must tell you that I cannot sleep at night for what my eyes have seen in Bosnia-Herzegovina. Please, Mr. President, you must do something to stop this terrible slaughter of innocents."

At that moment the television cameras panned to President Clinton, sitting on the dais behind the speaker. He was clearly moved by this appeal, his eyes glistened sympathetically, and he nodded with clenched jaw. But because he had not yet acted to thwart the unfolding mass murder of Bosnian Muslims, now two years in the making, I imagined hearing words that he never actually said: "But Elie, I am doing something about the Bosnian Muslims. I am here, with you, remembering the Holocaust." We were getting it all backwards. Not only did I fear that we were turning Holocaust memory into a kind of national self-congratulatory spectacle. But what if Holocaust memory was becoming a substitute for real action against contemporary genocide, instead of its inspiration? In the end we must recognize that memory cannot be divorced from the actions taken in its behalf, and that memory without consequences may even contain the seeds of its own destruction.

5 INHERITING THE HOLOCAUST

Jewish American Fiction and the Double Bind
of the Second-Generation Survivor

Andrew Furman

*My parents, no longer alive but continually reinvented, revised,
hostage to my own private therapy. The Holocaust survivor as
myth, as fairy tale, as bedtime story. I had created my own ghosts
from memories that were not mine. I wasn't there, in Poland,
among the true martyrs. Everything about my rage was borrowed.
My imagination had done all the work—invented suffering, without the physical scars, the incontestable proof.*

—Thane Rosenbaum

Whether or not the artistic imagination can ever be brought to bear upon the
Holocaust in a way that does not betray the feebleness of the former while simultaneously diminishing the true horror of the latter has been a source of
contention ever since news of the atrocity belatedly reached the widespread
public. Lionel Trilling put his finger on an often repeated moral quandary
when he noted that "there is no possible way of responding to Belsen and
Buchenwald. The activity of mind fails before the incommunicability of
man's suffering."[1] Given the incommunicable nature of the suffering experienced by the Nazis' victims, if we agree to accept Trilling's assertion for a moment, perhaps silence represents the only morally tenable response to the
genocide. Elie Wiesel ponders this question most directly in *The Oath* (1973),
but one might read Wiesel's entire oeuvre as a tortured meditation upon the
"power of silence" argument and, ultimately, a repudiation of it. While the
narrators of Wiesel's work are painfully aware of the ineffable nature of the
Holocaust, they find that they must bear witness through recounting their experiences. Language, as limited as it may be, is all they have.

That the questionable morality of depicting the Holocaust in literature has
dogged Wiesel, a survivor of the Nazi death camps, suggests how much

thornier the issue becomes when the Holocaust bestirs the imagination of Jewish *American* fiction writers. Artists who attempt to represent the Holocaust when their knowledge of the event is second- or third-hand, or transmitted by other cultural artifacts, can expect their work to elicit a special kind of scrutiny from academic and nonacademic readers alike. Cognizant, perhaps, of the slippery moral terrain, Jewish American writers proved especially reluctant in the wake of the Holocaust to dramatize the atrocity in their fiction. The role of the Holocaust in the work of Saul Bellow and Bernard Malamud exemplifies this reluctance. Bellow only dared to dramatize the Holocaust allusively in his 1947 novel *The Victim* before mustering up the artistic confidence to depict the atrocity more directly in *Mr. Sammler's Planet* (1969) through the horrifying recollections of his survivor protagonist, Artur Sammler. Bellow's Jewish American protagonist in *The Victim*, Asa Leventhal, must only endure the seemingly innocuous anti-Semitic barbs of a physically weak antagonist, Allbee. But as Lillian Kremer has observed, images associated with the Nazi persecution of European Jews—from asphyxiation by gas to resettlement trains—pervade the novel to suggest the relationship between Allbee's blithe anti-Semitism and its culmination in the Holocaust.[2]

Like Bellow, Bernard Malamud chose to approach the Holocaust from a safe distance in his novel *The Fixer* (1966). While the blood libel trial of Mendel Beilis fueled Malamud's plot most directly, critics were quick to recognize that through exploring the plight of Yakov Bok—a Jew rotting away in a czarist jail for a murder he did not commit—Malamud meant to dramatize the virulent and pervasive European anti-Semitism that would culminate in the Holocaust. Indeed, Malamud suggested as much himself: "To [Beilis's] trials in prison I added something of Dreyfus's and Vanzetti's, shaping the whole to suggest the quality of the affliction of the Jews under Hitler. These I dumped on the head of poor Yakov Bok."[3]

Given the reluctance of two such prominent Jewish American novelists to dramatize the Holocaust directly, it should come as little surprise that as late as 1966 Robert Alter could bemoan the dearth of Jewish American imaginings of this watershed event defining the twentieth-century Jewish experience: "With all the restless probing into the implications of the Holocaust that continues to go on in Jewish intellectual forums . . . it gives one pause to note how rarely American Jewish fiction has attempted to come to terms . . . with the European catastrophe."[4]

Since the 1960s we have enjoyed a rather steady outcropping of Jewish American fiction on the Holocaust—enough novels and short stories to merit book-length studies upon them, most notably Alan Berger's *Crisis and Covenant: The Holocaust in American Jewish Writing* (1985) and S. Lillian Kremer's *Witness through the Imagination: Jewish American Holocaust Literature* (1989). This is not to say that the controversy surrounding the Holocaust as subject for the Jewish American fiction writer has abated as the event recedes further and further into the past. Scholars and critics continue to cast a wary eye upon how Jewish American writers "imagine" the Holocaust. For example, upon reading Philip Roth's *The Ghost Writer* (1979)—wherein Nathan Zuckerman imagines that Amy Bellette, the assistant to his literary idol, is Anne Frank and, further, imagines bringing her home as his fiancée—Alan Berger, for one, had to say enough is enough. "Is Roth not utilizing the Holocaust to give himself legitimacy in the Jewish community?" Berger asked rhetorically.[5] More recently, he excoriated Roth's novel as a "literary exploitation" of the Holocaust.[6] While Berger did not use the term *Americanization,* what clearly raised his hackles was the way in which Roth (according to Berger's reading of *The Ghost Writer*) appropriated the archetypal human story of the European catastrophe for the self-absorbed purpose of bolstering his personal reputation in the American Jewish community.

I would argue that Berger overlooks an important element of the Bellette/Frank subplot and therein sells Roth's treatment of the Holocaust in *The Ghost Writer* far short. For if Zuckerman sees Bellette/Frank as a potential wife—talk about bringing home the Jewish girl!—she also emerges as Zuckerman's double. When he reads Anne Frank's diary, he is taken in not so much by the horror that looms over Frank's innocence as by her elegant use of the relative clause. "Suddenly she's discovering reflection," Zuckerman marvels, "suddenly there's portraiture, character sketches, suddenly there's long intricate eventful happening so beautifully recounted it seems to have gone through a dozen drafts."[7] He sees the diary primarily as a portrait of the artist as a young woman, the relic of a snuffed-out talent. Importantly, Frank's tragic fate, Zuckerman realizes, might have been his own had he been the Jewish artist cutting his teeth on the rattle and hum of Amsterdam's streets rather than Newark's. Thus, he projects himself into the drama he imagines for Bellette/Frank. Her preoccupations as a burgeoning artist startlingly parallel Zuckerman's. For example, Zuckerman's declaration of artistic independence to his mother—"I am on my own"—resonates in the declaration he imagines for Bellette/Frank: "*I don't feel in the least bit responsible to any of you . . . I don't have to give an account of my deeds to anyone but myself.*"[8] Zuckerman realizes that he entertains his own counterlife when he fashions one for

Frank—who takes on a new identity, Amy Bellette, and chooses not to reveal herself once she sees the impact that her diary has had upon the world. Would Zuckerman have sacrificed his identity for art? Would he have been selfless enough to choose the illumination of humankind over his own life? These, of course, are the questions that Zuckerman—and Roth, I believe—poses as he imagines a counterlife for Anne Frank, and for himself.

Additional controversies regarding the Jewish American writer's treatment of the Holocaust abound. For example, most scholars and critics lauded Art Spiegelman for his innovative and courageous artistic approach to the Holocaust in his Pulitzer Prize–winning *Maus*. Michael E. Staub's recent assertion that *Maus* presents a story of the Holocaust "that is much more accessible to a general audience than many other accounts, because it is particularly effective at inviting emotional involvement," exemplifies this critical approval.[9] Cynthia Ozick, however, cast a discerning eye upon *Maus* when she limned the metaphorical difficulty of Spiegelman's comic-book evocation of the Holocaust (he depicts Nazis as cats and Jews as mice). Ozick recognized that Spiegelman meant to invite the reader's visceral involvement through depicting the Jews as the Germans' prey. "But prey," Ozick perspicaciously argued, "is legitimate in nature; you can't argue with cats when they catch mice and kill them. It's killing, not murder. . . . The Germans were not cats and the Jews were not mice; both were human. And *that* is the *real* point in contemplating the Holocaust."[10] Small wonder, given the scrutiny to which Ozick holds Jewish American dramatizations of the Holocaust, that she shelved her own Holocaust story, "The Shawl," for several years before finally submitting it in 1980 for publication in the *New Yorker*.

In fact, Ozick has lamented the appropriation of the Holocaust by imaginative, rather than strictly historical, writers in America. Says Ozick, "I believe with all my soul that [the Holocaust] ought to remain exclusively attached to document and history. . . . If the Holocaust becomes commensurate with the literary imagination, then what of those recrudescent Nazis, the so-called revisionists, who claim the events themselves are nothing but imaginings?" Those familiar with Ozick's work might, at this point, be justifiably perplexed by her resolve. After all, the Holocaust has loomed large in several of her works. When Elaine Kauvar confronted Ozick with the apparent contradiction between her intellectual conviction and her artistic output, Ozick offered an intriguing response that cuts to the heart of the relationship, currently, between the Jewish American fictionist and the Holocaust: "Well, I did it in five pages in 'The Shawl,' and I don't admire that I did it. I did it because I couldn't help it. It wanted to be done. I didn't want to do it, and afterward I've in a way punished myself, I've accused myself for having done it. I wasn't there, and I pretended through imagination that I was."[11] Ozick's response illustrates, above all, how ineluctable the Holocaust has proven to be for the contemporary Jewish American fiction writer. As an American Jew, a nonwitness, Ozick does not believe that she has the right to depict the Holocaust in her work. However, the Holocaust pervades her consciousness and bursts upon her written pages: "It wanted to be done." As Ozick explained in an earlier interview, "I want the documents to be enough; I don't want to tamper or invent or imagine. And yet I have done it. I can't not do it. It comes, it invades."[12] Through deciding to publish the Holocaust fiction that "invades" her consciousness, Ozick affirms her belief in the revelatory power of art. Though ever wary of the imagination and its potential as a false idol, the facts alone (those "documents") are finally *not* enough, Ozick implicitly suggests.

Ozick's artistic stance concerning the Holocaust obtains for an ever-increasing cohort of Jewish American writers. Despite its seemingly insurmountable challenge to the American imagination and its concomitant moral land mines, contemporary Jewish American Holocaust fiction has carved out its own niche as a subgenre of Jewish American fiction. The Holocaust is a frequent theme in Ted Solotaroff and Nessa Rapoport's recent collection of contemporary Jewish American stories, *Writing Our Way Home: Contemporary Stories by American Jewish Writers* (1992). Isaac Bashevis Singer's "A Party in Miami Beach," Lore Segal's "The Reverse Bug," and Deirdre Levinson's "April 19th, 1985" represent particularly powerful Holocaust stories that Solotaroff and Rapoport chose from among "many, many others."[13] That Solotaroff, in his introduction to the collection, was compelled to refer to the Holocaust as "the subject that doesn't go away" illustrates the surge in Jewish American Holocaust fiction since Robert Alter's gloomy 1966 observations.

Indeed, some of our most promising young Jewish American writers have imagined the Holocaust significantly in their work. The most recent works to flash upon one's mental screen include Melvin Jules Bukiet's *After* (1996) and two stories in his earlier collection *While the Messiah Tarries* (1995), "Himmler's Chickens" and "The Library of Moloch"; and Rebecca Goldstein's "The Legacy of Raizel Kaidish: A Story," collected in *Strange Attractors* (1993), and her novels *The Late-Summer Passion of a Woman of Mind* (1989) and the dazzling *Mazel* (1995), which won the Edward Lewis Wallant award for fiction. As Lillian Kremer suggests, "Contemporary Jews increasingly feel that, geography aside, they were present at Auschwitz. American Jews carry the psychological burden of Auschwitz and Chelmno and Dachau and Bergen-Belsen and Treblinka and all the other Nazi death factories where their relatives died brutal deaths."[14] Kremer's observation complicates one of the principal arguments voiced by many who disapprove of "Americanizations" of the Holocaust: the atrocity didn't happen in America. While true in the literal sense, the assertion obfuscates the impact that the Holocaust had and continues to have within the Jewish American community. The Holocaust left an indelible thumbprint on the Jewish American ethos, forging the Jewish population in America as a "people of memory."[15] It forced Jews in America to reexamine their own Jewish identities and question the viability of a Jewish existence in *galut* (exile). Perhaps embracing an assimilated American identity was no guarantee against imminent persecution in America. After all, the Jews in pre-Holocaust Germany were, ironically, "the most privileged Jews on the continent—prosperous, fully emancipated, and largely assimilated into German society."[16] Perhaps assimilation was no longer desirable in the first place (why offer Hitler a posthumous victory?). Perhaps a Jew could be safe and spiritually whole only in a Jewish state. These are just some of the issues that faced Jewish Americans after the Holocaust.

While the European atrocity left a deep impact upon all Jews in America, the Holocaust affected and continues to affect the children of survivors in special and profound ways. The psychological burden to which Kremer refers above weighs most heavily upon this "second generation"—here I am borrowing Alan Berger's terminology—and has manifested itself in the current surge of novels and short stories that they have contributed to the burgeoning canon of Jewish American Holocaust fiction. These second-generation children of survivors engage the Holocaust with an unprecedented intensity as they grapple to come to terms, through their fiction, with both the seemingly ineffable horrors committed against their parents and the legacy of those horrors visited upon them.

Importantly, these second-generation works force us to reconsider our criteria for defining Holocaust fiction. One might notice that when Cynthia Ozick admonishes herself for "imagining" the Holocaust in her fiction, she only refers to that brief moment in "The Shawl" when she describes the actual experience of Jews in a concentration camp. Ozick, then, implicitly defines Holocaust fiction rather literally and in a way that excludes much second-generation fiction from the category. As one might expect, most second-generation writers explore not the European Jews' Holocaust experiences but largely the experiences of the second-generation child who grows up in the wake of the tragedy on more hospitable American terrain. It is my contention not only that such second-generation fiction must be considered Holocaust fiction but that it represents the most significant and poignant example of the continual "Americanization" of the Holocaust as the children of survivors illustrate how the Holocaust continues to inform—or haunt, rather—their cultural identities as Jewish Americans. Alan Berger, one of the few scholars to explore this second-generation work with any depth, has already brought to our attention the fine work by such writers as Thomas Friedmann, Barbara Finkelstein, and Julie Salamon.[17] For the balance of this essay, I will focus upon the fiction of an emergent second-generation writer, Thane Rosenbaum.

In his powerful first collection of stories, *Elijah Visible* (1996), Rosenbaum explores the special burdens of the second generation in America. To engage these burdens as thoroughly as he can, Rosenbaum creates a single protagonist, Adam Posner, but varies the details surrounding Posner's identity from one story to another. To wit, in one story Posner is a lawyer in an elite New York firm, in another story he is an abstract expressionist painter, in another a teacher; he grows up in Atlantic City in one story, in Miami in another, and in still another, New York. In Adam Posner, then, Rosenbaum creates a mosaic figure to capture the complex, nuanced, and above all diverse experiences of the Holocaust survivor's child in America. Through the many Posners, Rosenbaum dramatizes the second generation's vicarious psychological immersion in the Holocaust, their responsibility to reconstruct and remember the experiences of the survivor parents, and their struggle to maintain religious faith in a post-Holocaust America seemingly devoid of redemptive possibilities. Owing largely to the simultaneous breadth and depth of Rosenbaum's vision, his collection represents an invaluable contribution to the canon of Jewish American Holocaust fiction.

"HE CARRIED ON THEIR ANCIENT
SUFFERING WITHOUT PROTEST"

In the first story of the collection, "Cattle Car Complex," Rosenbaum tersely dramatizes the vicarious suffering of Adam Posner. While the name Adam suggests rebirth or regeneration, Rosenbaum chooses the name of his protagonist sardonically, for the overarching point of this opening story is that the past, specifically the Holocaust experiences of Posner's parents, bears down heavily upon this American Adam. The Holocaust has scarred Posner, precluding any meaningful relationships in his life. Not even a pet greets him at his barren apartment. More subtly, the Holocaust guides Posner's career choice. He reluctantly decides to become a lawyer to ensure his own safety: "He played the game reluctantly, knowing what it was doing to his spirit, but also painfully aware of his own legacy, and its contribution to the choices he was destined to make. Above all else he wanted to feel safe, and whatever club offered him the privilege of membership, he was duty-bound to join" (4). To be sure, the comfortable trappings of Posner's life and his relative physical safety in America contrast mightily with his parents' predicament during the Holocaust; they survive cattle cars and concentration camps.

That said, once Posner's elevator breaks down, trapping him indefinitely in the "hollow lung of the skyscraper," he suffers a psychological trauma that exemplifies the *presence* of the Holocaust in his life (3). The claustrophobia of the elevator transports Posner, psychologically at least, to a Nazi cattle car in Holocaust Europe. When a security guard, understandably confused, urges him to calm down and not make such a fuss over the mere inconvenience, Posner's psychic terror consumes him and he cries, "This is not life—being trapped in a box made for animals! Is there no dignity for man? . . . You are barbarians! Get me out! . . . We can't breathe in here! And the children, what will they eat? How can we dispose of our waste? We are not animals! We are not cattle! There are no windows in here, and the air is too thin for all of us to share" (8).

Rosenbaum takes pains to emphasize, in this story and in others, that Posner inherits the legacy of suffering from his parents. He "inherited their perceptions of space, and the knowledge of how much one needs to live, to hide, how to breathe where there is no air. . . . He carried on their ancient sufferings without protest—feeding on the milk of terror; forever acknowledging—with himself as proof—the umbilical connection between the unmurdered and the long buried" (5–6). To say, then, that Posner suffers "vicariously" for his parents might be to qualify matters overmuch. In Posner's mind, he does not suffer *for* his parents but assimilates their suffering into his own experience. As Posner finally emerges from the repaired elevator in his soiled rags, awaiting the pronouncement, right or left—an allusion to the Nazis' two lines at the Auschwitz train tracks designating either hard labor or immediate execution—we know that we have come a long way in Jewish American Holocaust fiction from Philip Roth's "Eli, the Fanatic," arguably the most incisive story of Roth's first collection, *Goodbye, Columbus* (1959). The thoroughly "Americanized" Eli Peck must aggressively seek out a fleeting identification with a Holocaust survivor by donning his Hasidic clothing. We know, more-over, that this merging of identities between Peck and the survivor is more il-lusory than real. The clothes, finally, do not make the man.[18] In Rosenbaum's story, Adam Posner does not need to seek out an identification with a Holo-caust survivor. He cannot expel the Holocaust from his psyche no matter how hard he tries. As the child of survivors, he grows up hearing his parents' screams at night and adopts their haunted past. The contrast between these two stories suggests, above all, that second-generation writers have begun to call upon their special experiences as children of survivors to forge their own special artistic contributions to Jewish American Holocaust fiction.

Rosenbaum's "Cattle Car Complex" goes a long way toward convincing one that the cultural identity of second-generation Jewish Americans remains inextricably bound to a legacy of Holocaust suffering. Now, few dispute that the Jewish American identity *earlier* in this century was tangled up in this web of suffering. Consider, for example, Leslie Fiedler's recollection of how his grandfather would respond when asked what was happening in the world: "Nothing new, *M'hargert yidd'n*. They're killing Jews. What else?"[19] While Jewish Americans in the late nineteenth and early twentieth centuries, like Fiedler and his grandfather, were fortunate enough to elude the Holocaust, the dogs of the Eastern European pogroms still nipped at their heels through memory, through vicarious suffering on behalf of those left behind to perish in Europe, or through manifestations of anti-Semitism in America. But given the postwar socioeconomic strides made by Jewish Americans—illustrated by Alfred Kazin's quip, "What's the difference between the International Ladies' Garment Workers' Union and the American Psychiatric Association? One generation"—many non-Jews cannot fathom today the persistent Jewish American ethos of suffering. As Julius Lester, an African American and a Jew-ish convert, observes, "From a black perspective . . . there is something jarring in hearing white-skinned Jews talk about suffering. No black denies that Jews suffered in Europe, but the Jewish experience in America has not been char-acterized by such suffering."[20]

The stories in Rosenbaum's *Elijah Visible*, "Cattle Car Complex" in partic-ular, challenge Lester's observations. While it is true that Jewish Americans no longer need endure the palpable suffering wrought by institutionalized anti-Semitism, Adam Posner in *Elijah Visible* still suffers from the horrors com-mitted against his parents. How could it be otherwise, given that he arrives home, in one story, to find them hiding from the Nazis in the dark corner of their bedroom? The second-generation child who observes his survivor parents trembling in their bedroom becomes the second-generation man with a "cattle car complex." The words of Fiedler's grandfather—"*M'hargert yidd'n*"—resonate, then, just as strongly for the Jewish child of survivors in contemporary America.

"MY IMAGINATION HAD DONE ALL THE WORK"

Still, if the Posner of Rosenbaum's collection inherits the Holocaust legacy of his parents "through his veins," it is just as true that experience itself cannot be inherited. A double bind, Rosenbaum suggests, plagues the second generation. Posner cannot get the Holocaust out of his skull; but at the same time he remains painfully aware that the treacherous imagination rather than memory burdens him. Thus, in several stories Posner must satisfy his inexorable desire to learn all he can about the Holocaust generally, and about his parents' experiences specifically. He must uncover the details that will sharpen the frustratingly nebulous images of terror that haunt him. The rub is that Posner's parents and other survivor relatives prove especially reluctant to share their stories with him. The memories are too painful, the truth too horrific for words. Besides, why burden the next generation with such stories?

One sees this relational dynamic emerge most poignantly in two stories, "The Pants in the Family" and "An Act of Defiance." The first might well be described as a meditation upon the incommunicable nature of the Holocaust. A short narrative of a dramatic moment in Posner's childhood frames a central narrative of the circumstances surrounding his mother's death during his adolescence. Through the acuity of a third-person narrator, Rosenbaum describes an episode on the Atlantic City pier when Posner's father abandons his son for a brief but scary moment. Baited by a barker at the shoot-out gallery— "Your kid will remember this day, when his pop chickened out of a fight" (39)—he releases Adam's hand and, replacing it with a rifle, shoots down every one of the animal targets with ease. The tale emblematizes the estrangement between the Holocaust survivor parent and the second-generation child. At the carnival, the father's past rushes upon him in a flash of memory and separates him from his confused son, psychologically and physically.

In the story's central narrative, Rosenbaum dramatizes the extent of the elder Posner's psychological disorientation as Adam, now the narrator, must make the final medical decisions for his dying mother. When the doctor tells Adam that he really should speak to his father, Adam cries, "Leave him alone, he won't be able to handle it . . . the man's been through enough. He's old and weak, and has been disappointed before by bad news. Just look at him . . . what else do you need to know?" (41). At sixteen, Adam must wear the pants in the family. His father, emotionally embattled and suffering from heart troubles to boot, simply does not have the strength.

Rosenbaum focuses, however, not so much upon the father's physical and psychological trauma as upon Adam Posner's continual struggle to penetrate the mystery of his father's agony. This proves especially difficult since his parents both suffer in silence, thus provoking Adam's frustrated curiosity. Adam's parents do not discuss their Holocaust experiences with their son; they attempt, understandably, to shield him from their pain and send him off to an elite preparatory school. Adam, then, must glean all he can through the silence: "I wanted to know more about what had happened to him during the war. It was always such an impenetrable secret—my parents, speaking in code, changing the passwords repeatedly, keeping me off the scent. And he was always so ill. There was never the occasion to catch them off guard, ask the big questions, holding out for something other than that familiar silence" (48). As Adam's father nears his own death, he becomes more communicative with his son and regrets having imposed a silent childhood upon him. Still, he does not understand why his son wishes to know about the past: "You think you need to know. . . . Do you want to know whether I ever killed someone? How will that change anything? What mystery will that answer?" (50–51). While one senses that certain experiences will remain forever in-scrutable, Adam's father does realize an emotional connection with his son through piercing the silence that had defined their relationship. Before he dies he opens his heart to his son, who embraces it (Adam clutches his father's ni-troglycerin pills). These pills, Rosenbaum suggests, represent the "final prize of the carnival" as Adam's father bridges the chasm between himself and the son he initially abandoned on the Atlantic City boardwalk (53).

Rosenbaum further contemplates the bridges that can and cannot be crossed in "An Act of Defiance." Here he presents us with an adult Adam Pos-ner who teaches a course on the Holocaust to a dwindling and increasingly apathetic group of students. Their lack of interest in the subject mocks Pos-ner's total immersion in it. That he teaches a Holocaust course bespeaks his need, like the younger Posner's need in "The Pants in the Family," to absorb as fully as possible his parents' experiences in the camps. This older Posner, a Ph.D., possesses a keener, more sophisticated understanding of the double bind that plagues him. As much as he strives to learn about the Holocaust experience, he knows that it will always remain an "Americanization," a product of his imagination that continually reinvents and revises his parents' European lives. "My imagination," Posner reflects, "had done all the work—invented suffering, without the physical scars, the incontestable proof" (59).

At the point that we meet Posner in "An Act of Defiance," his relentless imagination has left him emotionally fatigued, and he has begun to plot his escape from his Holocaust scholarship. He wishes to retreat to the "imperfect but amiable world" (59). Small wonder that he does not welcome the news that his uncle Haskell, a Holocaust survivor like his parents, plans to visit him for the first time to, as he puts it, "fix" his nephew's life (57). Posner fears that Haskell's arrival will only exacerbate his psychic torment, "feed my guilt, replenish my craving for the soul of survivors" (59). Interestingly, Haskell proves to be quite a different fish from Adam's father. Rosenbaum, to his credit, complicates our perception of the Holocaust survivor as silent sufferer. Haskell does not care to brood upon the past with his nephew: "I should come here, all the way from Belgium, to talk about the camps? This you need?" (65). Rather, he dates women he knows in New York, strolls through Central Park, coaxes his nephew into riding a tandem bicycle with him, and drags Adam along with him while he breaks a casino's bank in Atlantic City.

Haskell's yen for life, one must recognize, does not betray a lack of emotional depth on his part or a scant memory (the colostomy bag he wears serves as a perpetual reminder, certainly, of the physical ravages he suffered). Instead, Haskell embraces the joy of living to retaliate imperiously against the Nazis. He refuses to allow Hitler a posthumous victory by living a joyless life. As he explains to Adam, "I still know survivors who carry on this way, like your father did. Silent suffering. A private death that traveled with him, wherever he went, a ghost always on his shoulder, whispering into his ear, not letting him eat, work, rest. . . . You see, Adam, my life, with all the riches and pleasures that I allow myself, is an act of defiance. I am an assassin to their mission" (66). It becomes clear that Haskell means to "fix" his nephew's life by compelling him to adopt his own defiant outlook. He tells Adam that he must find a way to let go of the sadness that defines his existence. "There is *tsouris* [troubles] everywhere my boy," he writes Adam in a cautionary note, "but there is always more if this is all you see" (68).

To be sure, one of Rosenbaum's most persistent points in *Elijah Visible* is that the second-generation survivor in America has great difficulty seeing—or imagining, rather—anything else but the *tsouris* of the real survivors. Like the lawyer Posner of "Cattle Car Complex," the Posner of this story vicariously experiences the plight of the survivor when, en route to the airport to greet Haskell, he imagines his interrogation at U.S. Customs: "He fumbles excitedly. Nervous beyond sedation. A Jew with ethnically incriminating papers and a convenient scarlet letter—the shape of a Star of David—patched onto his lapel. Hands move in and out of his pockets. A mad search. Sweat builds on his forehead, then plunges into his eyes. . . . 'Sir, I must see your papers! Now . . . Jew!'" (61). Adam conjures the interrogation so vividly that he alarms his taxi driver by screaming "Stop!" at the imaginary Nazi interrogating his uncle (61). Given the absence of tangible memories, Adam cannot contain his rampant imagination; he continually reconstructs and reinvents their experiences. This, Rosenbaum suggests, is the special burden of the second generation in America.

Haskell evidently comes to appreciate his nephew's predicament, for he agrees to visit Adam's class to discuss his family's plight during the Holocaust. While ostensibly rendering the story to the class, Haskell reveals to Adam the horrible truths surrounding his family's Holocaust experiences. Through Haskell's terse, even matter-of-fact narrative, Adam learns that his father's parents were both murdered before the very eyes of all their children. They were shot after refusing to tell a Nazi where one of their sons, Adam's father, had stowed away weapons in the apartment. Thankfully, Adam's father managed to kill the Nazi with one of his concealed guns before the Nazi could proceed to kill the rest of the family. "There was more to the mystery of my silent father than I had dared realize," Adam reflects upon hearing the story (85). Finally, Adam learns one truth of his father's experience. A period can replace one of the many ellipses of Adam's imagination, offering him, one hopes, a modicum of peace.

"WE'RE NOT REALLY JEWS"

If the unbridgeable chasm dividing memory from imagination in *Elijah Visible* represents Adam Posner's greatest burden as a second-generation survivor in America, the waning of religious faith and adherence following the Holocaust also bears down heavily upon Rosenbaum's protagonist. Alienated from Jewish ritual and belief, Adam Posner cannot turn to religion for solace. True, this theological crisis, in the broad sense, is not peculiar to Americans or to the second-generation survivor for that matter. The God that died on the gallows in Elie Wiesel's first memoir, *Night* (1960), died not only in the eyes of a young Wiesel but in the eyes of many Jews and non-Jews worldwide. That said, Rosenbaum dramatizes in several stories the especially keen spiritual crisis of the second-generation American through Adam Posner, who must reckon not only with his own post-Holocaust religious doubts but with an American *Zeitgeist* of secularism and crass materialism that exacerbates his spiritual crisis.

In "Romancing the *Yohrzeit* Light," Rosenbaum evokes the crisis poignantly as Posner's religious alienation wars against a curious compulsion to commemorate his mother in a religiously meaningful way on the first anniversary of her death. The Posner of this story, an abstract expressionist painter, arguably represents the most disaffected Posner of the collection. Though Posner's mother, Esther, observes the Sabbath rituals and keeps a kosher home, Adam "ate all manner of spineless fish, and the commingled flesh of unhoofed animals. His hot dogs didn't answer to a higher authority other than his own whim of which sidewalk peddler to patronize" (17). He lives close to several synagogues in New York but avoids them at all costs "as though they were virtual leper colonies" (17). Not only does he ignore the high holidays, but he does not even know what time of year to expect them.

Posner's mother laments her son's renunciation of Judaism. She realizes that her son's refusal to observe Jewish rituals confers upon Hitler a posthumous victory, and she castigates Adam (who dons the obligatory black leather of the artist), "I didn't survive the camps so that you could walk around looking and acting like a camp guard. Look at you. Nothing Jewish that I can see" (20). She also does not hesitate to denounce the paganism of her son's art. She pleads with him to paint something Jewish, to abandon the gloomy nihilism that pervades his work. Pointing to one canvas in particular, she opines, "Thank God your father has been dead all these years—because *this* . . . would have killed him" (20). Importantly, Posner's mother does not encourage her son's identification with the Holocaust. A Jewish identity, Rosenbaum suggests, should be rooted not solely in one's remembrance of the European atrocity but in the rich legacy of Judaism that was almost completely snuffed out in the catastrophe.

This controversy surrounding the role that Holocaust remembrance should play in contemporary Jewish American life has recently made its way into Jewish American fiction. I will explore how Rosenbaum addresses the controversy in a moment. But it is worth pausing here to explore how the issue has emerged in the work of other recent Jewish American fictionists as well. For example, in Robert Cohen's recent novel *The Here and Now* (1996) a Hasidic character, Magda Brenner, admonishes the nominally Jewish protagonist for his ignorance of Judaism but easy identification with the Holocaust:

"Here you don't know the first thing about Judaism, not even the basic prayers. But put a number on a man's arm and suddenly you know all about them. . . . Thousands of years of history mean nothing to you, but five years of gas chambers, that means everything. It's perverse, no? The side that suffers and chokes and is defeated, that's the side that feels like a Jew. The healthy part is out playing with the *goyim*."[21] Magda Brenner argues convincingly that a healthy Jewish identity must be rooted in the thousands of years of Judaic history, not in a perverse identification with Hitler's victims. Earlier, Philip Roth challenged this cult of victimhood in *The Counterlife* (1986) through the "FORGET REMEMBERING" plan of Jimmy Lustig. Lustig wishes to dismantle Yad Vashem, Israel's Museum and Remembrance Hall of the Holocaust, since he believes that "we are torturing ourselves with memories! With masochism!" Although Roth portrays Lustig as more than a little bit nuts, the essential principles he articulates—"JEWS NEED NO NAZIS TO BE THE REMARKABLE JEWISH PEOPLE! . . . JUDAISM WITHOUT VICTIMS!"—enjoy an unmistakable currency in the Jewish American community.[22]

To return to "Romancing the *Yohrzeit* Light," Rosenbaum himself emphasizes the importance of Jewish ritual rather than Holocaust remembrance alone. Posner's memory of his mother's unwavering religious faith following her Holocaust experiences impels him to honor her on the first anniversary of her death by seeking out a *Yohrzeit* candle (the plain but long-burning candle that, in accordance with Jewish ritual, mourners light on each anniversary of a loved one's death). The lighting of the *Yohrzeit* represents, for Posner, his first attempt as an adult to reconnect with his Jewish heritage. Spiritually lost in New York, he abides by one meaningful Jewish ritual self-consciously to alleviate some of his pain following his mother's death. He wonders hopefully whether lighting the *Yohrzeit* might help him "find his own way back, too" (22).

Rosenbaum's narrative leads one to anticipate a hopeful conclusion. After Posner purchases the *Yohrzeit*, his art suddenly loses its characteristic dreariness. He paints discernible figures—including several portraits of his mother—in bright, warm colors. Rosenbaum, however, suddenly deflates one's anticipation of Posner's Jewish renewal (or *t'shuvah*) as carnal impulses compete with his theological stirrings. In short, his passion for a non-Jewish woman, Tasha—a Swedish fashion model, no less—interferes with his religious commemoration of his mother's death. Just after Posner lights the *Yohrzeit* for his mother, Tasha bursts through his apartment door and, sprawling kittenishly across the kitchen table, informs Posner that she wishes to consummate their relationship. As she attempts to blow out the *Yohrzeit,* unaware of its religious significance, Posner contemplates the choice that faces him: "He was unequivocally caught between two worlds—sandwiched between two competing desires. A small blond table had served up two irreconcilable courses on this most emotional of evenings: a Swedish smorgasbord of temptation, juxtaposed with a paltry three ounces of scrupulous wax" (30). As one might guess, Jewish observance stands little chance amid such temptation. Posner allows her to suffocate the *Yohrzeit*—that "paltry three ounces of scrupulous wax"—with a coffee saucer. His "need for Tasha's body had abbreviated the anniversary of his mother's death" (31). More disconcertingly, Judaism seems irretrievably lost afterward. First, his art reverts to its former gloominess. Then, the lure of the pagan realm, embodied by Tasha, proves too strong once again for Posner to resist. The story concludes as they celebrate a Swedish Christmas in Posner's apartment, replete with smoked ham, *julgrot,* and Swedish Christmas carols. The only candle lit is the one atop Posner's first Christmas tree. Importantly, these decidedly un-Judaic trappings remove Posner further and further from spiritual well-being. Tasha may have transformed Posner's apartment into her own, but Posner is left to wonder, "Where was *his* home?" (32). The second-generation survivor, Rosenbaum suggests, cannot embrace Judaism given the competing influences in post-Holocaust America and, tragically, remains hopelessly lost without Judaism.

Rosenbaum tempers the cynicism of "Romancing the *Yohrzeit* Light" somewhat in the titular story of the collection, "Elijah Visible." The story opens as Adam Posner, celebrating Passover with his cousins, bemoans the thinning of religion in their lives. Exasperated by the Elvis Costello music blaring in the background and the prosaic American fashion magazines littering the Passover table, he cries, "You call *this* a Seder?" (89). Later he elaborates upon the spiritual hollowness of their perfunctory Passover observance:

> To all those in the room, it was a seance of incomprehensible words, the mother tongue of orphans in the Diaspora, pig Latin for nonkosher Jews. . . . For the past ten years, ever since all the parents of these cousins had died, the Seder, which had once been a solemn and sanctified event, was reduced to a carnival. The informality was seductive, rampant—and everywhere. White yarmulkes lay folded on the table like crescent half-moons—untouched, unworn. The occasional mistake—the lighting of the menorah—inspired no alarm, no tremor of religious infraction. . . . The four questions went unasked, as though

the Posner family didn't want to know the answers, and were sapped of all curiosity. (89)

The desultory Seder illustrates, above all, the result of the silence between the generation of Posner Holocaust survivors and their children. The survivor parents do not discuss their Holocaust experiences, nor do they educate their children in Torah Judaism. Raised to "ignore the lineage that was unalterably theirs," Adam and his cousins cling to near-vacuous Jewish identities (95). Their lives exemplify the assimilatory trend in postwar America that Arthur Hertzberg so assiduously documents in *The Jews in America: Four Centuries of an Uneasy Encounter: A History* (1989). Especially disturbing, in fact, is the complacent manner with which Jewish parents, according to Hertzberg, directed their children's Jewish education: "What the mass of parents wanted, apart from a decent performance at bar mitzvah, was that the school impart to their children enough of the sense of Jewish loyalty so that they would be inoculated against intermarriage. . . . Once that inoculation had supposedly taken hold, the Jewish child could then be launched on his next task, to succeed in being admitted into a prestigious college."[23]

Adam and his cousins certainly appear to be the product of such an upbringing. However, a letter that Adam and his cousins receive from their cousin Artur, the last surviving relative of their parents' generation, jolts Adam from his spiritual complacency. Illustrative of the presence of the European past in the second generation, cousin Artur, who fled to Palestine after surviving Auschwitz, still lives and wishes to meet his cousins in America. He wishes to tell them about their family's history in Europe. Says Artur in the letter, "Your children should know what happened. They must continue to remind the world. . . . We must learn the lessons from the fire" (97). While Artur's letter moves Adam, his American cousins believe cynically that Artur intends only to exploit their sympathy so that they will foot the bill for his trip to the United States. Their convictions are rooted in their obscure knowledge of a longstanding feud over money between Artur and their parents.

The story harks back to Saul Bellow's "The Old System" (1968), perhaps the central postimmigrant story about Jews and money in America. In Bellow's story Dr. Braun remembers the bitter money feud between his two older cousins, Isaac and Tina. Their lifelong enmity offers him a glimpse into the maw of America as he observes how rampant materialism and sexual wantonness in America commingle dangerously with an "old system" of Jewish values that extols family cohesiveness above all.[24] In "Elijah Visible" the second-generation Posners must also revisit the money feud between their relatives.

However, the stakes are much higher in Rosenbaum's "Elijah Visible" than in "The Old System." Bellow's Dr. Braun, scarcely younger than his cousins, more or less shared their postimmigrant experience in America and struggles only to make sense of it. By contrast, the second generation of Rosenbaum's story did not participate in their relatives' European experiences, and moreover they possess only a limited knowledge of those experiences. Artur holds the key to a secret past that they can either claim, by embracing Artur, or eschew, by rejecting his overtures.

Adam's cousins, reflecting upon Artur's unpaid collect calls to their parents and other trivialities, initially choose to continue the grudge against him. They, like their petty and materialistic father, have embraced the "fat gods" of America (to borrow a phrase from Bellow) and perforce have little use for Artur. Their suspicions of Artur's motives aside, Adam's affluent cousins believe that they are doing just fine and cannot readily see how Artur might "save" them. It thus falls to Adam to describe to his cousins what they have indeed lost: "Listen to the music we play around here; we've lost our soul. We don't know who we are, where we come from, why we should care about tomorrow. Your kids are running around here like a couple of zombies; it could be Easter for all they know" (101). As Adam recounts the spare details he does know concerning their parents' Holocaust experiences, he forces his cousins to confront their family's painful history and to accept the burden of remembrance and their concomitant obligation to keep Torah Judaism alive. They realize that they cannot perpetuate the silence of their parents. "We can't afford," Adam argues, "to do that again. We owe it to the children, to ourselves—there's too much at stake" (102). Their cousin Artur, like Haskell in "An Act of Defiance," represents the final link to a past that they must claim. Even though Elijah does not make an appearance at the Posner cousins' Seder, Artur, by story's end, is on the way. The second generation, Rosenbaum suggests, might yet achieve *t'shuvah*.

In *Elijah Visible* Rosenbaum dramatizes the near rupture of Jewish existence, but he also envisions the restoration of Jewish continuity through the piercing of the silence between Holocaust survivors and second-generation children; through the defiant humor of Haskell, who uses the numbers of his Holocaust tattoo to triumph at an Atlantic City roulette wheel; through the similar defiance embodied in the Holocaust survivors' mantra at Cohen's summer cottages—"Leisure *Macht Frei*"; and through the sizzle of a match that poignantly triggers Posner's memories of his mother over the Shabbat candles.

As a second-generation writer, Rosenbaum realizes painfully the unimaginable nature of the Holocaust. That he can never truly comprehend the horrors experienced by his parents is both his burden and his muse. Most importantly, perhaps, his protagonist's psychological immersion in the Holocaust raises questions that face both the children of survivors and the broader Jewish American community today: How and to what extent should Holocaust remembrance inform the contemporary Jewish American ethos? Can Holocaust education and Torah Judaism peacefully coexist? Might they even bolster one another to forge a stronger Jewish American identity? Rosenbaum does not offer answers to these questions. The stories in *Elijah Visible* suggest, finally, that it is in the fervent search for answers, rather than in the answers themselves, that the key to a meaningful Jewish American identity lies.

6 SURVIVING REGO PARK

Holocaust Theory from Art Spiegelman to Berel Lang

Amy Hungerford

In the final frame of Art Spiegelman's comic book *Maus I,* the protagonist, Art, calls his father a "murderer."[1] Vladek has not actually killed anyone; indeed, Art doesn't exactly believe that Vladek has killed anyone. What Vladek *has* done is burn the diaries of his dead wife, and it is this act of destruction that Art calls murder, as if the destruction of Anja's record of her experiences at Auschwitz were somehow equivalent to the kinds of destruction that took place at Auschwitz. And although the equation between the destruction of representations (the diaries) and the destruction of persons (the Jews)—the equation more generally between persons and representations—may seem at best hyperbolic, it is, I want to begin by suggesting, characteristic of a certain contemporary discourse of the Holocaust. The equation plays a role not only in imaginative representations of the Holocaust like *Maus* but also in critiques of the very idea of an imaginative representation of the Holocaust.

Berel Lang argues in his essay "The Representation of Limits" that all literary representations of the Holocaust are violations of the facts of history, and that the violation of the facts of history is immoral in the same way that the violation of persons is. Literary representations violate the facts of history because the mere idea of such "imaginative representations" makes the implicit claim "that the facts do not speak for themselves, that figurative condensation and displacement and the authorial presence these articulate will turn or supplement the historical subject (whatever it is) in a way that represents the subject more compellingly or effectively—in the end, more truly—than would be the case without them."[2] So the facts that would otherwise "speak for themselves"—facts that, Lang claims, "do not depend on the author's voice for their

The final page from Maus I: My Father Bleeds History.

existence" (RL, 316)—are silenced by imaginative representation, or, more precisely, the historical representations through which the facts should be allowed to speak are silenced by imaginative representation.

Thus, Lang describes the treatment of facts in literary representations in terms of oppression, oppression that mirrors what Jews suffered during the Holocaust: "The denial of individuality and personhood in the act of genocide; the abstract bureaucracy that empowered the Final Solution, moved by an almost indistinguishable combination of corporate and individual will and blindness to evil, constitute a subject that in its elements seems at odds with the insulation of figurative discourse and the individuation of character and motivation that literary 'making' tends to impose on its subjects" (RL, 316). The historical fact that is here "at odds" with literary representation is that Nazi brutality reduced people to nonpersons, denying them the marks of personhood; since "figurative discourse" endows the victims with personhood— with "motivation" and "individuation of character"—it thus "defies" the historical facts that might otherwise have "spoken for themselves." And so these marks of personhood become an *imposition* upon the subjects of literary representation, who are in this case the very persons who were also imposed upon by the Final Solution. Literary representation denies the historical facts their specific content, their individuality; in essence, it denies them the marks of personhood. As we shall see, such treatment of historical representations—of the facts that those representations contain—is understood by Lang as a kind of murder, not simply a denial but a repetition of the Holocaust.

Once we put the point in this way, we can see more clearly how Spiegelman's personification of Anja's diaries and Lang's personification of historical representations can be located within a larger cultural project. Indeed, the very idea of culture may be understood in terms of this project. For the most common site upon which we relocate the pathos that ordinarily belongs to the human victim—the victim of murder—is neither the diary nor the history but the culture. What worries many who are invested in the future of certain cultural groups is that, as Eddy Zemach puts it in his essay "Custodians," "cultures can die."[3]

Expressions of this anxiety cross the generic spectrum from popular fiction to scholarly essays and can refer to almost any culture. In the Native American community, for example, the threat to the continuance of the culture has historically taken the form of adoption of Indian children by white families. Thus, the plot of Barbara Kingsolver's best-selling *Pigs in Heaven* pits a loving and well-meaning white woman who adopts—illegally, it turns out—an abandoned Cherokee child against an equally well-meaning Cherokee lawyer who sees such illegal adoptions as a threat to the survival of Indian culture.[4] Kingsolver gives us a solution that only fiction could provide: the adoptive mother turns out to be part Cherokee after all, and by the end of the book *her* mother marries a man who turns out to be the child's grandfather. Yet the very structure of the solution, improbable as it may seem, is not far from the kind of solution scholars such as Eddy Zemach advocate to counteract what they and others see as the impending death of Jewish culture.

For the Jewish community the threat to continuance has not been adoption but assimilation and intermarriage. Sociologists of the American Jewish community divide up into "optimist" and "pessimist" schools, or "accommodationist" and "assimilationist" schools, according to how likely they think it is that there will be in the future as there has been in the past something identifiable as a Jewish ethnic group in America. The essays in *The Americanization of the Jews* are mostly of the "pessimist" bent. Paul Ritterband, for instance, cites declining fertility, increasing intermarriage, and increasing geographical dispersion of Jews in America as "emblematic of the devolution of the Jews in our time." "Jewishness," he writes, "is attenuating."[5] Charles Liebman is equally skeptical about the viability of what he calls "a group that defines itself as Jewish and that is recognizably Jewish" in America. He fears that although in the future a group might continue to "define itself" as Jewish, the group might nevertheless "become so assimilated that they are culturally unrecognizable as Jews."[6] The historian Arthur Hertzberg points to the decline of anti-Semitism and the increasing distance of present-day Jews from the immigrant generation as forces that could result in the disappearance of the ethnic community.[7]

In the face of this outlook, advocates of continuity feel compelled to step forward and offer rationales for resisting such change. Zemach, one such advocate, argues that "the question is not whether one is to accept a culture; it is what culture, and what group that incorporates it, with which one chooses to associate oneself. That decision is most significant: Choosing not to align oneself with a group, say, not to join the local Jewish community, shapes the community's destiny, for one makes it an even smaller minority. . . . Cultures can die."[8] Against the possibility that a culture will "die" or be lost, people must be recruited to propagate the culture. If in Kingsolver's novel the death of culture is warded off by the enrollment of "new" Cherokees, we can see that for Zemach the solution is similar. Cultural death can be warded off by recruiting Jews to the practice of a Jewish cultural tradition; indeed, cultural death can be avoided by the enrollment of "new" Jews.

But the question remains, Why should any culture survive? Why should Jewish culture in particular survive? If recruitment to an identity is *possible* because we think of cultural identity as something that can be claimed and lost, as something that is not simply equivalent to one's present beliefs and practices, it can only be *necessary* insofar as we also believe that certain cultural practices are not only ephemeral but also inherently valuable, and in fact more valuable than those that threaten to replace them. This is always a difficult case to make, as advocates of recruitment rarely wish to denigrate other cultural practices in the process. Thus, while Zemach notes that certain desirable practices such as philanthropy or intellectual achievement have become associated with Jewishness, and that Jewish liturgy serves as the container for a valuable "anthology of hundreds of years of literature," his rationale for recruitment turns on the notion that cultural practices are inherently valuable in the same way that we think human life is inherently valuable; he implies that we should strive to avert the death of most any culture (not just Jewish culture) simply because it is a death.[9] Though this may provide a rationale for *adopting* any particular cultural practice, and especially any "dying" minority practice, it cannot provide a rationale for *abandoning* whatever practice the new one replaces, for that abandonment would always mean contributing to a cultural death, albeit a different one.

In his controversial book *Why Should Jews Survive?* Michael Goldberg takes on this objection while continuing to argue for the survival of Jewish culture.[10] He answers his title question in a way that is at once historicist and religious. Goldberg points out that cultures rise and die out all the time without significant losses to humanity as a whole, and he argues that the only coherent reason for Jews to resist this cycle—to consider themselves exceptional as a people—is the covenant relationship that the Jewish people traditionally claim with God. Goldberg thus argues against both those like Zemach who find inherent value in perpetuation and those who argue that Jewish culture in particular must perpetuate itself in order to both mourn for and defy the Holocaust.

It is this latter group with which he is most concerned, because he believes that the Holocaust—and not the interest in perpetuation—has structurally replaced God in the Jewish community. Goldberg traces how traditional religious characteristics of the Jewish people—such as the belief in chosenness or uniqueness—are secularized by transferring those characteristics to the experience of the Holocaust; hence the intense scholarly interest in theorizing its uniqueness. He claims that when the Holocaust is simultaneously heralded as the death of God, it comes to fill the place of God and thus constitutes an instance of idolatry that parallels the ancient Jews' worship of Ba'al. Why should Jews survive, then? According to Goldberg, the Jews as a people should survive in order to fulfill the Messianic promise God has made through them to all the world.

Although his account is a coherent one, to a generation of thoroughly secularized Jews in America Goldberg's rationale for survival sounds at best old-fashioned and at worst absurd. But most would admit that Goldberg is right on one count: the Holocaust has indeed become a cornerstone of Jewish identity in America (Israel is different in this regard.)[11] In light of this, the passing of the generation who actually experienced the Holocaust presents a problem for the construction of Jewish identity. If the answer to the question, Why should Jews survive? is going to remain centered on the Holocaust, and if one's connection to the Holocaust rather than one's commitment to Judaism stands at the center of American Jewish identity, the passing of that generation threatens to sever the community's ties to an important source of its identity. That new ways of connecting to the Holocaust are being constructed is obvious as we watch the proliferation of movies, books, classes, and museums that tell the Holocaust story, and as we witness the separate efforts of the Yale Video Archive and moviemaker Steven Spielberg to collect videotaped testimonies of survivors. Since the new connections remain independent of the life of individual survivors for their future existence, they promise to remain available to all for all time.

What is less obvious, and more interesting, is *how* these representations of the Holocaust forge connections between that event and present-day people, and by what discursive technologies this recruitment to identity occurs. As we examine how these technologies work in some of the best-known historical and imaginative representations of the Holocaust—Spielberg's *Schindler's List*, the United States Holocaust Memorial Museum, the *Maus* books, and the writings of Berel Lang—we will begin to see that they invite not only Jews but also non-Jews to connect to the Holocaust. If, as Goldberg's argument suggests, Jews are, through the story of the Holocaust, recruited to what has become the center of Jewishness, what can the technologies by which that recruitment takes place tell us about the nature of Jewish identity? When non-Jews are recruited to identify with the Holocaust, are they being recruited to the same thing as Jews? These questions have no single answer. By analyzing how recruitment works and the technologies on which it relies—which is the main concern of this essay—we will uncover a range of possible answers. I will begin with a recruitment technology that relies on the equation between persons and representations sketched above: the technology of the list.

FROM HISTORY TO THE LIST

In "The Representation of Limits" Berel Lang works to build a theoretical structure upon which all representations of the Holocaust can be based and against which they can be judged; he explicates and argues for a formula meant to help writers and readers think about the moral aspects of any particular project (though all of Lang's examples involve discussions of the Holocaust). Lang calls the formula and its product "the moral radical of representation."[12] To illustrate the use of the moral radical, Lang proposes that there is a moral difference between the functionalist and intentionalist accounts of the Final Solution.[13] The former, he claims, assigns responsibility to a system, thus exculpating the individual and rendering the Holocaust "collectively unintended" (RL, 309), while the latter holds the individual responsible and maintains that the Holocaust was intended in all its extremity. Though everyone would agree that the difference Lang describes is a historical one—a difference between one version of how things happened and another—we might at this point want to ask what makes the difference between functionalist and intentionalist versions of the Holocaust distinct from other divergent versions of history. Why does the difference become a moral issue for the interpreter? While functionalist and intentionalist versions of history certainly point to different moral judgments of Hitler and his officials, it is not clear why the historian becomes less moral if the judgment against Hitler—based on an analysis of historical events—becomes less severe.

Lang contends that the morality of any historical account rests upon the "consequences" of the particular version of history; presumably, divergent accounts of the Holocaust are distinct from divergent accounts of other events—consider, for the sake of argument, the 1980 presidential election—because any given interpretation of the Holocaust means more or is somehow more powerful in the culture than any given interpretation of the presidential election. But while Lang asserts that "it is clear that differences on this issue [of intention] have significant moral and social consequences" (RL, 308), he never specifies what these "moral and social consequences" might be. What does become clear is Lang's preference—and a moralized one—for connecting events or statements as tightly as possible with nameable individuals and their intentions. What is at stake, then, between functionalist and intentionalist accounts is perhaps not so much the existence of consequences as the existence of intentions—intentions upon which judgments about moral responsibility can be built. In this case it is Hitler's intentions that are at issue; at this point in Lang's argument it is not the historian's intentions that appear to be at issue but rather his response to unspecified "social consequences" of his work. But in the next stage of the argument the question of intention appears to shift from Hitler to historian, and the object of responsibility shifts from the community—from a group of people—to representations.

This shift takes place through Lang's second example of the formula's application, in which he uses it to judge histories of the Final Solution that insist that there was no systematic killing of Jews by Nazis. The (again unspecified) risk calculated by Lang's moral radical increases dramatically with this kind of denial. He argues that the degree of risk incurred justifies an equally extreme response from what he calls a "moral community." The "moral community" Lang invokes in his example of a justified response is a conference of Holocaust historians meeting in Boston. During the question-and-answer period following a presentation by Saul Friedlander, the notorious Holocaust denier Arthur Butz challenges Friedlander's version of history, implying or claiming—Lang does not print Butz's question—that the Holocaust as Friedlander represented it did not occur. Friedlander refuses to answer the question, and Lang reads that response as a moral decision. According to Lang's gloss on the incident, Friedlander acted as the voice of a moral community that wisely resists the kind of risky history for which Butz was arguing (RL, 312). Though Lang's example centers on a community of scholars, Butz's failing is importantly not a scholarly one; Arthur Butz is, according to Lang, a person who has "separated himself" from the moral community (RL, 312); he is not simply an incompetent historian. Since Lang seemingly cannot account for the "social and moral consequences" of Butz's version of history, what is the risk he runs and whom does he stand to harm by producing incompetent history? Why, precisely, is Butz not mistaken but immoral?

Lang suggests that if Friedlander were to have answered Arthur Butz's question, he would have had to believe that "questions can be detached from people," and that "historical representation has no intrinsic or necessary moral standing" (RL, 312). His refusal rightly, according to Lang, resisted not simply the question but also these assumptions. Lang believes that these assumptions "are rightfully disputed, not uniquely in their bearing on accounts of the 'Final Solution.'" For the same reason that he favors the intentionalist over the functionalist account of the Holocaust, Lang believes that statements as well as actions must, of moral necessity, be attached to people and their intentions; for Lang this is a question of social responsibility. But by implying that the whole "moral community" recognizes that historical representations have "moral standing" in and of themselves, he transfers morality from the relation between persons—social responsibility—to the relation between persons and representations. If these two relations become nearly indistinguishable in Lang's essay, it is because persons and representations are nearly indistinguishable. By the end of the essay Lang has moved from the attachment of representations to persons (through intention and responsibility), to the "intrinsic moral standing" of facts, to the "moral presence" (RL, 313) of facts. Thus, the moral indictment against Butz will not be the seemingly commonsense one—that Butz is immoral because his revisionist history serves anti-Semitic aims. Lang does not in fact need to impute to Butz anti-Semitic intentions (intentions to harm people) if he can cast Butz's history as an anti-Semitic act (actually harming the equivalent of people).[14]

We can understand in a new way, then, why scholars such as Lang—not to mention the general public—are outraged over Holocaust revisionism as if it were a form of murder, and why historians have made concerted efforts to suppress it despite their profession's allegiance to the idea of free speech.[15] We can also make sense of Lang's claim that artistic representations, in obscuring morally present facts, also obscure or erase the real (historical) victims and therefore reenact the genocide. Thus, the responsibility that Lang wants to assign to historians is not—since Lang never specifies precisely how it could be—a responsibility toward present society. After all, figures like Arthur Butz are so marginal in their beliefs that they pose little threat to social order even if they do spark public debate. Rather, the risk a historian or anyone runs in discussing the Holocaust is that of harming these morally present facts.

Because Lang is committed both to the moral presence of facts and to the immorality of imaginative representations of those facts, he advocates the chronicle as the most moral form of history for the Holocaust; it is a form that simply lists historical events in chronological order, leaving only the selection of events to the discretion of the historian. This form is supposed to allow the facts "to speak for themselves" and is meant to remove the agency and voice of the historian as much as possible from the scene of representation. Lang is not so naive as to think that the chronicle avoids questions of the historian's agency altogether, but he considers debate about which events to include to be taking place on the safest moral ground. But the idea of the chronicle is most interesting not because it raises questions about the historian's agency; rather, it is interesting because on the theoretical level the chronicle lists facts in the same way that—in an increasingly popular form of Holocaust memorial—the ritual reading of names lists victims. Indeed, insofar as the facts are endowed by Lang with the "moral presence" of persons—and it is because they are so endowed that they must be chronicled rather than narrated—the chronicle already is a list of names. The history that Lang reduces to chronicle is a history that he has transformed into memorial.

So if history becomes chronicle and chronicle becomes memorial, the historian assumes the position of the mourner as he "remembers" the events and the people lost. The technology of the list thus connects the historian to the event not only as a scholarly mind thinking about a subject but more importantly as a relative grieving for a lost family member. This same connection is constructed and encouraged by another repository of Holocaust history, the United States Holocaust Memorial Museum, an institution that has also managed to merge the practice of history and the practice of memorial.[16] The purpose of much of the museum's design is to bring the visitor into a personal and emotional relation with the events the exhibits describe.

Most obviously, this personal relation is constructed through the "identity card" each visitor is given before entering the permanent exhibit. From the main concourse of the museum an usher directs visitors into the cordoned-off space in front of elevators that take them to the opening of the exhibit on the fourth floor. In that space is a table piled with booklets labeled "Identity Card" and sorted by gender that each contain the photograph and story of a Holocaust victim. The usher encourages visitors to take an identity card according to their gender—initially these booklets were to be matched with visitors according to age as well—and instructs them not to open it until the end of the first level of the exhibit. The four pages of the identity card tell the story of the featured person in chronological order, each page of the story to be turned at the end of the corresponding level of the exhibit. Because the visitor is invited to identify with the victim not only by reading his or her story (by learning about the victim) but also by carrying identity papers (by behaving like the victim), the visitor becomes both a mourning family member and the double of the person whose story he or she carries. The visitor can then search for his or her "own" name among the memorial lists that cover the museum's interior windows.[17]

This process surprises us far too little. At the Vietnam War Memorial, just up the Mall from the Holocaust museum, if visitors look for a specific name among those listed on the black marble, it is because the name is one they know from their town or is their own surname. It is a name they knew before they arrived. Experience, not a pamphlet, provided them with it. Those of us who did not know the dead, who have no personal connection to them, may scan the names for a while or simply take in the grim impersonality of the list. The Vietnam memorial—and in fact most public memorials—is designed to be both personal and impersonal. In contrast, the Holocaust museum provides for every visitor a familial or personal connection to the victims that most of us lack. This works, of course, for Jews and for non-Jews.

While lists at the Holocaust museum can, with the help of identity cards, provide the visitor with "ancestors" who experienced the Holocaust, Steven Spielberg's film version of the novel *Schindler's List* takes the technology of the list and runs it backwards in time, providing Jewish descendants for a non-Jewish moral hero.[18] In fact, much of the film is taken up with maneuvering the list into the position where it can perform such work, since list making begins as a thoroughly repressive tool. In the opening scene we see the registration—the listing—of rural Jews in a Krakow train station as the first stage of their journey toward Auschwitz; later, Itzaac Stern is almost carried away on a train to the death camps because his name was accidentally put on a deportation list. But whereas these scenes of list making explore how the list gives or denies power to individuals—those who are on the list are powerless, those making the list powerful—the final, and definitive, scenes of list making cast the list not as a repressive tool but rather as a genealogy. When Schindler makes his final list of the Jews he is to buy name by name from the horrible Amon Goeth, Schindler says to Goeth, "I want my people," to which Goeth replies, "Who are you, Moses?"

Lest the viewer miss the implication, the final scenes of the film expand upon the biblical paradigm: Spielberg moves from a black-and-white scene of the survivors from Schindler's factory marching across a field into a color picture of the real, present-day descendants of those now announced on the screen as "The Schindler Jews." One by one these descendants place stones on the grave of Oskar Schindler. Text appears over the scene of the graveyard telling us that there are fewer than a thousand Jews left in Poland today. In the next frame the viewer is told that there are over four thousand "Schindler Jews" and their descendants living today. Spielberg thus invokes both the genealogical representations of Genesis and the real persons to which the film refers, blurring the boundary between representation and reality to produce his final interpretation of the Schindler story: by making a list, Schindler claims "his own people"; by saying their names and laying their stones, the Schindler Jews claim him—a Gentile—as their ancestor, the man who gave them life.

The last image of *Schindler's List* takes that point yet one step further. The last hand to touch Schindler's gravestone at the end of the film places a flower there, not a stone, and it is not, like the other hands, named as belonging to one of the "Schindler Jews." The unnamed hand is reputed to be Spielberg's, but in its anonymity it stands for any hand, for the reverent viewer's hand. Though Spielberg may rest his connection to Schindler on the fact of his own racial Jewishness, the hand we see is in no way marked as Jewish.[19] In the end, anyone can form a connection to Schindler in this way, regardless of his or her relation to Schindler's acts during the war and regardless of race; anyone can lay a stone or a flower on Schindler's grave and thus claim him as a forefather.

It is clear that *Schindler's List* and the Holocaust museum, insofar as they recruit both Jews and non-Jews to identify with the Holocaust victims, cannot be said to recruit to a specifically Jewish identity; if they do recruit Jews to identify with their race, they do not do the same for non-Jews. The purpose of devices that produce identification with the victims in the film and the museum is a moral one; the film invites any viewer to honor the morality of Schindler's efforts to save lives, and the museum invites the visitor to a historical awareness that will inevitably result in his or her commitment to prevention, to the slogan "Never again." In other words, we are invited to honor Schindler and abhor Hitler, not because one saved Jews and one killed Jews, but because one saved lives and one took them. The film and the museum share the assumption that—as the generality of "Never again" implies—the Holocaust could happen to anyone, to any group. The non-Jew could be a victim, too. If the line thus blurs between Jewishness and non-Jewishness in these particular presentations of the Holocaust, then recruitment looks only incidentally like recruitment to Jewish identity. In Spiegelman's *Maus*, on the other hand, because the line between Jewishness and non-Jewishness is dramatized by the animal heads, we see a version of the recruitment phenomenon that can tell us more about what it might mean to recruit to a more specifically Jewish identity through a representation of the Holocaust.

The technologies of connection we see in *Maus* in fact do, like the Holocaust museum, recruit both Jews and non-Jews to identify with the Holocaust. The very device that governs the drawings—the device that makes the books so distinctive—demonstrates the ways in which anyone can come to identify with the event.

For example, when, at the beginning of *Maus II*, Art considers which animal to use in drawing Françoise, his French and non-Jewish wife, she reminds him that she converted to Judaism and so must be a mouse, too.[20] Although Françoise's conversion is religious, Jewish faith is not represented as part of her character; her mouseness finally connects her not to a religion or even a cultural practice but simply to the family of her husband, to various Holocaust survivors, and most importantly to the mouse victims of the story Vladek tells and Art draws. Conversion brings not a new faith or a new culture but a new body contiguous with the Jewish bodies populating the story. In this case, Jewishness—signaled by the mouse head—is inseparable from connection to the Holocaust: because Françoise has a mouse head even as Art

From Maus II: And Here My Troubles Began.

is deciding how to draw her, it is not even clear whether she is connected to the Holocaust because she is Jewish or whether she is Jewish because, through her husband, she is connected to the Holocaust.

It is important to note that although Françoise's conversion and her resulting identity as a mouse give her relation to the past a certain pathos (she is identified with the victims), any of the options we see Art doodling in his sketchbook (a frog, a moose, a rabbit, a French poodle) would have given her some relation to the event, as the animal heads do for all the characters regardless of their personal relation to the Holocaust. The boys who abandon little Artie in the flashback scene that opens *Maus I* are depicted as dogs, a choice of animal proleptically motivated by the Holocaust story Art will eventually draw. Even American place names must be read in relation to the Holocaust: Vladek's vacation house, flanked by a house owned by another survivor couple, is located in "the Catskills." All important aspects of the present take their identity from the past event, though these identities differ from those constructed by the Holocaust museum's identity cards. Identification with the victims—something assigned to everyone at the museum—is in *Maus* reserved for those who are Jewish (what that term means in *Maus* must remain an open question for now). *Maus* finds the source of present-day identities not only in the victims of the Holocaust, then, but also in other participants in World War II.

Although Françoise argues successfully for her identification with the victims—her logic convinces Art to make her a mouse—*Maus* as a whole provides no consistent system by which such eligibility can be established for all characters. Even when Art chooses Françoise's identity, it appears that the choices between identities—choices about which animal heads designate which identities *and* choices about which characters get which heads—are motivated primarily by the cartoonist's imagination. The sketchpad full of other possibilities for Françoise's character foregrounds these as imaginative and perhaps arbitrary choices in spite of her protestations to the contrary. Art made her a mouse, but perhaps not because of her conversion. Indeed, some Jews in *Maus* may not be identified with the victims at all: in *Maus II*, when asked how he would draw Israeli Jews, Art suggests porcupines, which in its very humor also draws attention to the choice as choice rather than necessity. Humor, not Holocaust history, makes the suggestion seem right.

While these passages seem to suggest that one's connection to the past is the product of imagination—here, the cartoonist's imagination—Spiegelman is in fact committed to a connection based on the facts of history. The central choice of mouse heads for the Jews is motivated by a very specific history: by the ways in which Nazis represented Jews prior to and during the war. The epigraph to *Maus II* makes that motivation explicit by quoting a German newspaper of the mid-1930s: "Mickey Mouse is the most miserable ideal ever revealed. . . . Healthy emotions tell every independent young man and every honorable youth that the dirty and filth-covered vermin, the greatest bacteria carrier in the animal kingdom, cannot be the ideal type of animal. . . . Away with Jewish brutalization of the people! Down with Mickey Mouse! Wear the Swastika Cross!" (*II*, 3). All persons in the present are in effect identified in relation to the Holocaust—to the paradigms of Nazi discourse—rather than in relation to some other source of identity in the present; for example, present-day Germans in *Maus* have identities linked with Nazism rather than with the political parties to which they might plausibly belong in the present. And Jews remain mice in present-day America, retaining with that identity all the connotations of victimhood that made the identity appropriate for Vladek's Holocaust story.[21]

While the epigraph thus suggests that *general* identities in Maus—German cats and Jewish mice—are motivated by history rather than imagination, other features of the text suggest that even *particular* identities—a mouse named Mala and a cartoonist-mouse named Art—are motivated by history, albeit a family history. The dedications and credits at the opening of each *Maus* volume emphasize this motivation. The acknowledgments in *Maus I* list people—Paul Pavel, Mala Spiegelman, Françoise Mouly—who later appear as characters in the strip; the opening of *Maus II* reads like a note about the author as it describes how "Art Spiegelman, a cartoonist born after WWII, is working on a book about what happened to his parents as Jews in wartime Poland" (*II*, 6). Though the opening of *Maus II* serves as a summary of *Maus I*, it also serves to blur the distinction between the author and his character, Art, between other characters and their real counterparts, and between the inside and the outside of the cartoon itself.

Occasional photographs also contribute to this blurring of boundaries between the cartoon characters and real people. *Maus I* contains just one, and that one photo is actually part of a cartoon within the cartoon. When Art's mother commits suicide, he draws a comic entitled "Prisoner on the Hell Planet" in which the characters are represented in distorted, but human, forms. In its upper left-hand corner a hand grips a snapshot of Anja with her son next to her. The comic itself, actually produced by Art Spiegelman after his mother's suicide—it first appeared in *Short Order Comix*, no. 1 (1973)— and the photo within it remind the reader that this is a true story, that the characters represent real people, that the comic is, as Spiegelman has insisted outside as well as within the covers of *Maus*, nonfiction. In *Maus II* a photo of Vladek and Anja's lost son Richieu produces the same effect. Far from disrupting narrative, as Marianne Hirsch has suggested, the photographs attempt to make history and comic one seamless reality within narrative.[22]

Though the analysis above makes the logic of Spiegelman's drawings appear to be fairly simple—they relate the present to the past, the real to the artificial—the theoretical work that enables these relations is as complicated as Berel Lang's historiography. Since people do not in fact have mouse heads, how does *Maus* argue for the truth—the biographical and autobiographical genre, and the nonfiction status—of its story? Why does Spiegelman go to the trouble of consistently calling attention both to the figurative aspect of his work and to its transparent connection to real persons and real events? We can begin to formulate answers to these questions if we look at chapter 2 of *Maus II*, where Spiegelman interrogates the relation of the animal head to the identity of his characters by introducing a new element into the drawings: the

Family photo of Art and his mother, inserted into the short comic (included in Maus I) about Anja's suicide.

mouse mask. The head and the mask, it turns out, are not the same thing, and it is precisely in the distinction between them that *Maus*'s claim to non-fictionality and its central claims about identity lie.[23]

Chapter 2 opens with a human-headed Art wearing a mouse mask, sitting at his cartooning desk feeling depressed and incapable of continuing with his book. In by now familiar Holocaust-history fashion, he recounts the dates of certain events as if they were part of a chronicle: "Vladek died of congestive heart failure on August 18, 1982," "Françoise and I stayed with him in the Catskills back in August 1979," "Vladek started working as a tinman in Auschwitz in the spring of 1944." The events of the present and past, of Holocaust history and family history, are mixed up together, creating a confusion of time frames that finally produces the ambiguous phrase, "We're ready to shoot!" (*II*, 41): is it the cameraman ready to start filming an interview or a Nazi guard ready to shoot a prisoner? Outside the window of Art's studio we see the guard tower of a concentration camp; on his floor lie piles of naked mouse-headed bodies. From frame to frame Art shrinks in stature, becoming childlike in the face of remembered events and present commercial success.

What binds the events and images of present and past together is, of

Art wearing the mouse mask, from Maus II.

course, Art's mental state, his depression. In the cartoon, as in most popular psychology, depression is the disease of being controlled by a traumatic personal past, a disease of being unable to forget painful experiences. But Art's depression links him not only to events he himself experienced, such as his mother's suicide, but also to tragedies he did not experience, such as the murder of Jews at Auschwitz. Depression, here indistinguishable from the structure of remembering, becomes another technology through which a person's identity transcends the limits of that person's current experience and personal past to encompass experiences—like the Holocaust—that are historically remote from the individual. Though depression looks here like the disease of too much connection with the past, the fact that Art's malady is signaled by the mask would suggest otherwise.

If depression makes Art feel distant from the person—or mouse—he is in the rest of the comic, if it makes his and even other people's historically grounded identities feel like masks, the cure for depression will be not less connection to the past but more. In other words, Art's problem turns out to be not the past but his inadequate connection to the particular past that his organic mouse head embodies. Art's session with Pavel, his survivor-psychiatrist—conducted in masks—will solve this problem by forging a new kind of connection between Art and the experience of the Holocaust. Instead of being connected to the past by depression, Art will be able to connect through narration, through telling a true Holocaust story. We will see that in *Maus* the narrative connection is in turn imagined as a bodily one; when narrative is restored, the mouse mask turns back into the mouse head. To put my initial formulation another way, what appears at first to be the symptom of depression—Art's inability to write—turns out to look like the cause of depression, for the session with Pavel suggests that the restoration of narrative in fact cures depression.

One part of the session with Pavel, then, is dedicated to solving the kinds of philosophical problems with narrative that also trouble Berel Lang: How, both Art and Pavel wonder, can Art accurately represent such extreme suffering? Should Art really speak for the victims? Pavel suggests that "the victims who died can never tell THEIR side of the story, so maybe it's better not to have any more stories" (*II*, 45). Initially Art agrees. "Samuel Beckett," he points out, "once said: 'Every word is like an unnecessary stain on silence and nothingness'"; but a frame of unproductive silence causes both of them to reconsider Beckett's point. "[Beckett] was right," Pavel says. "Maybe you can in-

Art growing taller as he walks home from his session with Pavel, from Maus II.

clude it in your book." Once they agree that one can, ethically, tell Holocaust stories, the practical problem of access—that Art can't imagine what it was like in Auschwitz and can't visualize the tin shop clearly—can be solved by using the narration they have just endorsed. Through narrative, experience and memory are transferable between persons: Pavel shouts "Boo," startling Art. "It [Auschwitz]," he says, "felt like that" (*II,* 46). Then Pavel provides from his own memory, not of the camps but of his childhood, the details Art needs in order to draw the tin shop in which his father was forced to work. In the practical work of forging narrative connections with the past, then, one's *own* memory becomes irrelevant; someone else's narrative provides the material for one's own.[24]

The relation of Art's story to Pavel's story can thus be characterized as use: Art uses Pavel's story in order to tell his own. But the relation between Art's story and the story of the most important survivor—Vladek—looks quite different although it is built on the same assumptions about transferability that enable Pavel to graft his experience onto Art's. Initially what troubles Art is the apparent difference between his story and Vladek's (the stories of their experience), and that is what first keeps Art from telling his story (his cartoon story, which is, of course, a story of his and Vladek's and now Pavel's experience). He feels that his own life story is less important than his father's: "No matter what I accomplish," Art complains to Pavel, "it doesn't seem like much compared to surviving Auschwitz."

Pavel's response to Art's complaint is crucial to *Maus,* for Pavel—and, as I will show, psychotherapy itself—provides the link that will connect Art firmly and finally to the Holocaust. Though Pavel reminds him, "You weren't in

Auschwitz . . . you were in Rego Park" (*II*, 44), the psychiatrist goes on to suggest that Vladek, perhaps feeling guilty about surviving, had to insist that he was always right in order to make sense of his survival, "and he took his guilt out on YOU," he tells Art, "where it was safe . . . on the REAL survivor."[25]

But how can Art be a survivor? How can the children of survivors be survivors themselves? Trauma theory—as articulated by both literary critics and clinical psychologists—has provided the answer, the technology by which the trauma of the Holocaust can be transmitted between persons. The belief in specifically intergenerational transmission of trauma turns out to be a powerful technology for recruitment to Jewish identity; we can see its power not only in imaginative representations like *Maus* but also in the clinical literature that attempts to address what many therapists believe are problems unique to the children of Holocaust survivors. Dina Wardi's account in *Memorial Candles,* for example, demonstrates both the assumptions that underlie the belief in intergenerational transmission of trauma and the practical ways—the technologies—by which therapists and their clients construct "healthy" means of connecting to the traumas that the parents suffered. Her work centers around group therapy sessions in which young adults—many of them the children of Holocaust survivors—produce personal narratives that, more often than not, construct the Holocaust as the source of their pain.

First it is instructive to note that debate on the issue of "second-generation" survivors has centered on the question of whether all children of survivors or only those who become ill—"the clinical population"—are afflicted with the traumas their parents experienced, which amounts to a question not so much about whether "intergenerational transmission of trauma" is possible but about how that transmission works.[26] But Wardi takes the idea of transmission beyond just the children of survivors. Although she admits in the introduction to *Memorial Candles* that her own parents are "not actually Holocaust survivors, nor did any member of their extended families meet his death in the Holocaust, except for a distant relative of my father's," she nevertheless claims that "like every member of European Jewry of that period, I too am a daughter of survivors in potential." "Indeed," she goes on to ask, "which member of the Jewish nation is not a child of survivors in potential? It therefore seems to me that the problems raised in this book touch the essence of the Jewish nation in the post-Holocaust generation."[27]

The problems raised in *Memorial Candles,* the problems that Wardi sees as crucial to Jewish identity, appear to be an elaboration of the problems we see condensed in Art's session with Pavel. For example, many in Wardi's therapy group, like Art, lack concrete information about their parents' Holocaust experience; also like Art, they fill in the gaps with bits and pieces of other people's stories. In a chapter focusing on problems with sexuality, Wardi argues that the *possibility* that some of the survivor-mothers were sexually abused in the camps—none of the participants in her group are recorded as actually knowing that their mothers were sexually abused—becomes part of the trauma that is transmitted to the children. In their discussions the therapists and participants use what they have learned from films and books to fill in the details of what might have happened to their parents. These details seem to allow them to come to terms with the imagined trauma; that is, the details help them respond emotionally to possible or imagined events.[28] The therapy group thus provides a context in which the memories of other people can be grafted onto the memories of the "second generation" in order to help this generation "identify" properly with survivors. To put it another way, the group becomes a context in which the members can see themselves, as Art is encouraged to do, as "survivors."

The idea that trauma can be "transmitted" intergenerationally is not new, nor is it new in its application to Jewish identity. Freud's *Moses and Mono-theism* posited a similar transmission of guilt—in this case guilt for the murder of Moses, the Jews' primal father—but Freud is specific both about the ways in which he needs the transmission to work in order to account for his conclusions and about the problems with the idea of transmission.[29] Wardi, on the other hand, embraces an unspecified notion of transmission without registering the slightest strain: sometimes she says that children "absorb" the traumas of their parents, sometimes that they "internalize" them, sometimes that the children fail to learn that they are not their parents and therefore become their parents (it becomes the job of therapy to teach them what parts of themselves are not in fact themselves but are rather their parents, and which of their feelings are "theirs" and which are "their parents'").[30] Indeed, it is clear that what interests Wardi and Spiegelman is not transmission itself but how transmission can be used—or to put it more neutrally, what transmission *does*. Spiegelman uses the phenomenon of transmission to resume narration and, in the work as a whole, to build a Jewish identity around the Holocaust. Wardi uses the idea of transmission both for therapeutic purposes—to encourage in a clinical population the behaviors that we think are "healthy"—and, as we have seen, to account for the "essence of the Jewish nation."[31]

In *Maus*, then, we can see that belief in "intergenerational transmission of trauma" means not only that the survivors of the camps can produce the survivors of Rego Park, but also that the survivors of Rego Park can be understood as being survivors of the camps. The relation to the past that psychotherapy thus enables—that helps Art "feel better" (*II*, 46)—replaces the depressive relation to the past with what *Maus* imagines as a healthy, true relation to the past. This new relation makes Art's cartoon story ("A Survivor's Tale") *his* in the sense that the story of his father's experience is his father's. When Art becomes a survivor, the story of his father's experience becomes the story of Art's experience, which is why the session with Pavel transforms the mouse mask into a mouse head. The mouse identity is no longer *his* but *him*. So, to reformulate again the relation between narration and depression, if depression appears to be caused, and not simply signaled, by a failure of narration, and if the cure for depression is in fact the resumption of narration, it is because narration—the survivor's tale—produces the "real" person, the "REAL survivor." To put this in Wardi's terms, telling your story in therapy ideally results in turning the parts of yourself that were not in fact you ("feeling your parents' pain") into parts that are you ("feeling your own pain"). That narrative—in therapy or in comics—produces a real person should come as no surprise; it is simply the inversion of the logic by which Art can contend that the destruction of Anja's diaries was an act of murder.[32]

Once we see how narrative—how telling *true* stories, in Spiegelman's case—works in relation to identity, we can see why Spiegelman argues that *Maus* must be classified as nonfiction, why it must be taken as literally true, why Jewish mice are the product not of imagination but of history. Spiegelman's letter to the editor of the *New York Times Book Review* protesting the placement of *Maus I* on the fiction bestsellers list makes the point even clearer. Spiegelman makes two distinct arguments as to why *Maus* is not fiction. First, he appeals to the facts included in his book: research, he claims, has ensured that the facts included in the story are true to history, and thus the content of the story—as distinct from its "novelistic structure"—must be nonfiction.[33] But this appeal to research and to the precedence of content over form cannot by itself produce the conclusion Spiegelman is looking for. Plenty of fiction writers conduct research to ensure the verisimilitude of their novels, and many base their narratives on true stories, but this does not turn fiction into nonfiction; *Anna Karenina* is still fiction despite its verisimilitude and despite the fact that it was based in part on a true story. Rather, Spiegelman's conclusion rests on his claim that to put *Maus* on the fiction list is to participate in Holocaust denial. He writes, "It's just that I shudder to think how David Duke—if he could read—would respond to seeing a carefully researched work based closely on my father's memories of life in Hitler's Europe and in the death camps classified as fiction." His cartoon cannot be classified as fiction, then, because to do so is to make the Holocaust a fiction and to make oneself, like David Duke, racist—which is also to say it makes the *Book Review,* like Arthur Butz, immoral rather than incompetent. The *Book Review* is in danger not of being wrong about genre but of being anti-Semitic. When telling true stories has the power to turn the artificial person (Art in the mouse mask) into the true person (Art with the mouse head), calling the true story artificial threatens to cancel the true person. In other words, there is more than one way to kill the diaries: you can burn them, or you can call them fiction.[34]

Why, then, does Spiegelman flirt with fictionality by populating his nonfiction with fantastical animal-persons? The answer is that in *Maus* Spiegelman aims at a literal truth that photographs or realistic drawings would fail to convey: the truth that not only Jewish identity but all identities arise from the Holocaust and, more specifically, from telling Holocaust stories, for it is Holocaust-centered identity that the animal heads make visible, make literal, and it is telling Holocaust stories that makes the heads themselves "REAL."

7 "THREE THOUSAND MILES AWAY"

The Holocaust in Recent Works for the American Theater

Joyce Antler

The Holocaust was a defining event of the twentieth century. To many Americans, however, its atrocities happened somewhere far off, "three thousand miles away," as a character in Arthur Miller's new play, *Broken Glass,* observes.[1] So too in the history of American theater, the Holocaust appears almost entirely as a drama that, while enormously tragic, occurred elsewhere. In some plays, moreover, the people who were its primary victims are not even designated as Jews. Presented as a universal event affecting hapless Europeans, the Holocaust on the American stage appeared distant from the conscience, memories, and conflicts of American Jews.

The phenomenally popular *Diary of Anne Frank* set the pattern. This Broadway hit, which opened in 1955 and garnered all the top critics' awards, including a Tony and the Pulitzer Prize, turned the story of the young victim into a life-affirming triumph. "*The Diary of Anne Frank* is not in any important sense a Jewish play," wrote John Chapman in the *Daily News,* in a typical comment. "It is a story of the gallant human spirit."[2] Audiences did learn about the Holocaust from this strangely exuberant drama, one of the earliest artistic works in the United States to address the subject, but they were more likely to be inspired by Anne's courageous struggle than to confront the horrors of the Holocaust itself. Americans might empathize with the young girl's plight and blame the Nazis—though none appeared in the play—but they certainly did not need to implicate their government, or their own communities, or themselves, for playing any role in the tragic drama overseas, nor did they necessarily see themselves suffering from its consequences.

In linking the Holocaust directly to the American psyche, and especially in exploring its relation to American Jews, Arthur Miller's *Broken Glass* helps breaks new theatrical ground. The play premiered at New Haven's Long Wharf Theater and then opened to mixed reviews at New York's Booth Theater in the spring of 1994, enjoying a smashing success in London's National Theater later that summer. That the play came at roughly the same time as the opening of the United States Holocaust Memorial Museum—symbolically located on the Mall close to our other national monuments—may be an indication of a significant shift in perspective, one that struggles with the Holocaust as an American as well as a European phenomenon.

America as a context for the Holocaust has been given dramatic shape in several other recent plays, including *Blue Light,* by the celebrated novelist Cynthia Ozick. Her first foray into theater, *Blue Light,* which premiered at Sag Harbor's Bay Street Theater in the summer of 1994, is a chilling and provocative examination of Holocaust revisionism. The emotionally paralyzing consequences of denying Holocaust memory are also revealed in *Unfinished Stories,* by Sybille Pearson, which premiered in 1992 at Los Angeles' Mark Taper Forum, and in a British play, *Kindertransport,* by Diane Samuels, performed at the Manhattan Theater Club. In these plays the poison of denial lingers over several generations, distorting family relationships and retarding individual growth. Each probes the dilemmas of being Jewish, specifically the need to acknowledge the pain of the Holocaust and the existence of anti-Semitism—even Jewish anti-Semitism—in the contemporary world.

Of course, plays that represent the Holocaust as an exclusively European experience have not lost their salience. Recent productions of Romulus Linney's *2* (about the interrogation of Hermann Goering before the Nuremberg Tribunal) and Charlotte Delbo's *Who Will Carry the Word?* (a starkly realistic drama about women inmates of a Nazi death camp written by an Auschwitz survivor) bear this out.[3] These various plays suggest that fifty years after the Holocaust, as the success of *Schindler's List* also reveals, artists and audiences are newly ready to probe material that bears direct and accurate witness to the Holocaust.

Arthur Miller is no stranger to the subject of the Holocaust. Several of his plays, including *After the Fall* and *Incident at Vichy,* both written in 1964, and his 1980 telescript *Playing for Time* explore its ethical implications. *After the Fall,* an expressionist drama centering on the stream of consciousness of the Jewish lawyer Quentin, focuses, in Miller's words, on a trial by a man's "own conscience, his values, his own deeds."[4] Quentin has witnessed several catastrophes, among them the stock market crash, the Holocaust, and the McCarthy witch-hunts, and has experienced two failed marriages, including one to a self-destructive starlet modeled on Miller's real-life wife, Marilyn Monroe, who committed suicide. Addressing an unseen "Listener," who has been variously interpreted as God, the audience, a judge, a psychiatrist, or a clergyman, Quentin sifts through the evidence of his life as he asks himself whether he is entitled to become involved with Holga, an Austrian woman who survived World War II and fought the Nazis.

The link between Quentin's moral culpability and the evil of the Holocaust is made visible through the only realistic piece of scenery in the play: a large stone tower, representing a German concentration camp, which dominates the stage. "Who can be innocent again on this mountain of skulls?" Quentin asks himself at the play's conclusion. "I tell you what I know! My brothers died here."[5] Using the Holocaust as the symbolic measure of evil, Miller establishes a universal brotherhood whereby all men and women must accept responsibility for the fall from innocence, both personal and public. "The same destructive force that wreaks havoc with one's personal life," writes one critic, "causes wholesale slaughter when left unchecked in the community of which the individual is a small but representative part."[6] The self-pitying, guilt-ridden Quentin, Miller makes clear, is any man and all of us.

Miller wrote *Incident at Vichy*—completing it in only three weeks—at the request of Robert Whitehead and Howard Clurman, who had produced *After the Fall* at the new theater at Lincoln Center in New York. The play continues to explore the theme of *After the Fall* but presents it in realistic rather than symbolic terms. In Miller's words, the main idea of *Incident at Vichy* is that "when we live in a time of great murders, we are inhabiting a world of murder for which we share the guilt. . . . We have an investment in evils that we manage to escape, that sometimes those evils that we oppose are done in our interest. . . . By virtue of these circumstances, a man is faced with his own complicity with what he despises."[7] The play is set in a waiting room in Vichy, where a young Nazi major and French authorities question ten suspects, calling each into an interrogation room; some will be released, the others not heard from again. The drama focuses on the last two detainees, an assimilated Jewish French doctor, Le Duc, and a Catholic Austrian prince, Von Berg, arrested by mistake. Le Duc, who has failed in his attempt to enlist the other detainees to fight the authorities, convinces Von Berg of his own complicity in the Nazi atrocities. "Each man has his Jew," he tells Von Berg; "it is the other."

Finally Von Berg hands his document of safe passage to Le Duc, who reluctantly accepts it and escapes Auschwitz; Von Berg will take his place. Again Miller strikes the note of universality: the play concerns the "question of insight—of seeing in oneself the capacity for collaboration with the evil one condemns. It's a question that exists for all of us."[8]

Miller's interest in the philosophical aspects of the Holocaust reemerged some fifteen years later in his adaptation of Fania Fenelon's memoir *Playing for Time*, presented on television in 1980, where it was hailed as one of the medium's best dramas. Five years later Miller did a stage version of the story of this Resistance fighter who winds up leading an orchestra in Auschwitz. In Miller's hands Fenelon too is portrayed as an existential figure who acts bravely and responsibly in the face of certain death.[9]

When Miller began his career, it was with the intention of playing the "psychological role of mediator between the Jews and Americans, and among Americans themselves as well."[10] Art, he believed, could express "the universality of human beings, their common emotions and ideas."[11] Nonetheless, Miller's continuing concern with the Holocaust and his acknowledgment that his ethical principles derive from Old Testament values indicate this "American" writer's deeply Jewish roots.[12] But it was not until *Broken Glass*, Miller's first play to deal directly with the issue of being Jewish in a non-Jewish world, that he joined his probing about the universalist meanings of the Holocaust with the actual experience of Jews in the United States.[13]

Broken Glass projects the agony of the Holocaust and related issues of moral responsibility onto the unhappy lives of an American Jewish couple struggling with their ethnic and sexual identities in the 1930s; with its American setting and its sharp focus on issues of home-grown anti-Semitism, the play in many ways resembles Miller's powerful first (and only) novel, *Focus* (1945), more than it does his Holocaust dramas.[14] The idea for *Broken Glass* actually came from a story Miller had read in the 1930s about a woman whose legs became mysteriously paralyzed; the image of the woman, and another of her husband, who always dressed in black, "as if he were in mourning for his life," stayed with Miller for half a century.[15] Miller also kept abreast of other mysterious cases of paralysis, particularly those of Cambodian refugees. He noted that an equally compelling inspiration for the play was his reaction to recurring headlines about "ethnic factionalism" in the contemporary world.[16]

The play, set in 1938, takes its title from Kristallnacht, the Night of Broken Glass, when in a terrifying display of cruelty and barbarism, Nazi Party members and SA Brownshirts set fire to more than one thousand Jewish synagogues. Over the next day and a half, thousands of Jewish businesses, cemeteries, schools, hospitals, and homes were attacked and looted, often by neighbors, as police and fire companies stood idly by, encouraging and abetting the destruction. Hundreds of Jews were killed or injured, tens of thousands arrested. In a final humiliation, the Jewish community as a whole was fined 1 billion reichsmarks ($400 million) for damages. Kristallnacht, as the pogrom came to be called, horrified the Western world, for it marked the first time since Hitler's accession to power five years earlier that anti-Semitic violence had occurred nationwide and in full public view. And it shattered hopes that Jewish existence in Germany might continue undisturbed. Within weeks after Kristallnacht, Jews were expelled from schools, denied access to public places, and prohibited from owning businesses.

Yet Kristallnacht did little to convince the West of the need for swift action against Germany's aggressions. In America the press focused on Kristallnacht as a way of extorting money from Jews, not on Germany's volatile anti-Semitism; national leaders worried about foreign entanglement; and the public continued to separate ordinary "good" Germans from Nazi thugs, erroneously believing that Hitler did not enjoy broad support. The possibility of systematic, scientific annihilation of the Jews remained as yet beyond imagination.

Kristallnacht held a special terror for many American Jews. In the 1930s, anti-Semitism was even more virulent and well organized than it had been in the nativist 1920s, with over one hundred organized hate groups and a wide public audience; Father Coughlin's weekly radio addresses, well laced with anti-Semitism, were said to reach fourteen million listeners alone. Despite the remarkable progress of American Jews, discrimination in business, the professions, and education was commonplace (signs reading "Christian Tourists Only" were a common sight at vacation resorts). Commenting on the state of Jewish anxiety, a well-known 1936 study in *Fortune* magazine observed that the quieting of Jewish apprehensions ought to be the "first order of business." Although not openly acknowledged, that alarm grew even more intense after Kristallnacht.[17]

While these events form the backdrop of the play, the action takes place in Brooklyn, where Miller spent his boyhood. In her novel *Leaving Brooklyn* Lynne Sharon Schwartz describes Brooklyn as a place where the savage passions of human life were deliberately "kept at bay"; conformity, the denial of risk, and the repression of dark secrets were in fact "the very reason for Brooklyn's existence."[18] Miller's siting of his play in the heart of Brooklyn is uniquely appropriate. With 850,000 Jews at the end of the 1930s—one-third of the borough's population, and half of the city's total number of Jews— Brooklyn was home to the largest gathering of Jews in America.[19] Many of these were second generation, eager to leave behind the teeming immigrant ghettos where they had been raised. Those who could afford it settled in middle-class neighborhoods like Flatbush, with its clean, wide boulevards and suburban atmosphere.

Miller's Brooklyn differs from the Bronx portrayed in *The Rise of the Goldbergs*, the 1930s family drama starring and written by Gertrude Berg, which remained one of radio and television's top shows for three decades. Comfortable in their Jewishness, secure in their community life, and generally untroubled by anti-Semitism, the Goldbergs easily bridged their ethnic past with the new opportunities of American life.[20] The world of Miller's protagonist Philip Gellburg (nee Goldberg) is much more alienating. Like many of the immigrant sons and daughters who became secular Jews and assimilated Americans, Gellburg struggles to find a foothold between the older familiar verities and the beckoning appeal of American pluralism. Some Jews of this transitional generation jettisoned ethnic heritage completely; others retained selective elements of tradition or community. And many, like Gellburg, found themselves caught between their perceptions of anti-Semitism and their own rejections of Jewishness. According to historian Lucy Dawidowicz, this became the profile of the self-hating Jew, "warped by the misery of his enforced identity with Jews, obsessed by a desperate wish to be someone else."[21]

To acknowledge their links with the wider community of Jewry might reveal the tenuousness of American identity; denying such bonds, however, could result in inauthenticity and spiritual isolation. The relationship of ethnic identity to moral and ethical choices is one important question raised by Miller's play. Another concerns sexual tensions between men and women and the nature of gender identity: how the performance of masculinity and femininity is shaped by interlocking personal and social forces. Using the broken-glass metaphor, the play reveals the shattering of three illusions: the end of the innocence of Western democracies about fascism; the end of innocence about the idea of assimilation and the melting pot; and the end of sexual innocence and of the romantic view of love and marriage. At the end of the nineteenth century, Freud's studies in hysteria—which ushered in the new field of psychoanalysis—marked another end of innocence, this one about the nature of female illness. Through Freud, hysteria was revealed to be a complex response to a shock, or fright, resulting in a "trauma." The connections between trauma, paralysis, and politics lie at the mysterious core of Miller's play and link the various aspects of the death of illusion and innocence.

After viewing newspaper photographs of Kristallnacht, the once vibrant Sylvia Gellburg—played brilliantly in New Haven and New York by Amy Irving—is stricken with a mysterious paralysis that leaves her unable to walk. While her family and Harry Hyman, the sympathetic doctor called in to treat her, downplay the events of Kristallnacht, Sylvia feels personally identified with the Jewish victims; looking at pictures of elderly German Jews on their knees in the street, she imagines the horrifying events to come. Sylvia is not hysterical but prescient; her inability to move others to empathy or action is one source of the paralysis.

For Sylvia, the smashing of glass, the beating of children, and the arrest and internment of Jews are an immediate emergency. "What will become of us!" she cries in fright to Hyman. "You've got to do something before they murder us all!" (104–5). Sylvia seems to know exactly where it will end. (Arthur Miller has recalled his mother as being just such a clairvoyant who could predict tragic events; there is evidence too that it was Jewish women in Germany who noted the danger signals first, sometimes urging their husbands to emigrate from the Nazi regime.)[22]

While the "broken glass" of the play's title connotes German violence against Jews, it also represents the end of Sylvia Gellburg's sexual innocence and the destruction of her marriage. Philip Gellburg, a self-hating Jew who takes offense if he's mistakenly called Goldberg, has been impotent for twenty years; Sylvia's infirmity, which gives her new power in their marriage, is rooted in her husband's physical and emotional numbness. Like many of the immigrant sons and daughters who became secular Jews and assimilated Americans, Gellburg finds himself caught between his sharp sensitivity to anti-Semitism and his distance from his own Jewish identity. Self-hating and inauthentic, he takes out his frustrations on Sylvia, occasionally becoming violent; Sylvia fears him, even dreams of him as a German mutilating her breasts. Only at the end of the play, after suffering a heart attack upon discovering that his anti-Semitic WASP boss distrusts him, does Gellburg confront his own self-loathing.

It is possible that Sylvia responds to Kristallnacht because she herself has been degraded, brutalized, trivialized, in her sexual relationship and her marriage; she is a victim who has given her whole life away "like a couple of pennies" (110). Looking at pictures of old Jews on their knees in the street, she knows something is wrong but has no words for it. It is something in her, she says, "like a child," but a "very dark thing" (69); perhaps it is her dead dreams, her abortive ambition. She is unable to talk about this to anyone; even the sympathetic Dr. Hyman tells her that the "Nazis can't possibly last" (68). Although the cause of Sylvia's paralysis is ultimately unknowable, we do understand that it is in some ways a response to her unspoken fright. Unlike Nora in *A Doll's House*, she can't walk out on her husband, so in the end, after Kristallnacht, she doesn't walk at all.

French novelist and theorist Hélène Cixous claims that because all women suffer gender oppression, they therefore all resemble Freud's famous patient Dora, the eighteen-year-old whom Freud treated for hysteria.[23] Up through the end of the nineteenth century and even into our own time, hysteria was considered a disturbance of femininity, associated with emotional or somatic weaknesses common to women. Freud's revolutionary formulation of hysteria as a disease of "psychical" origin—manifest in such symptoms as sudden paralysis, fits, tantrums, uncontrollable sobbing, and the like—connected female trauma to deep-seated sexual drives and problems of gender formation. Contemporary theorists, including many feminists, highlight the transformative power of the illness; hysteria became personal theater, a way for women to express and challenge relationships of power and control embedded in the social world.[24]

The presentation of hysteria was a distinguishing feature of turn-of-the-century realist drama as well as of the new field of psychoanalysis. Henrik Ibsen, author of three plays that some critics associate with female hysteria (*Rosmersholm*, *The Lady from the Sea,* and *Hedda Gabler*), along with playwrights such as A. W. Pinero and Henry Arthur Jones, opened up the genre to the presentation of complex female characters troubled by "double" natures and repressed sexual desires. In the heroines' somatic sufferings, female spectators detected their own powerlessness; the dramas conveyed a tense world of masculine/feminine conflict that seemed to replicate the gendered spaces of their own lives. "Hedda is all of us," commented Elizabeth Robins, an American actress who played several major Ibsen roles in the 1890s.[25]

In the contemporary period, the trope of the hysterical female has been reclaimed. This time it is not the purveyors of realism but feminist playwrights such as Hélène Cixous, Maria Irene Fornes, and Joan Schenkar who find the figure paradigmatic.[26] No longer simply a victim but a heroine of resistance, her subversion of patriarchy is clear. Interestingly, Miller's *Broken Glass* recalls the dramatic inheritance of the realist masters while at the same time expressing a recognition of gender oppression—and resistance—common to contemporary feminist playwrights.

Sylvia Gellburg, the paralyzed character who speaks in a "Jewish woman's tone of voice" (109), had many counterparts in reality. Bertha Pappenheim, the celebrated late-nineteenth-century hysterical case "Anna O.," became a leader of the Jewish women's movement in Germany. Henrietta Szold cured herself of severe depression and went on to organize and lead Hadassah, one of the most powerful women's organizations in the world; in the 1930s, Szold established Youth Aliyah, which rescued thousands of German Jewish children from extermination by arranging their transport to Palestine.[27] In the United States, Jewish women of all backgrounds were noteworthy for their early mobilization to aid the resettlement of refugees. And women's heroic resistance in the concentration camps is now well known.[28]

While Miller's portrayal of Sylvia's hysteria as a product of her husband's failures—and thus of gender oppression rather than female weakness—links him to several contemporary feminist playwrights, the brush strokes of Sylvia's characterization are too airily applied to give her post-Kristallnacht paralysis (or the play's resolution) the depth it needs. Notwithstanding an unusually strong performance by Amy Irving as Sylvia and a generally strong cast, Broken Glass received mixed reviews on Broadway during its month-long run. Critics lauded the seriousness of Miller's vision but wondered if the play's creaky structure had overwhelmed the metaphysical revelations that lay at its core. It was a different story in London, where Miller is much celebrated as a playwright, and Broken Glass garnered the usual accolades there.[29]

The heart of the play, tautly directed at the Long Wharf and Booth Theaters by John Tillinger, lies in the scenes between Philip Gellburg (Ron Rifkin) and Harry Hyman (David Dukes), assimilated Jews who reflect opposite parts of Miller's own identity. The woman's story, while drawn as a personal, psychosexual counterpoint to the public terror of Nazism, is less fully developed (which accounts for the trouble Miller had in ending the play—sometimes letting Sylvia rise in triumph after Gellburg's death, at other times having her attempt to stand, albeit feebly).

Philip Gellburg's identity problems emerge more clearly than his wife's. But just as her private sufferings are tied up with the very public revelation of Kristallnacht, so too are his. And so too is Gellburg's sexual malfunction—his own sexual paralysis—connected to larger questions of identity, culture, and politics.

A hard worker doing a distasteful job, Gellburg is proud of what he has achieved: he is the first Jewish officer in an important Gentile firm, heading the Mortgage Department of Brooklyn Guarantee and Trust. But in his obedience to what the firm demands, he has begun to hate his own people and to hate himself. Gellburg loves Sylvia but can't express that love. Like her, he combines an instinct for kindness with one of domination; it is not clear whether he wants to help or humiliate her. Hyman tells Gellburg, "You helped paralyze her with this 'Jew, Jew, Jew' coming out your mouth and the same time she reads it in the paper and it's coming out of the radio day and night. . . . You hate yourself, and that is scaring her to death" (126–27).

Perhaps it is his inability to function as a husband that makes Gellburg try all the harder to succeed at work. He covers up his failure at home with his efforts to assimilate, to demonstrate the outer certainty of his success. When that illusion is broken by Sylvia's paralysis and by his implication (as he wrongly believes) in a Jewish "double-cross" (119) at the office, he is left exposed; his fragile image of himself collapses and he dies. Gellburg's fatal heart attack makes an interesting, gendered contrast with Sylvia's paralysis.

In his downfall we see the perils of living an inauthentic life, of distancing oneself from one's people, of refusing to see the signs of danger, the denial of humanity; only Sylvia can see them. Miller makes an insightful point about the connection of power and empowerment to identity and sexuality. Although Gellburg reveals that he has lost sexual interest in his wife because he feels that her silent protest against domesticity has unmanned him, at the end of the play, in his conversation with Dr. Hyman, we learn that his self-denial as a Jew has been equally problematic. He confesses that although he wanted "to be an American like everybody else," now he doesn't know who or where he is. He wonders about God, about whether he wouldn't have been happier in a Jewish firm, and recalls his connections with the old religious Jews of the Lower East Side but admits that he is ashamed of them. "Why must we be different?" he asks Hyman. "Why is it so hard to be a Jew?" (122). All this gets little response from Hyman, the socialist-idealist, who insists that Jews are like everyone else, a part of a greater humanity. Hyman's aloofness suggests a certain kind of paralysis as well—an inability to make connections not only to his roots but to the troubles of the world. Appearing in boots and riding clothes, Hyman, like Gellburg (who always wears black), seems to have put on the outfit of the enemy, or perhaps he is merely living his life as a pose.

In his autobiography Miller has written about growing up Jewish in an assimilated world. Living first in Harlem, and then, when the depression made things tougher, moving to Brooklyn, the Millers should have melted in the proverbial pot, yet Miller for the most part felt himself to be an "undissolved lump" floating on the surface, feeling his apartness yet denying it. He grew up programmed "to choose something other than pride in my origins." In his private reveries he was not the "sallow Talmud reader" but Tom Swift, hero of military courage, who dreamed of entering West Point (as Gellburg's son does). Later, when he married his first wife, a Catholic, he believed, with her, that they were "leaving behind parochial narrowness of mind, prejudice, racism, and the irrational." He would henceforth identify himself "with mankind, rather than with just one small tribal part of it."[30]

Miller tells us, though, that as it turned out, Jews like himself were "building a fortress of denial" that would be cracked only after Hitler's war. Although (unlike Gellburg and Hyman) Miller recognized Hitler's threat quite early because of the Nazi intervention in the Spanish Civil War—he dreamed about Nazis for seven years before the Final Solution—nonetheless, when he met Jewish refugees in Italy waiting for a boat to Palestine after the war, he distanced himself from them, denying their common origins. Whenever he thought about that encounter, he was ashamed. This kind of detachment is the "very soul of the matter": "a failure to imagine will make us die," Miller wrote.[31]

Miller does not blame American Jews for their attempt to "deny . . . the world's reality," for he understands that the anti-Semitism that ran rampant in the country at the time—and that explodes on the pages of his 1940s novel *Focus*—severely limited their options. "Escape and denial," he remarks, "are hardly the monopoly of the Jews." This makes it all the more urgent, he believes, for American writers "to reveal what has been hidden and denied, to rend the veil."[32]

Of all his Holocaust plays, Miller does this most fully in *Broken Glass*, coming to join the universalist theme of social and ethical responsibility for the Holocaust with the particular experience of American Jews. Linking the personal tragedy of the Gellburgs—the denial of identity and consequently the denial of love—to the political horrors of fascism, *Broken Glass* reveals that to be blind to oneself, as Gellburg and even Hyman are, makes us blind to the world about us. In that regard Sylvia's paralysis is a metaphor for the paralysis of the whole society, which is unable to act in the face of Nazi terrors.

As always, Miller makes it clear that he abhors such moral nihilism. He continues to see tribalism—the denial of the ethnic, religious, or national identity of others—as a major crisis of contemporary times, when once again the world seems perilously divided among warring groups based on particularistic lines. But in the sympathetic, clear-sighted figure of Sylvia Gellburg and the tragedy of her marriage, he expresses a profound regret and understanding of the plight of American Jews while exposing the inadequacy of their response.

The premiere of Cynthia Ozick's *Blue Light* at the Bay Street Theater in Sag Harbor, New York, in August 1994 was a significant theatrical event. Directed by Sidney Lumet, returning to the stage after a thirty-year absence, and with strong performances from Dianne Wiest and Mercedes Ruehl in the roles of Holocaust survivors Rosa Lublin and her niece Stella—characters who appeared in Ozick's stunning fiction "The Shawl" and its sequel, "Rosa"—*Blue Light* is an impressive, often startling work, despite some obvious problems. Ozick went through eleven drafts of the play before its Long Island debut.

Although *Blue Light* is Ozick's first play, she has been repeatedly drawn to the subject of the Holocaust. "I cannot *not* write about it," she admits. "It rises up and claims my furies."[33] Among her most powerful stories, "The Shawl" and "Rosa" concern the devastating effects of the Holocaust on victims and survivors. She wrote the stories in 1977 but put them away for several years, believing that the Holocaust must not become the subject of fiction. She continues to hold this belief yet "constantly violates" the tenet: "My brother's blood cries out from the ground, and I am drawn and driven."[34]

"The Shawl" tells of a magic shawl that helps Rosa, the main character, nurse her baby daughter, Magda, in a concentration camp. Stella, Rosa's fourteen-year-old niece, takes the shawl, and when Magda, who until now has been kept hidden, goes searching for it, she is discovered by guards and brutally murdered. "Rosa" finds the main character, now fifty-nine, living in a home for the elderly in Florida. Supported by Stella, who lives a repressed and lonely life in Queens, Rosa still mourns Magda; she writes her letters and talks to her and finds some solace in the shawl, which has become her obsession; while her reveries let her imagine Magda in various stages of the life she never had, they also take her back to happier times in the Warsaw Ghetto, where she grew up. Published separately in 1980 and 1983, "The Shawl" and "Rosa" were joined under one cover in 1989 as *The Shawl: A Story and a Novella*, but they remain separate, if related, stories.[35]

Although in writing the play, Ozick "borrowed 2½ characters" and the notion of the shawl from these stories, *Blue Light* cut her "umbilical cord" to them. But Ozick accepted Lumet's transformation of the shawl as item of

clothing "into the fabric of the idea of the play—sometimes it is a baby, sometimes it is a ball gown, sometimes it represents the past, sometimes joy or very
deep sorrow. It is protean and everything imaginable."[36] Representing Rosa's
attachment to the memories of her past and the destruction of her future, the
shawl expresses the inconceivable horror and tragedy of the Holocaust. But it
is also symbolic of the illusions Rosa and Stella live with. When a Holocaust
denier enters their lives, those illusions are painfully shattered; there is a moment of reconciliation when their own denials are no longer possible.

Blue Light is set in 1979 in Miami, where Rosa has been sent by Stella after
smashing the windows of her Brooklyn junk store. Rosa is as much a misfit at
the Buckingham Apartment for Seniors in Miami as she was up north.
Outfitted in the shabby clothes of a refugee, she is churlish and isolated, en-
meshed in memories of her dead daughter, who appears to her in an apparition when she throws on the shawl that Magda had loved. While these reveries carry some of the playwright's most vivid language and were given a
powerful and moving performance by Wiest, they were not fully integrated
into the present life of Ozick's characters. Ozick revised the monologues for
the play's Broadway run.[37]

The most fully realized tensions in the play lie between Rosa and Stella,
now a spinster who wears long-sleeved dresses—ostensibly to cover up her
concentration camp number, although they are also an emblem of her repressed desires. Choosing to bury the past, Stella considers Rosa mad for
dwelling on it. Mercedes Ruehl's characterization of Stella's repressed desire,
and her triumphant act 2 rebellion against her own victimization, are revelatory. Secondary characters, including Simon Persky, a resident of the retire-
ment home who tries to draw Rosa out, Mr. Peterfreund, another retiree, and
Hortense, the mindless blond receptionist, carry important elements of
Ozick's theme about memory and denial yet are subsidiary to the dramatic
action.

Garner Globalis—a dapper, smooth-talking young man in white suit and
shoes who, we later learn, represents the Institute for Historical Review (an
actual Holocaust "revisionist" group)—is the playwright's most provocative
creation; he did not appear in the earlier fiction. Globalis's sinister purpose
unfolds over the course of the drama. He first seduces the affection-starved
Stella in order to gain access to Rosa, whom he then manipulates in what is
no less an act of seduction. Pretending to listen to her stories about Magda,
which everyone else is tired of hearing, he fraudulently obtains her signature
to a confession that she had made Magda up—that her baby was a fantasy just

as stories about Nazi gas chambers and the annihilation of the Jews were "collective fabrications . . . mass delusions."[38] Although Globalis walks away with the signed document, his betrayal leads to a reconciliation between Rosa, who has blamed Stella for her baby's death, and Stella, who has internalized her own guilt. In a riveting speech Stella denounces Globalis's deceptions and names him for the Nazi that he is.

While this play, like Miller's, ends in forgiveness, Ozick's vision is more dire. With the signed document he carries away, Globalis carries the future, a point emphasized by the receptionist's naive willingness to spread the false word of his institute. Not knowing history leads to blindness; it is Stella who realizes that this kind of not-seeing becomes Nazism. Holocaust denial, Ozick warns, may be another kind of Kristallnacht.

The word echoes earlier, at the start of the play, when Stella berates Rosa for breaking the windows of her junk shop. "You've crossed the line," she tells Rosa. "You've made your own *Kristallnacht,* that's what. *They* smashed store windows, *they* smashed glass, now you're doing it to yourself! What the Nazis did, you're doing it to yourself!" But as the play unfolds, we see that no Holocaust survivor—not even Stella, who tried to erect a new life by hiding her scars from herself—can escape the past. Their experience separates them from all others, even sympathetic onlookers like Persky. And it is this experience that must be remembered. Rosa's recollections of her past—which she sees in her reveries through the "blue light" of words, words that bring back her mother, a poet, and the family's elegant lifestyle in pre-Holocaust Warsaw—make that past, the "before" of her life, more of a reality to her than the present. The truths of the Holocaust are painful. Survivors, in an unlikely parallel of interest with deniers, have a stake in forgetting. Ozick's art is perhaps best expressed in this disturbing insight about Holocaust denial. Despite the current building boom in Holocaust memorials, Ozick's characters epitomize the allure of forgetting. Which of us, after all, wants to define ourselves in the context of the century's most barbaric and least understood crime?

Like Sylvia Gellburg's paralysis, a response to her almost clairvoyant vision of Nazi terror, Rosa Lublin's "blue light" hallucinations separate her from family and community. Neither woman, however, is mad; it is the rest of us, who deny the truth of terror and of history itself—or who aid those who would deny—who have lost our senses. Ozick readily admits that her play is a "thesis play," written to expose the problem of Holocaust denial as a cancer affecting American life as much as it has affected Europe. Like Miller, she shows that private humiliations and personal tragedies cannot be separated from larger public ones. The events surrounding both the remembrance and the denial of the Holocaust must be seen on this dual plane.

The denial of heritage, like the denial of history, has been at the forefront of other playwrights' recent incorporation of the Holocaust experience. The *Unfinished Stories* of Sybille Pearson's play relate to the interlocking lives of three generations of a family living on New York's Upper West Side. The secret in this family has been kept by eighty-year-old Walter, a German refugee doctor and intellectual who fled the Nazis as a young man. Only when Walter, ill with cancer, is preparing to die does he pass on to his grandson Daniel the story of his own escape, at the cost of the life of Erich Muhsam, a German Jewish radical intellectual whom Walter idolized. Walter's Holocaust past has nonetheless shaped his family in ways none of them understands. "If you can't absorb the meaning of the Holocaust in your own life," says Pearson, the child of a Jewish father much like Walter, "it will forever affect your relationship with your own children, and with their children."[39] For Walter himself, the Holocaust—the "before" of his life—remains ever present, as it did for Rosa and Stella. Walter explains the order of his books to his son: "The first shelf. The authors who died before Hitler. Second. Those murdered by Hitler. The third. The exiles who lived out their lives. The last shelf. The exiles who took their own lives."[40]

In Diane Samuels's *Kindertransport*, a young refugee girl, Eva, transported out of Germany and given a safe home in England, grows up as an Englishwoman, Evelyn. When given the opportunity, she refuses to join her mother, Helga, who survived the concentration camps, and she hides her past from her own daughter, Faith, now grown. Aware of frightening secrets in her mother's life but unable to discern them, Faith feels unfinished, in limbo. Only when the mystery is revealed and her mother's Jewish birth and Holocaust past are acknowledged as a part of her own history can Faith begin to take responsibility for her own life. Telling the truth about her identity begins the healing process as well for Evelyn and her English foster mother, Lil. *Kindertransport* reveals the damaging emotional costs of the repression of memory and identity, not only for Holocaust survivors but over a family's continuing life cycle.

Like *Blue Light* and Barbara Lebow's 1984 hit, *A Shayna Maidel* (1984), still in constant production, Pearson's and Samuels's plays reveal the Holocaust as an experience that cannot be erased from the consciousness of survivors. "We are not normal," Stella acknowledges at the conclusion of *Blue Light*, "I don't think it will ever come to an end. It will never go away, never." With the coming to voice of a new generation of playwrights who are beginning to explore the impact of the Holocaust experience not only on survivors but on their children and even grandchildren, the Holocaust as a dramatic event has increasingly been situated outside the more typical settings of concentration camps, train depots, or courtrooms, and inside the memories and imaginations of survivors and their offspring.

The half-century that has passed since Hitler's Final Solution has enabled Americans to reappraise their involvement in the Holocaust in a variety of other media. Exhibits at the United States Holocaust Memorial Museum and a recent PBS documentary, "America and the Holocaust: Deceit and Indifference," reflect this ongoing reassessment. Developed as an interpretive space that would give visitors a "visceral" experience of the horrors of the Holocaust while alerting them to the dangers of America's passive response, the museum provides a bridge between the European experience and the United States' more remote implication in the catastrophe. Its location adjacent to the Washington Mall places Holocaust memory within American public space; quotations from American presidents and State Department officials along with American newsreels and exhibits addressing the failure of American foreign policy emphasize American involvement in the Holocaust. At the same time, visitors are immediately removed from American geography: they are given identity cards, taken through crowded, narrow exhibit corridors, put on cars resembling German transport trains, and, through a variety of photographs, artifacts, and oral and filmed interviews, asked to confront the stark reality of the lives of Holocaust victims and survivors—people much like themselves.

The fundamentally theatrical nature of the museum was expressed by museum designer Ralph Applebaum, who acknowledges that his team intended to present the Holocaust as "a play in three acts"—"Nazi Assault," "Final Solution," and "Last Chapter"—that would directly engage visitors in the ongoing drama of events, reducing their distance from the murderous atrocities in Europe and the flounderings of their own policymakers. Like the recent crop of Holocaust plays, the museum warns spectators about the dangers of remaining aloof from genocidal possibilities in their own society.[41]

In her 1987 anthology of Holocaust plays, Elinor Fuchs persuasively argues that collective catastrophe rather than individual suffering is the most authentic theatrical expression of the Holocaust.[42] Through the carefully coordinated design of architectural and visual space and the incorporation of a variety of exhibit materials dealing with ordinary Holocaust victims and survivors, the United States Holocaust Memorial Museum attempts to bridge this dichotomy. In contrast, the new "Americanized" Holocaust plays limit Holocaust representation by portraying its effects within the framework of family melodrama. But despite this narrow canvas, the best of these plays, like Ozick's and Miller's, incorporate an urgent warning against the distancing of time and geography. Viewed not as a single, isolated event, however horrific, but as one that blends past, present, and future—not as an event geographically limited to war-scarred Europe but as one that also implicates America— the boundaries of Holocaust memory are paradoxically expanded even as theatrical representation is diminished.

"I refuse to write a play that reduces the Holocaust to an image or myth," Ozick says. "*Blue Light* is about Holocaust denial, not the Holocaust."[43] Ozick turned to theater because she was incensed by the betrayal of history by Holocaust revisionists. "It used to be that imagination would create what had never been there—a world of make-believe. But now we have the imagination [of Holocaust deniers] pretending that something that is there never happened. This is an entirely new thing in the world." Ozick wishes that her play might become obsolete, so that the need for its warning about Holocaust denial—like the thesis of denial itself—could "be thrown into the trash."[44] But she doubts that this will happen soon.

Like *Broken Glass* and other new American plays that deal with Holocaust issues, *Blue Light* expresses the hope that historical memory may be a prophylaxis against the failure of imagination, courage, and human connection; remembering becomes both a moral obligation and a political necessity. It is a message that Americans, too often neglectful of history, might well ponder.

8 THE CINEMATIC TRIANGULATION
OF JEWISH AMERICAN IDENTITY

Israel, America, and the Holocaust

Sara R. Horowitz

The screening of a new Hollywood movie about the Holocaust provides critical clues in *The Cutting Room*, a 1993 English-language detective novel written in Israel by Robert Rosenberg, an American-born Israeli and journalist.[1]
In this mystery novel, former police detective Avram Cohen, a Holocaust survivor, journeys to Los Angeles, where the high-powered Hollywood director
Max Broder has recently completed a major film about the Holocaust. The
friendship between Broder and Cohen dates back to the war, when both engaged in acts of armed resistance and sabotage and together survived the
deathcamp Dachau. To avenge Nazi atrocity, Broder formed a group called
the *nokmim* (the avengers) and soon came to live in the United States. Cohen,
on the other hand, decided to leave the war and its hatreds behind him. He
withdrew from Broder's group and went to Palestine, to build the nascent
state of Israel and to regain a sense of normalcy. Through the respective life
choices of Cohen and Broder, Rosenberg's novel posits differences between
Israeli and American responses to the Jewish past, and the concomitant place
of the past in contemporary Jewish identity. Broder's movie, *The Survivor's
Secret*, gradually revealed during the course of the narrative, is the fulcrum by
which Rosenberg critiques American uses of the Holocaust and the meanings
that the Nazi genocide acquires in American cinema.

Max Broder's private nickname is "der Bruder," the brother. Thrown into
a brotherhood of sorts by their shared Holocaust past, Cohen and Broder ultimately go their separate ways, follow separate Jewish destinies. Since their
postwar separation, Broder has utilized international connections to propel
his movie career. He amasses a fortune and for years nurtures a dream of pro-

ducing a definitive Holocaust movie, the story of his past. Broder seeks out Cohen, repeatedly urging him to leave the hardships of Israel for the good life in Los Angeles. Cohen, by contrast, makes a strong effort to bury the past, his tormenting memories emerging only in nightmares. The completion of the movie and Broder's suspicious death reawaken the past for Cohen.

The posthumous screening of Broder's film is a major event for the Los Angeles Jewish community. *The Survivor's Secret* is a sentimental, heroic war film, which focuses on Nazi atrocity and Jewish resistance and revenge. In it, Broder also depicts his own Nazi-hunting after the war as vengeance against former Nazis and their families. Broder's powerful international connections keep his bloody vendettas beyond the law. The film evokes in viewers a lawless hatred. Even the vaguely anti-Semitic Irish American policeman assigned to investigate Broder's death is won over to the director's version of history and justice after seeing the film: "Don't get me wrong. I'm an American. I believe in due process. But sometimes when you know what the fucker's done, and you can't touch him? 'Cause he's protected? I gotta admit, I envied you" (242).

The Los Angeles Jews who gather to view the film know little of the Holocaust or of Israel, except for some predictable clichés that they repeat unthinkingly. They reiterate an unexamined version of the Holocaust that relies on a sense of perpetual Jewish victimization. Ironically, this sense of beleaguerment is at odds with their economic and political security, as depicted in the novel. Rosenberg's American Jews utilize a past they know only dimly to legitimate self-interest and to perpetuate a state of suspicious hostility in the world. Moreover, other than this shared focus on the Holocaust as an emblem of the Jewish condition, past and present, these Jews show neither a collective nor an individual sense of Jewish values, Jewish meanings. The novel depicts them as religiously hollow and crassly materialistic. Only an imagined sense of beleaguerment unites them and fuels their sense of Jewish identity.

By contrast, in the Israel that Cohen inhabits, the Israel of the novel, there is less obsession with the Holocaust and less distortion of contemporary life with its resonances. His belated encounter with Holocaust memory in America plunges him into despair, from which he is rescued only by the arrival of his Israeli lover, Ahuva (beloved), a Jerusalem magistrate judge. "We are not *nokmim*," Cohen keeps repeating to American Jews who insist on seeing in him and in his country a tough machismo that both avenges and redeems the murdered Jews of Europe. The narrative undercuts this familiar American representation of the Israeli by repeated references to Cohen's aging body, his paunch, his heart condition. Indeed, *The Cutting Room* pointedly contrasts American and Israeli Jewish bodies. American Jewish bodies are indistinguishable from other American bodies; the novel portrays both as either innately ugly or grotesque in their doomed pursuit of youth and beauty. The first American Jewish woman Cohen meets has "taut orange skin that bespeaks expensive sun and surgery" (12); another woman wears tight clothing "advertising either a beauty club or a surgeon, but not authentic youth" (14). Even of a young woman, Cohen observes, "Diets and exercise controlled her body" (48). By contrast, "Ahuva's pale skin and its even paler lines of age" (17) mark Cohen's Israeli lover as a woman at peace with her authentic self. One Jewish American man is a "roly poly" in a metallic Lycra running suit, with "barrel thighs, balloon belly, and weak chest" (46); another has a "small grey ponytail that only [accentuates] the absurd fight against old age" (47). By contrast, Cohen has a paunch and "an unruly lock of hair . . . more white than black" (15). The novel thus unravels the popular American portrayal of the Israeli as the "new Jew," youthful, virile, and vigorous. Instead, it suggests that the American pursuit of physical perfection is a mark of inauthenticity and insecurity. The Israeli Jew's ease with aging marks him (or her) as the authentic Jew, living out the Jewish destiny and ensuring the Jewish future. Thus, Ahuva shows no alarm at the pale lines on her face but worries about overrunning her biological clock.

As imagined in this mystery novel, American Jewry is rootless and shallow. Without an inner sense of meaning, American Jews forge a shaky sense of identity and destiny out of a rigidly reconstructed memory of a horrific past. This obsessively ritualized memory draws them together as Jews, substituting for other, more nourishing communal Jewish values. The novel suggests that by keeping alive the memory of the Nazi genocide, American Jews have also kept alive the Nazi, have internalized him in their vacuous sense of a Jewish identity that can lead only to its own destruction. This internalization is symbolized by a key figure in the mystery, a fugitive Nazi war criminal who has adopted a Jewish alias. More correctly, he has developed a Jewish persona—a Holocaust survivor who coexists with and struggles against his Nazi persona. The former Nazi succeeds in suppressing his Nazi self until Broder begins filming the Holocaust. The movie triggers a shift in his fragile psychic balance so that the Nazi self reemerges. "Don't you see? . . . [You] made him come back with all your questions." Moreover, the Jews themselves evoke classic anti-Semitic stereotypes, highlighting the bankruptcy of Jewish life in diaspora, however comfortable. Broder, for example, exemplifies the anti-Semitic figure of the Protocols of the Elders of Zion in his powerful international connections and his bloody vendettas that are somehow beyond the law. In Rosenberg's novel, then, American representations of the Shoah reevoke anti-Semitism both outside and within the body of the Jews in America. Israel, by contrast, is the place where Jews flourish unselfconsciously, so that they need not linger in the painful past—a place where love and justice (Ahuva the magistrate) redeem and transform the Jewish past.

While Cohen and Broder share a European past rooted in the Nazi genocide, they embrace divergent visions of the Jewish future. Although the two men were once like brothers, Rosenberg puts to question the relationship between the American and Israeli Jewish communities. The depiction of American Jews as obsessed with the Holocaust and with physical appearance suggests that the two communities have so diverged that their continued connection cannot be guaranteed. By turns sentimental, paranoid, materialistic, and hollow, the American Jew contrasts negatively with the authenticity of the Israeli in relation to the Holocaust, and hence in relation to Jewish identity.

One might read in *The Cutting Room* an articulation of the author's autobiographical choices as an American-born *oleh*, an immigrant who has chosen to be an Israeli rather than a diaspora Jew. At the same time, the novel offers a credible critique of the way that popular representations of the Holocaust—and in particular its cinematic portrayal—have functioned as a vehicle for the working out of Jewish American postwar identity. Popular culture constructs and promulgates what might be called a folk discourse of history. It is here, to the chagrin of historians and professors, that most people learn what they "know" about history. The Holocaust too has taken its place in American historical consciousness as much through the vehicles of television, movies, mystery novels, romances, and espionage thrillers as through literature, memoirs, and the work of historians. Cinema in particular has come both to shape and to reflect popular understanding of the Nazi genocide. While scholars and intellectuals continue to argue whether the Holocaust can be "represented," and whether those historical events can be assimilated into art and literature, popular culture has already evolved sets of mythic memories about the Holocaust. Examining the representations of Holocaust remembrance in popular culture provides a touchstone to contemporary interpretations and ideological uses of the Holocaust; the recounting of the events of the Nazi genocide is as much about the present as about the past. Cinematic versions of the Shoah comment not only on the murdered Jews of Europe but also on the ideological climate in which the films themselves are produced, distributed, and reviewed. These films generate sets of interlocking meanings about the nature of evil, anti-Semitism, racism, the Jew, and Jewish destiny.

In different ways, both Israeli and American popular representations of the Holocaust present the Nazi genocide as the site where issues of contemporary Jewish identity are worked out with relationship to the Jewish past. Israeli representations of the Shoah are largely self-sufficient. That is, for the most part they do not require the presence of America or American Jews to narrate the tragedy of European Jewry. Quite to the contrary, an effacement of America facilitates the narration of the predominant version of the Holocaust, which depicts a certain progression from the European Jew to the Israeli Jew with nowhere to exist but Zion. On the other hand, America seems increasingly unable to represent the European catastrophe as a Jewish Holocaust without in some way implicating Israel. In most popular American accounts of the Shoah, and in the predominant Jewish American folk theologies, a triangulation occurs among Israeli, American, and European Jews.

The concept of *ha-shoah ve-ha-gevurah*, destruction and heroism, which governs Israeli popular understanding of the Holocaust, opposes the presumed passivity of European Jewry, described as going *ka-tson la-tevah*, like sheep to slaughter, to the self-reliance of the state of Israel. On one level, *Shoah* refers to the murder of the Jews of Europe, and *gevurah* to the successful defense of the nascent state. On another level, *Shoah* and *gevurah* are both terms internal to an account of the Holocaust: *Shoah* refers to murdered, compliant Jews while *gevurah* refers to the heroism of Jewish partisans, the rebellions in the Warsaw and Vilna ghettos. Early on, these narratives of heroism were the narratives most frequently recounted in Israel about the Holocaust. Behind this version of history was a sense of shame regarding the Holocaust victims and also a fear for one's own vulnerability to catastrophe. By selecting and retelling tales of heroism, this early mode of recounting the Holocaust elided the figure of the ghetto rebel with the figure of the pioneer soldier. These narratives retroactively create for the new Jews of Israel a set of ancestors who are fighters and survivalists, obviating the difficult and ambivalent burden of claiming the "passive" murdered Jews as ancestors. In this retrospective, narratives drive a wedge between the victims and the heroes. The victims become representative of diaspora Jews, and thus diaspora as a condition *(galutiyut)* becomes responsible for the Shoah. Yad Va-Shem, where the vista of Jerusalem opposes the memorials, and Beit Ha-Tefutsot, the Tel Aviv museum of the diaspora where all roads of persecution lead only to Zion, concretize this reading of history. In order to blame *galutiyut* generally—rather than the particular conditions in Germany and Eastern Europe in the 1930s and 1940s—this representation must minimize, discredit, or efface the image of a thriving contemporary Jewish American community and the function of America as a refuge for Jewish immigrants. Repeated recounting in public ceremonies, school plays, and other popular vehicles prioritized partisan and ghetto fighter stories; this, and a suppression of survivor testimony that was not about "heroism," shaped the popular understanding of the Shoah. The tragedy of ghetto fighters who battled against overwhelming odds and perished was elided with the story of Masada, where Jews chose death with dignity over defeat and enslavement. The struggle of ghetto fighters was also seen as another version of the battle of the few and ill-equipped Zionists against the massive and well-armed Arab enemies. In this light, not only did the Israeli fighter redeem the shameful and tragic Jewish past but the two enemies—past and present—were mythically united. Embedded in this is a distrust of the "world" that did not come to the aid of the murdered Jews of Europe and that would also let the vulnerable Zionist state founder, as well as a sense of the precariousness of one's own existence, which only narrowly and provisionally escapes the fate of European Jewry.

While there is little focus on the Holocaust for the first decades of Israeli cinema, the destruction of European Jewry always resonates, implicitly or explicitly, in early Israeli films that depict the building of the nation. The refugees from Nazism underscore the need for a Jewish state, its motivation and its justification. The 1954 film *Giv'a 24 Eina Ona* (Hill 24 Doesn't Answer), for example, is representative in its depiction of the Israeli struggle for a strategic hill in the 1948 War of Independence against the background of illegal immigration of Holocaust survivors into British-controlled Palestine. The Arab enemy forces are elided with the Nazis as eliminationist enemies of Israel, overwhelming in number and determination; this association is concretized by the presence of a Nazi among the wounded Arabs. The film's protagonists—who all die defending the hill—link the fighters in the War of Independence with resistance fighters during the Holocaust, offering a paradigm for Jewish destiny preferable to the presumed passivity of the Holocaust victims. As in many other films of this early period, the presence of an American Zionist engaged in defending the nascent state links the Israeli struggle with democracy, modernity, and civilization and—by implication—links the Arab with fascism, backwardness, and barbarism. In the decades following the 1967 Six-Day War, Israeli film begins to deal in a more complicated and nuanced way with the Arab presence in its midst and the effect of that presence on Israeli Jewish identity and values. Both the evocation of the Holocaust past and the presence of the American become increasingly marginal. In the late 1980s and 1990s, Israeli cinema turns at last to confront Holocaust memory directly, through feature films such as *Kayits shel Aviya* (The Summer of Aviya), short art films such as *Ma Kara* (What Happened), and documentaries such as *Ha-behira ve-hagoral* (Choice and Destiny). These films do away altogether with the American presence in grappling with the Holocaust past in an Israeli context.

American popular interpretations of the Holocaust have followed a different trajectory, resonating with shifting attitudes about Jewish American identity. Eventually the Nazi genocide becomes the vehicle by which to explain American Jews to themselves and to others. While America is extraneous to Israeli reconsiderations of the Shoah, American popular representations of the Shoah have evolved to figure Israel in important ways. In early American cinematic responses to the Holocaust, not only was the Jewish homeland notably absent but so was the Nazi genocide itself. The postwar film *Gentleman's Agreement*, for example, probes the phenomenon of genteel anti-Semitism in America without once mentioning the European catastrophe. The 1947 film, based on Laura Z. Hobson's novel of the same name, responds to the Holocaust by tackling the delicate subject of this prejudice. That the Holocaust was both the backdrop and the motivation for this exploration, however, is made clear in publicity released for the film, as well as by the implicit contrast between the polite and bloodless discrimination practiced in New York and Connecticut and the brutal persecution in Europe a few years earlier. While the movie's Jews encountered "no yellow armbands . . . no Gestapo, no torture chambers," as one press release noted,[2] the historical events that featured those manifestations of anti-Semitism made that attitude shameful in America.

In *Gentleman's Agreement*, journalist Skylar Philip Green determines to write an exposé of anti-Semitism from the inside out. By posing as a Jew, Green hopes to learn—and so to write about—how it feels to be the target of bigotry. As the movie progresses it exposes a variety of anti-Semitic attitudes and practices, ranging from Jewish self-hatred to understated Gentile superiority; from hostile remarks by drunken restaurant patrons to ejection from posh resorts; from restrictive hiring practices to taunting children. Because all of these manifestations attack the dignity rather than the body of the Jew, one might be tempted to dismiss them as unpleasant but relatively harmless. But the unspoken backdrop of the Holocaust makes clear that these actions fall along a continuum whose extreme culmination is genocide. In this light, all anti-Semitism resonates with Nazism and so cannot be tolerated in America.

Early American responses to the Holocaust universalized its meaning to encompass all forms of bigotry, all hatred, all social injustice, all evil. Here too *Gentleman's Agreement* repeatedly insists that its concern with anti-Semitism extends to prejudice generally. For example, Green chides his self-hating Jewish secretary for her use of the derogatory *kike:* "Words like yid and kike and nigger and coon make me rather sick no matter who says them."[3] Moreover, anti-Semitism is repudiated not only because it is wrong, in and of itself, but also because it embodies the antithesis of American values. After an exclusive hotel refuses to honor Green's reservations, thinking him Jewish, he rails, "They're persistent little traitors to everything this country stands for and stands on and you have to fight them. Not just for the 'poor, poor Jews' . . . but for everything this country stands for." Green's fiancée, Kathy, an upper-class northeastern divorcée, harbors a genteel form of anti-Semitism, manifested first as a discomfort with Phil's masquerade, then a reluctance to introduce him as her "Jewish" fiancé. Eventually Kathy grudgingly acknowledges her delight in being Christian rather than Jewish, just as one is glad to be "good looking instead of ugly, rich instead of poor, young instead of old, healthy instead of sick."[4] By the film's conclusion, a remorseful Kathy repudiates these attitudes and determines never more to allow an anti-Semitic remark to pass uncontested. She even offers her Connecticut summer home to a returning Jewish GI and his family, offering to help him face down the inevitable hostility of the upper-crust Gentile neighbors. In so doing, Kathy affirms the American ideals of tolerance, equality, and democracy. Although the GI never names the vanquished enemy overseas, the war against Nazism and fascism is suggested to be continuous with the war at home against bigotry and discrimination, which similarly threaten American values. The GI calls it "a different kind of war," one fought socially rather than militarily. In accepting and assimilating its Jewish citizens, then, America becomes more itself and assumes its proper destiny.

As the film charts this other kind of war on the home front, it engages with a question of definition: What is an American Jew? The film ambivalently puts forth several versions of Jewish identity, which correspond to the ways in which American Jews see themselves, and also to the ways in which they are seen—or would like to be seen—by other Americans. In its argument against anti-Semitism, *Gentleman's Agreement* minimizes the difference between Jews and others. The movie announces this theme early on, as Phil Green struggles to find the right angle for the series he has been assigned to write on anti-Semitism. His young son asks over breakfast, "What's a Jew?" In answering, Green offers the first of a number of shifting benchmarks for Jewish identity. The journalist reminds his son that they have seen several churches in New York, that each of those churches represents a particular religion, and that Jews are people who go to a particular church called a synagogue. Thus, a Jew is a member of a particular religion—one of many, each with its own distinct site on the American urban landscape. Each religion is different, but at the same time, all are similar. Additionally, Green points out, anti-Semitism is only one of a variety of hatreds targeted at members of a particular religion. As Green explains this, he and his family seem to stand outside of the religious question altogether. Although much later in the film Green refers to himself and his family as Christians, this early breakfast conversation seems to position the Greens as neutral. While some people hate Jews and some hate Catholics, Green's son reasons, "no one hates us because we're Americans!" The boy's remark allows Green to hammer home the point that religion is one's private, domestic business within the context of a shared public domain. He explains to his son that a Jew is as American as anyone else: "You can be an American and a Protestant, or an American and a Catholic, or an American and a Jew." At the same time, the unexpectedness of the son's response to the idea of religious hatred—"we're American" rather than "we're Christian"—and the boy's apparent lack of familiarity with houses of worship of any sort prior to arriving in New York signal that membership in a religion is, after all, a mark of difference in America.

For the audience, this conversation reinforces the Enlightenment response to the centuries-old European Jewish question: religion as distinct from nationality. By implication, Germany's repudiation of its Jewish citizens is a repudiation also of democratic values, and hence an example to be rejected. Green observes, "One thing is your country . . . but the other thing is religion. . . . That doesn't have anything to do with the flag or the uniform or the airplanes." In defining the Jew's nationality as American through the national symbols of flag, uniform, and airplanes, Green also sets aside the suspicion of dual loyalties for the American Jew—a specter raised briefly by the film's only mention of the Jewish homeland in Palestine. When queried by Green about Zionism, a noted physicist archly asks whether the journalist refers to "Palestine as a refuge, or Zionism as a movement for a Jewish state." Both men agree that some "confusion" exists about that issue.

While the movie's initial definition of the Jew falls under the category of religion, to pose as "a Jew" Green need only declare himself as such without assuming any recognizable religious or ethnic or cultural markers. "I'll be Jewish. . . . I can just say it. I can live it myself for six weeks, eight weeks, nine months, no matter how long it takes." In fact the very absence of such visible markers is precisely the point the movie wishes to make: a Jew in America is as American as anyone else. In planning the series, Green wishes to know how his old friend Dave Goldman feels about anti-Semitism: "Can I think my way into Dave's mind? He's the kind of fellow I'd be if I were a Jew, isn't he? We grew up together. We lived in the same kind of homes. . . . Whatever Dave feels now . . . would be the feelings of Dave not only as a Jew but the way I feel, as a man, an American, as a citizen." Green's musings emphasize the similarity between the two men—their shared Americanness, their shared citizenship, their shared maleness. A Jew cannot, in fact, be distinguished from his fellow citizen. Green scrutinizes his own face in the mirror: "Dark hair, dark eyes, sure so does Dave. So do a lot of guys who aren't Jewish. No accent, no mannerisms. Neither does Dave."[5] Green does not assume any of the Jewish religious practices that in the 1940s (and even now) might cause discomfort: he eats what others eat, does not request time off for Jewish holidays or for the Sabbath. To "live it"—to live as a Jew—means to live as the target of anti-Semitism, rather than to live differently in any other way. Embedded in this idea is the contention that as much as the existence of anti-Semitism depends on the existence of the Jew, the existence of the Jew also depends on the existence of anti-Semitism. This Sartrean notion is given more explicit expression by Professor Lieberman, a world-renowned physicist meant to represent Albert Einstein, who contends that since there is no Jewish "race" or type, and since he is not Jewish by religion, only anti-Semitism keeps him Jewish. He is a Jew, in short, because "the world still makes it an advantage not to be one." Thus, being Jewish is a moral posture, whether assumed by a Jew like Lieberman or a Gentile like Green. At the same time, Jewishness becomes emptied of meaning, a cipher.

The film is careful not to identify American Jews too closely with the decimated Jews of Europe. As a returning GI, Dave is always seen in American military uniform; in the battle for social justice too he is a soldier rather than a victim. "There's a funny kind of elation about socking back," he tells Kathy. Thus, American Jews are distinguished from the victims of the Nazi genocide, the murdered, "passive" Jews who remain outside the framing of the film but provide its unacknowledged backdrop. This careful distancing of the American from the European Jew shores up the insecurity of American Jews in the 1940s. At the same time, it marks a turning point for Jewish Americans, who have proven themselves in battle and need no longer fear rejection and discrimination in their country. In this light, Dave's forthrightness contrasts favorably with the earlier response of the older Irving Weinberg, a Jewish friend of Green's publisher, who urges the magazine to reconsider the planned series on anti-Semitism: "It'll only start it up more. Let it alone. . . . We know from experience that the less talk there is about it, the better."[6] Dave's uniform stresses the successful absorption of the Jew into American society. For non-Jewish viewers, the uniform provides reassurance that one need not fear the Jew, whom the movie reveals not as an unassimilable alien but a defender of American values at home and abroad. Indeed, Dave explains to Green, it is worth fighting anti-Semitism not because of "the poor, poor Jews" who suffer on its account but because America needs to be kept to its own standards of social equality for all.

The film's inner contradictions regarding the definition of a Jew correspond to ambivalences and difficulties regarding the nature of Jewish identity in the 1940s, which has been gradually evolving from the language- and culture-based distinctions of the immigrant generation and now is beginning to absorb both the implications of the Holocaust and the opening up of economic and social opportunities. In *Gentleman's Agreement* Jewish identity is worked out with the noticeable absence of mention of the Holocaust. But the film remains uncertain about what constitutes Jewish identity. Just as Green insists on his similarity to Dave, "as a man, as an American, as a citizen," the film stresses similarity among all Americans. Through Dave and through Green's protracted masquerade, Jews present themselves to an American audience as compatriots. We are just like you, they seem to say; you need not fear our presence. In presenting Jews as such, however, the film shows a discomfort with anything that marks a difference between Jews and others: a different religion, a different appearance, different values.

The absent but implied Holocaust backdrop of *Gentleman's Agreement* is a precursor to early cinematic portrayals of the Holocaust in America. Like *Gentleman's Agreement*, these films universalize the Jewish catastrophe, so that the Nazi genocide becomes a metaphor for social injustice of all kinds. In this first phase of American Holocaust films, the European Jewish catastrophe stands metaphorically for the treatment of minority groups in the United States and for oppressed people globally. While the primary victims of Nazism were Jews, the films warned against the dangers of racism generally. This universalizing reflects a reluctance among American Jews to call attention to themselves as different. It suggests a desire on the part of American Jews to remember and memorialize the Holocaust, but also to distance themselves from the murdered Jews of Europe, from the grotesque corpses of documentary newsreels and from the influx of postwar refugees. The absence or presence of Israel in these cinematic representations marks the extent to which the films suggest embracing Jewish American identity, however reconfigured, or letting it go in favor of an American universalist vision. The contrast between Otto Preminger's 1960 film *Exodus* and Sidney Lumet's 1965 film *The Pawnbroker* exemplifies this difference in approach.

The Pawnbroker, based on Edward Lewis Wallant's novel, juxtaposes flashbacks of Holocaust memory with scenes of contemporary Harlem. On one level, the recurrent flashbacks depict the ongoing trauma of the Holocaust survivor, whose past intrudes uncontrollably into present life. Thus, the protagonist, Sol Nazerman, rides the New York subway at rush hour and finds himself transported in memory to the crowded boxcars that took European Jews to concentration camps. On another level, the Harlem events that trigger these flashbacks suggest that American racism represents the continuation of the Holocaust into the present. Thus, as Nazerman considers the value of a diamond ring brought to his Harlem pawnshop, he recalls the Nazi seizure of such rings from many Jewish fingers; as he views the breasts of a Harlem prostitute who offers herself to him, he recalls seeing his wife in a Nazi brothel. These flashbacks represent both the thawing out of frozen Holocaust memories for Nazerman and the dawning realization of his complicitous role in exploiting the inner-city underclass. Having numbed himself emotionally in order to live beyond the brutal murder of his wife and children, Nazerman has become bitter, cynical, shut off from others. More damningly, he has allowed himself to remain willfully ignorant of the exploitative practices of the powerful African American slumlord who owns not only his pawnshop but also a ring of brothels in Harlem. In fact, Nazerman prospers because the pawnshop launders the profits from the other man's illegal operations, suggesting a parallel with Aryans who profited from and remained willfully ignorant of the Nazi genocide.[7]

At the same time that Nazerman's unwanted memory flashes bring the past back to him and to the viewing audience, the film demonstrates that memory of the Holocaust has faded in America. Other than Nazerman, a well-intended social worker, and the Harlem boss who taunts Nazerman with knowledge of his past suffering, no one seems to recollect the Nazi genocide. A mere two decades after the Holocaust, Nazerman's American-born niece and nephew ask him for money for a pleasure trip to Europe, with no acknowledgment of the resonances of their request for Nazerman, for whom Europe can be only "a cemetery." Pawnshop patrons show no recognition of the concentration camp number on Nazerman's forearm; Jesus, the eager young Puerto Rican man who works for Nazerman, thinks it a mark of membership in an esoteric society.

As it melds the European past with contemporary social unrest in America, Lumet's film argues for the relevance of the Holocaust for American audiences, reconfigured not as a Jewish event but as an archetypal human one— indeed, the archetypal Christian event. In the film's concluding segment, Jesus regrets his part in an armed robbery of the pawnshop and is killed by a bullet intended for Nazerman. In an evocation of the stigmata, the pawnbroker mourns the death of his assistant and pierces his own palm with the spindle that holds the shop's receipts. Thus, the film recasts the Jewish catastrophe as an emblem of human suffering and human injustice everywhere. The Jewish victim and the Puerto Rican Jesus are equated, and Nazerman himself, whose name resonates with both Nazi and Nazerite, is shown to be simultaneously a creation of Nazi atrocity, a collaborator in Nazi-like exploitation, and a redemptive sufferer, like Jesus of Nazareth. The insularity of Nazerman's Jewish memory, whether of the Holocaust or of other episodes of persecution, fosters only disconnection—from American-born Jews who do not see themselves in embittered Jewish refugees such as Nazerman, and from other Americans, who struggle with their own social problems. It is significant that *The Pawnbroker* is one of the few American films to focus on the Holocaust in which the state of Israel does not figure in any way.[8] There is merely the European Jewish past, which burdens the Jew, and the American present, in which Jewishness has little significance in the shared civic arena.[9] Although it focuses on the resonance of the Nazi genocide in the contemporary world, the film suggests the need to let go of the Jewishness of the Holocaust in favor of a Christianized version in order for Holocaust memory to become meaningful and, ultimately, redemptive on the American landscape.

In contrast to Lumet's treatment of the Holocaust, which removes the Nazi genocide from its Jewish specificity, *Exodus* treats it as a distinctly Jewish event—indeed, the quintessential Jewish event. Like Lumet, Preminger universalizes the Holocaust as the symbol of ultimate evil. But unlike *The Pawnbroker*, which shows a discomfort with the particularity of Jewish history and identity, *Exodus* pairs the Jewish catastrophe with the Jewish triumph. The Holocaust and the creation of the state of Israel are shown in the film as the two pillars by which Jewish Americans come to define their sense of identity. The predominant folk theology of the Shoah—out of the ashes of Auschwitz, the birth of Israel—entered into mythic American consciousness in large measure through *Exodus*—both Leon Uris's immensely popular novel and the subsequent film. The representation of this theology, however, also masks the nativization of the Holocaust in these works.

The protagonist, Ari Ben Canaan, is portrayed as a powerful, handsome, and virile Sabra. *Exodus* contrasts the modern Israeli (strong, aggressive, and self-reliant) with the old Jew of Europe (weak, short, and feminized in popular European folk images). An unarticulated but important triangulation exists among the remembered old Jew, the new Israeli Jew represented on screen, and the American Jew offscreen, external to the film's plot. Through the film's portrayal of Ari Ben Canaan, played by Paul Newman speaking an unaccented American English, the film asserts a distance between the American Jewish viewer and the "old Jew." The identification of the American Jew with the new Israeli Jew is encouraged by the American English dialogue in both the book and the film. Although Ari personifies the young Israeli man, he also stands for the American Jew—that is, the American Jewish male.

Ari articulates his understanding of Jewish identity within the context of his relationship with the lovely American Christian nurse, Kitty. Jewish difference in *Exodus* is always expressed through gender—through the idea of miscegenation. On the one hand, *Exodus* presents Jewish-Arab difference as unbreachable; Ari will not permit his sister Jordana to marry her Arab friend. Moreover, the connection between the Arab enemies of the Jewish homeland and the Nazi murderers of the Jews of Europe—asserted not only metaphorically but by revealing the Grand Mufti's German connections—justifies the insistence on this difference. On the other hand, Jewish-Christian difference pressed into sexual liaison has a different valence. Kitty's attraction to Ari confirms that the new Jew, whether Israeli or American, is different from the old Jew. Frequently in literary and cinematic representations of Jewish Americans of the 1960s, 1970s, and early 1980s, the non-Jewish woman's desire for the Jewish American man asserts the Jewish male's acceptance into the dominant culture. Correspondingly, these works figure America as an alluring female to be conquered, to be entered.[10] Thus, as much as Ari asserts his difference from his Christian lover, the film erases difference between Americans and Jews. In perhaps the best-remembered scene in *Exodus,* a British military officer boasts to Ari, who sports a British uniform, that he can always detect a Jew, that some ineffable difference in their eyes distinguishes the Jew from others. Ari immediately asks the officer to help him remove a speck of dust that has flown into his eye. In a protracted scene in which the officer scrutinizes Ari's blue eyes from a variety of angles, the film makes clear that although Jews have a particular history that distinguishes and even ennobles them, they are no different from anyone else.

Exodus is representative of popular American representations of Jewish history that, in depicting the state of Israel as the culmination and redemption of the Shoah, conflate the American and the Israeli Jew. In this sense, the twinned stories of the European catastrophe and the birth of Israel turn into an internalized discourse about American Jewry. The imagined Israel is not the actual Israel, then, but an Israel of the mind. In Israeli culture this progression from a devastated European landscape to Israel suggests that Jewish continuity has no viability except in Israel. But in its American versions the relationship of the Holocaust to Israel does not suggest that American Jews leave home for Zion. Rather, the old Jew destroyed in the Shoah comes to represent a vision of Jewish impotence that American Jews wish to cast off, while the virile Israeli represents the healthy and sexualized body of the American Jew.

This triangulation of Israel, America, and the Holocaust in working out Jewish American identity is even more explicit in *QB VII,* a 1974 made-for-television movie also based on a novel by Leon Uris. If in *Exodus* the birth of the state of Israel cannot be told without reference to the Holocaust, in *QB VII* the story of the Holocaust cannot be told without reference to Israel. Loosely based on an incident in the author's life, *QB VII* follows the libel suit brought by the Polish-born physician Adam Kelno against Abraham Cady, a Jewish American writer. In his magnum opus, *The Holocaust*, Cady refers briefly to Kelno's participation in the notorious medical "experiments" at Jadwiga, a fictional concentration camp. Kelno, who has been knighted and has led a life of altruism, ministering medically in third-world countries and London slums, sues Cady for defamation of character after the book's release in England. Cady's need to gather proof of Kelno's collaboration in order to acquit himself of libel permits the movie to represent the Holocaust to its American television viewers, through the testimony of former victims, actual photographs and Nazi film footage shown as part of a visit to Yad Va-Shem, and conversations among the film's other characters.

The film culminates in the protracted trial sequence, which enables the Holocaust to be narrated at length and justice to be served. As in other American movies, the meaning of the Holocaust is universalized to enfold a "common meaning"—in this case to encompass all political oppression. Cady's closing speech warns against "those who hate and bomb and starve other people because they fear the color of their skin because it is different from theirs, or their politics because it is different from theirs, or their religion because it is different from theirs" and urges viewers to an unspecified commitment to fight evil: "What happened between 1939 and 1945 in Europe is still happening in half-a-dozen countries across the world. And it will continue to happen as long as evil men remain organized and good and gentle men are deceived and put upon and paralyzed by them."[11] Since Cady has just received notification that his son has been killed in the Six-Day War, his warning—as in *Exodus*—links the Arab threat to Israel with Nazi terror. But Cady's oration also implicates American racism and Soviet oppression. However, more than a call to arms, the film is an extended exploration of Jewish American identity, negotiated through the Holocaust past and the post-1967 Israeli present. Moreover, Cady's ability to universalize the Holocaust so that its meaning points to other atrocities and other oppressions serves as proof that the Jew is no longer victim but warrior for justice.

In a departure from Uris's novel, the film introduces Cady as a popular American writer thoroughly alienated from his Jewishness. Cady is shown in perpetual conflict with his father, Morris, who first appears in Beverly Hills, incongruously wearing a black yarmulka over his stylish haircut. The older Cady speaks with a slight European accent and in the cadences of Yiddish ("I want you should see the pool"). For twenty years he lives with his son, his Gentile daughter-in-law, and their son. The film contrasts the father (depicted as Jewish but not American) with the son (American but no longer Jewish). Because he is an immigrant, marked by language and dress, Morris's Jewishness is presented as part of his essence and need not be negotiated.[12] But the American-born son—precisely because he is American-born—must reinvent Jewishness if he is to have a Jewish American identity. To Abraham Cady's dismay, his father holds *minyans* (Jewish prayer services) in their home to mourn the death of elderly Los Angeles Jews. Morris berates his son in the name of Judaism for his moral failings: "You were brought up to love God and to obey his commandments and you are turning out to be a bum and I want you should stop!" For his part, Cady becomes increasingly dissolute, engaging in a chain of adulterous affairs, drinking excessively, insulting his wife and his father, and squandering his gift as a writer. Ironically, in rejecting Jewish values, in creating himself *de novo* as a modern American man, Cady is portrayed both as morally empty and as an embodiment of the anti-Semitic stereotypes of the vulgar, avaricious, carnal Jew. He tells his wife, "I don't believe in the Jewish thing. Or the Christian thing, or the Moslem thing, or the Buddhist thing. . . . I believe in myself. And I believe in money."

While *Exodus* predates the 1967 Six-Day War, *QB VII* was filmed after the Israeli victory that galvanized widespread public affirmation of Jewish American support for the state of Israel and a concomitant groundswell in public pride at being Jewish in America. A visit to the dying Morris, who has moved to Israel, awakens in Cady a commitment to Jewish identity. The gathering of European immigrants and younger Sabras who pray at his father's deathbed in Tel Aviv unifies the old and the new Jew, the European past and the Israeli present. Cady can understand neither the Hebrew of prayer nor the Yiddish of his father. He must have his father's dying words translated, and at his father's burial he reads the words of the prayer for the dead, the Kaddish, from a transliteration. Despite these signs of alienation from Jewish culture, Cady resolves to honor his father's memory and reclaim his own identity as a Jew by finally writing a great book about the Nazi genocide.

Cady's attitude to the state of Israel reflects the growing public attachment of American Jews to the country in the wake of the 1967 war. Cady takes great pride in Israel's military prowess, symbolized for him and for the viewers by an Israeli Air Force formation flying above Cady and his non-Jewish mistress soon after the Six-Day War. This military prowess not only assures the continued existence of the state of Israel amid hostile neighbors, it also symbolizes a transformation of the image of the Jew from passive victim to active defender. The quick and decisive victory of the Six-Day War and its favorable portrayal in American culture thus permit American Jews to open themselves up to an exploration of their Holocaust past and pre-Holocaust roots. In this vein, Israel and the Holocaust are yoked together in the post-1967 sense of Jewish American identity. Indeed, although Cady titles his book simply *The Holocaust*, the story of Nazi atrocity is interwoven with the story of the evolution of Israel from Jewish homeland to Jewish state. As Cady describes his book, it relates "the testing of the Jewish people by the Lord God of Israel . . . from the ovens of Jadwiga to Sinai and Suez. . . . I want the reader to be there when they hoist the Star of David over Jerusalem, then rekindle the Eternal Flame." Not surprisingly, given the autobiographical origins of *QB VII*, Cady's *The Holocaust* sounds a lot like Uris's *Exodus*. By implication, the two narratives of Cady's novel—the destruction of European Jewry and the triumph of the state of Israel—are not only inseparable, they are identical.

Israel is implicated in *QB VII* in yet another way. During the years immediately following World War II, Kelno practices medicine in the British-controlled Middle East and Arabian North Africa. Replete with camels, sheiks, nomadic tribes, and veiled women, the movie portrays an exotic oriental landscape already made familiar cinematically both by colonialist films such as *Lawrence of Arabia* (1962) and by Zionist films such as *Exodus* and the Israeli *I Like Mike* (1961). In both types of film the implied audience identifies with the Western visitor who brings to a benign but primitive people the benefits of Western technology, medicine, and civilization. The Arabian landscape of the movie *QB VII* represents a curious departure from the Uris novel, which places Kelno in Sarawak, Borneo. What accounts for this change in locale, which seems to work against the grain? In assisting the friendly but backward Arabs, Kelno evokes the figure of the Israeli in many early Zionist narratives and films, who brings to the Middle East the promise of Western advances. The Zionist settler thus hopes to win for himself a welcome in the region that will benefit from his presence.

This association so established between Kelno and the Zionists works against the thrust of the film on two levels. First, it links the Zionist presence in Palestine/Israel with the British colonial occupation. Rather than arguing for the ancient Jewish roots of Zion, the film thus casts the Zionists as yet another group of European outsiders. Jews appear not as Europe's victims but as the arm of European colonialism. Second, the association casts Kelno in a favorable light, wherein he functions as a stand-in for the Israeli Jew. At the same time, the Arabian scenes serve to further certain cinematic purposes. The dramatic tension of the film depends on the viewer's uncertainty as to whether Cady is correct in accusing the seemingly noble Kelno. This association with a familiar trope (that of the Westernized Israeli helping the more primitive Arab) makes his innocence credible, thus extending the movie's suspense. The sequence also serves to reinforce the working out of Jewish American identity even during the lengthy section of the movie devoted entirely to Kelno's history, in which Cady does not appear at all. The contrast between the technologically advanced Westerner and the backward Arab reinforces American identification with the Israeli.

In melding together the Holocaust past, the Israeli present, and the identity struggles of the Jewish American author who was personally involved in neither, *QB VII* transforms the recovery of Holocaust memory into a contest of manhood between Cady and Kelno. This is signaled by the movie's opening voice-over, which explains, "This is the story of the lives of two men who fought each other in one of the most fascinating trials in modern history." Because Kelno's libel suit focuses on whether or not he brutally castrated Jewish men as part of Nazi medical "experiments," both the libel trial and an earlier deportation hearing feature a series of Jewish survivor-witnesses who narrate their own castration. Thus, the Holocaust itself becomes synonymous with forced sterilization, with a ghastly unmanning of Jewish men. On a metaphoric level, this characterization of the Holocaust recaptures both the anti-Semitic stereotype of the Jew as effeminate and the impotence of the Holocaust victim against the forces of genocide. Cady's recovery of Jewish identity involves a restitution of Jewish American manhood. In the movie's opening sequence, Cady and Kelno face off in front of the courthouse. As they glare at one another across a crush of reporters, Cady announces, "This is one Jew you're not gonna castrate, Kelno." This brief scene is repeated two more times, so that Cady's declaration introduces each of the movie's three segments.

As the trial progresses, the movie depicts each man as seen and judged through the eyes of his only son. In the transformation from novel to film, the shape of each man's family changes to effect this gendered, father-son focus. Cady's daughter Vanessa in the novel does not exist in the film, nor does Kelno's protégé Terry, who is replaced by a physician-son. In the movie, each son decides whether to reject or to emulate his father. Kelno's son flees the courtroom in horror and leaves his father's home permanently, while Cady's son declares his love for his father before dying as a paratrooper in the 1973 Yom Kippur War.

Throughout the film Cady exemplifies an exaggerated masculinity. Introduced as a daring war hero, volunteering for the RAF during World War II, he continues to be feisty and combative in personal relationships. Even in a diminished condition—temporarily blinded and bandaged after his plane is shot down—he manages to have sexual relations with his nurse. In his numerous extramarital affairs he is depicted not only as libidinous but also as highly attractive to women. Cady's behavior—which brings happiness neither to him nor to his intimates—is revealed to be a response to an insecurity, an attempt to shore up the emasculated image of the Jewish male by rejecting Jewishness and embracing a hypermasculinity. His exposure to Israel enables him to reclaim a Jewish manhood—symbolized both by the Israeli Air Force formation overhead and by his son's wearing of an Israeli uniform. Cady suddenly finds that he can exist first "alone"—that is, with his writing and without women—and then in a monogamous relationship. In contrast, Kelno's masculinity is always undermined or displaced. In response to the overtures soon after the war of the nurse who will become his wife, Kelno warns, "I cannot give you what you want to give me. . . . I haven't been with a woman in five years." In his work among the Arab tribes, Kelno helps women to give birth. Most notably, he cures the sheik's son of impotence and sexual underdevelopment; the young man is then able to marry and to sire a child. Kelno's brutal wartime participation in castration experiments is revealed, in this light, as an attempt to compensate for his own shaky masculinity by emasculating others. Thus, Kelno is depicted as repeatedly defining and reaffirming his masculinity through what he does to and for others. In the final analysis, the movie depicts not the Nazi but the Jew as the "real man."

Two decades later, in Steven Spielberg's movie *Schindler's List* (1993), Israel is represented as the historical culmination of Jewish destiny. When the Schindler Juden awaken the first morning after their liberation, they learn that no one likes the Jews. A Russian soldier tells them they can't go east, and they can't go west. As they begin walking to the nearest town looking for food, we hear Naomi Shemer's Six-Day War hit song, *Yerushalayim shel zahav* (Jerusalem of Gold).[13] The Jews crest a hill in a line extending from one edge of the screen to the other. The film changes from black and white to color, implying a movement from past to present, and suddenly we are no longer viewing 1945 Czechoslovakia but contemporary Jerusalem. The film ends with a lone man (presumably Spielberg) praying or meditating at Schindler's grave. As the film sets up this sequence, the Schindler Juden arrive in Israel because they can go nowhere else. The only possible topographies in the film are Europe and Israel; American is left unimagined. It is not that the film argues against going to the United States; it is simply that in the universe of the film, no America exists to go to. This allows *Schindler's List* to put forth a view of history consonant with the prevailing Israeli interpretation of Jewish history, which views diaspora life as untenable for Jews. In the depiction of Jewish history in Beit Ha-Tefutsot, for example, the persecution of Jews in many countries culminates in (and is solved by) an ingathering of exiles to Zion. The museum's representation of Jewish history does not include the history of Jews in America, seeking and finding refuge and freedom. One can readily understand this depiction from the vantage point of an Israeli museum. But from a Jewish American director whose financial success and artistic freedom affirm that here too is a place for Jews?

Michael Berenbaum, former director of the Research Institute of the United States Holocaust Memorial Museum, has stated that as Americans come to view the Jewish past, they inevitably Americanize it—that is, give its events an "American" meaning in the civic arena. What American uses has Spielberg made of Israel? Unlike *Exodus, Schindler's List* does not offer the young Israeli fighter as the paradigm for the new Jew. The Jews we see in Israel are old; they are Schindler Juden, almost fifty years after liberation. In the historical part of the film, the Jews conform for the most part to anti-Semitic folk images of the Jew. The Jewish men are short, unattractive, and money-grubbing, contrasting visually with the clean good looks of the tall Schindler. While the camera portrays the Schindler Juden of the past as aging and invalid in the present, the image of the virile and handsome Schindler during the war years is never displaced by a later image. Although a legend on screen informs the viewer that after the war Schindler failed at business and marriage, the film preserves the visual image of Schindler in his prime, not only physically but morally and spiritually.

Elsewhere Spielberg has said that he modeled his Schindler on his mentor and father surrogate, Steve Ross, head of Time Warner. Liam Neeson, the actor who plays Schindler, studied home movies of Ross to learn his mannerisms. While *Exodus* imagines the American Jew onto the Israeli soldier, and *QB VII* actually transforms an American Jew into an Israeli soldier, *Schindler's List* imagines the American Jew onto the Aryan savior. Thus, *Schindler's List* distances the American Jew not only from the old Jew of Europe but also from Israel, which exists in the film solely as a place for Holocaust survivors and cemeteries—a repository, in other words, of Jewish memory. In the film's reconstruction of the Nazi genocide, many of the European Jews actually speak with an identifiably Israeli accent, thus further conflating the old Jew with the Israeli. Like the culture of the European Jew—emblematized by the Sabbath candles that begin and end the genocide—Israel is viewed sentimentally and nostalgically. But Jewish life is redeemed ultimately in America through identification with and emulation of the successful Christian.[14]

In the most recent wave of Holocaust films, the triangulation of Israel, Holocaust, and Jewish American identity has begun to break down. Both in Israel and in North America, the past decade has introduced a number of intimate, private films made primarily, but not only, by children of Holocaust survivors, where Jewish identity and its connection with the Holocaust past are explored solely in an Israeli or an American context. In different ways this trend reflects a sense of identity secure enough to allow for the unpredictability of survivor testimony, less ideologically and psychologically safe. As utilized in these films, survivor testimony opens up a multiplicity of memories and viewpoints, often in conflict with official and public interpretations of the Holocaust.

In *Ha-behira ve-hagoral* (Choice and Destiny; 1993), for example, Israeli filmmaker Tsipi Reibenbach interviews her parents, both survivors. Her father's testimony, which occupies most of the film, interrupts the popular clichés about survival, heroism, and martyrdom. He tells his daughter that he wishes that the man who saved his life in a camp had died and thus had not been able to save him. His own death would not have been a catastrophe, he explains to his daughter: "You would not have been born, but I would have suffered less." He relates other details about the struggle to survive conditions of atrocity: drinking urine when thirsty or cannibalizing bodies from the Mauthausen gas chamber if any flesh remained on them. These gruesome details prevent survival from being construed as glorious and heroic, and the film thus breaks with narratives of the past wherein the new Israeli Jew saw himself in the exceptional Shoah hero. Throughout the film the mother silently busies herself with cooking and cleaning chores while the father speaks. Bursting with emotions and memories that she wants to reveal but cannot, she is visibly in internal conflict. Only at the film's end does she speak up. She tells her daughter that she cannot stop the flow of memories, the resurfacing of losses. Since the filming began, the mother cannot fall asleep. When alone, she walks around the apartment calling the dead by name. All these years, she says, she has not wanted to speak about her experiences. But now, suddenly, she finds herself compelled to do so. The entire family, her children and grandchildren—all born in Israel—watch her emotional outburst.

In essence, this film is not only about the memory of European-born Shoah survivors but also about the younger generation of Israelis seeking and accepting the history of their elders. The mother's long-deferred speech takes place in a room full of young Israelis; their willingness to listen to unbridled testimony makes her act of witnessing possible. Implied in this is a rejection of the earlier, simpler, and more ideologically determined narratives of *Shoah ve-gevurah*. The father's admission that he would rather have died during the Holocaust, even if it meant that his daughter—the one making the film— would never have come into existence, interrupts the theological/political discourse that sees the suffering of European Jews redeemed by the birth of the state of Israel. The willingness of the Israeli family to listen to the grandparents' story represents the willingness of contemporary Israel to look at the Jewish past. Although the film depicts the listening posture of the family as the necessary catalyst for a reexamination of the past, in fact the film could be made—the family was ready to listen—because the narrative of heroism had already begun to unravel.

Avraham Heffner's short 1988 film *Ma Kara* (What Happened) exemplifies and politicizes this unraveling. The film opens with a depiction of young Israeli soldiers in conflict with rock-throwing Arab boys in the West Bank. As the soldiers pursue the boys across rocky terrain and winding alleys, the camera focuses on one soldier and one Arab. The soldier's face betrays indecision and emotional conflict. Will he kill the boy if necessary? The boy trips, and the camera closes in to reveal his vulnerability and fear.

Suddenly the scene shifts to a middle-aged man whose dream about the Israeli occupation we turn out to have been watching. The man drives to work with a neighbor, a woman who is a Holocaust survivor. The two argue about Israeli-Palestinian relations and about the lessons of the Shoah. The man fears that his son, serving on the West Bank, will be forced to compromise his political and ethical ideals. The woman responds by narrating her own Holocaust memories. Her experiences convince her that Israel is perpetually on the verge of destruction. This precariousness constitutes the condition of the Jew. In response, one must be tough or be killed. The man argues that things have changed, that Jews are no longer victims but victors, that one must not be abusive of power, that the occupation should end. Together these two middle-aged neighbors represent the spectrum of political meanings of the Holocaust in Israel. The woman identifies Arabs with Nazis, with the Holocaust as the paradigmatic Jewish event. The man senses uncomfortable resonances linking European anti-Semitism with Israeli anti-Arabism. The woman survivor tells her neighbor, "I am your nightmare." When they arrive at the workplace, the man's son—the soldier of his dream—awaits in uniform. "I killed an Arab woman today," he says. The film thus incorporates the Holocaust past in asking what it means, after the Six-Day War, the Yom Kippur War, and the invasion of Lebanon, to be an Israeli Jew.

In his 1989 avant-garde film *Everything's for You,* Abraham Ravett explores his father's Holocaust memories and the ghost presence of the family who died during the Nazi genocide, whose existence Ravett only recently learned of. Ravett focuses on the personal impact of these events—memories he cannot himself remember but must recover from others. Through conversations with his father Ravett explores the dimensions of his father's past in his own life. Father-son conflicts become comprehensible and are ultimately resolved and forgiven in light of the father's traumatic experiences and deep bereavements. The son learns belatedly that his father had a wife and children before the war, a family that perished under the Nazi genocide. Interspersed with conversations with his father and animated reconstructions of their past troubled interactions are scenes with Ravett and his own young son, a toddler whom he diapers, entertains, and showers with. The film communicates a loving father-son relationship as implicated in a complicated, composite sense of identity—as a Jew, as a man, as an American, as an artist.

In contrast to most earlier films about Holocaust meaning and Jewish American identity, Ravett's film engages issues in a private, rather than a public, discourse. It is representative of a generation of Jewish Americans that has been characterized as the first to be able to choose whether or not to be Jewish,[15] and to choose from an array of Jewish possibilities. The film personalizes Holocaust memory as a family affair, not a focalizing point for Jewish destiny, Jewish community, or Jewish survival.[16] The film finds American meanings for the Holocaust by looking at its very private resonances for an American filmmaker. As such, it does not require the implication of Israel in its memory work. Several sequences in the film utilize spoken Yiddish, sometimes untranslated. For example, as the film shows original film footage of Jews in a European ghetto, Ravett's voice repeatedly questions his father— who by now is no longer alive—"Vas hat dein kinder getin, Pop?" (What did your children do, Pop?). Thus, the diasporic Yiddish is the language of the Jewish past, and also the intimate language between father and son.

While these new, private ways of examining the resonances of the Holocaust have not displaced the more communal, triangulated representations, they exist alongside them in a growing body of cinematic representations of Holocaust memories and meanings. The range of these representations enriches and deepens our understanding of the Holocaust past and the shaping and reshaping of Jewish identity.

9 REFLECTIONS ON THE HOLOCAUST FROM NEBRASKA

Alan E. Steinweis

On April 16, 1996, more than twenty-five hundred Nebraskans crammed into the Lied Center for Performing Arts on the campus of the University of Nebraska in Lincoln. They had come to see and hear Elie Wiesel, who on this Yom HaShoah (Day of Remembrance of the Holocaust) had been scheduled to speak about "The Seduction and Danger of Fanaticism." The event had attracted the largest audience in the history of the Lied Center, which in the past had played host to many of the finest orchestras, ballet companies, and traveling Broadway companies. Hundreds of people had to be turned away from the Wiesel speech; many of them opted to watch it on a closed-circuit TV monitor that had been set up at the other end of campus. Wiesel himself arrived over an hour late. His flight from Chicago had been delayed, and airline connections to Lincoln, a city of about two hundred thousand inhabitants, are not frequent. In the packed Lied Center, however, people waited patiently. Upon Wiesel's appearance on the stage, the crowd rose to its feet and gave him an extended ovation.

The speech itself was typical for Wiesel: rambling, disjointed, at times platitudinous, but nonetheless compelling, forceful, and profound in a way that is not quite explicable. Members of the university faculty who were in the audience—like professors elsewhere, duty-bound to cultivate an air of skepticism and nonchalance—rolled their eyes and smiled at each other smugly as they endeavored to extract substance from the speech. But they knew that Wiesel was not there for their benefit. He is the bearer not of intellectual analysis but of a moral message. And, indeed, when Wiesel finished speaking, the audience again jumped to its feet, where it remained for many minutes as it showered the embarrassed Wiesel with applause and cheers.

For Wiesel, who is arguably the most admired Jewish person in the contemporary world, this was a moment of triumph in the Heartland of America. In many respects Wiesel's appearance at the University of Nebraska was typical of similar visits to countless American university campuses. But in this case the typical is made remarkable by the fact that it occurred in Nebraska. What possible connections could people here have to the terrible fate that befell the Jews of Europe over fifty years earlier? In fact the connections are numerous and profound. They derive not merely from the simple fact that Nebraskans share in a media-driven national popular culture in which the Holocaust has been ubiquitous for almost two decades, but also from regionally specific cultural, ideological, religious, and ethnic factors.[1] By exploring how the Holocaust has attained significance in this most middle part of "middle America," we can gain important insights into the broader phenomenon of the "Americanization" of the Holocaust.

The state of Nebraska has a population of about 1.5 million people, about half of whom live in or around the two cities of Omaha and Lincoln, which lie fifty-five miles apart along Interstate 80 in the southeastern corner of the state. The other half of the state's population live in small cities and communities in farm and ranch country. While by the standards of American society as a whole the population of Nebraska can fairly be characterized as homogeneous, the population being overwhelmingly white, there are visible minorities of African Americans, Native Americans, and recently arrived Mexican and Asian (mainly Vietnamese) immigrants. Moreover, there is a good deal of diversity with respect to national origin among the European American population. The largest segment of European settlers in Nebraska in the late nineteenth century was German, but there were also significant numbers of Czechs, Swedes, and Danes. One also finds denominational diversity within the Christian population. Protestants of various stripes form the majority, but there is a very large Catholic population as well.

There has been, and continues to be, a considerably greater Jewish presence in Nebraska than many New Yorkers, Californians, or Floridians might realize. About eight thousand Jews live in Nebraska, the vast majority in Omaha. Earlier in the century the Jewish population in Omaha had been considerably larger, the city having been an important regional place of settlement for Jewish immigrants from Russia and Poland. Jews have played important roles in the commercial development of the state, in education, in the professions, and in politics. In recent decades two of Omaha's mayors have been Jewish, as have a United States senator, a chief justice of the state supreme court, and two chancellors of the flagship campus of the state university. Into the 1960s the university had two Jewish fraternities and a Jewish sorority, although in the past quarter-century the Jewish component of the student body has diminished considerably.

Although the absolute numbers of the Jewish population are small, Jews have been a visible segment of the population for about a century. Genteel anti-Semitism persists, although it is less of a problem than it used to be, and of course the Heartland has more than its share of crude, militant anti-Semites, who usually, although not always, are to be found on the margin of society. But integrated as they are into the commercial and professional classes, Jews have come to be treated respectfully by most elements of the non-Jewish bourgeoisie. Owing largely to the development of Holocaust consciousness in American society as a whole, deference to Jews has assumed a variety of institutionalized, even ritualized, forms. These have included the insertion of a Judaism component into the multicultural curricula of schools and universities, newspaper and local television features about Jewish holidays and festivals, and workshops for hospital nurses on how to deal with the special needs of Jewish patients.

But it is in the commemoration of the Holocaust that the ritualized deference to the Jewish minority is at its most conspicuous.[2] In Nebraska the "official" commemoration takes place in the spectacular state capitol building in Lincoln, usually in the presence of the governor and other important state and local officials. Middle-school pupils, few or none of whom are Jewish, recite Holocaust-related poems they composed as a class assignment. The choir of a different middle school movingly performs Hebrew and Yiddish songs. A guest speaker, usually a prominent scholar invited for the occasion by the university, delivers a short address. The ceremony culminates in a candle lighting by Holocaust survivors and the children of survivors. (As of this writing, in 1997, about a half-dozen survivors live in Lincoln, and perhaps four times that many in Omaha. In the past the numbers had been greater, but time has taken its toll.)

This official Yom HaShoah ceremony, which is duplicated in an essentially similar form in many of the statehouses of the region, signifies the acknowledgment by the non-Jewish elite of a central concern of the small Jewish minority. As such, it constitutes a compelling public recognition of the existence of diversity in a region that thinks of itself, and is perceived by outsiders, as extremely homogeneous. In a region that remains socially and culturally traditional and politically conservative, the impact of such an overt gesture of solidarity with a small religious minority should not be underestimated. On the other hand, it should be noted that this gesture also reflects the acceptance of Jews into the mainstream of society, which cannot be said with respect to the African American, Mexican, and Native American minorities in the region. Notably, there is no equivalent ceremony commemorating the dispossession and brutal treatment of Nebraska's Native Americans in the nineteenth century, even though these events were far more closely connected with the history of the state, and even though twice as many Native Americans as Jews live in Nebraska. One of my students put her finger directly on this particular point when she mentioned in class that for young Nebraskans like herself, studying the Holocaust is a "safe" means of learning about "other peoples' victims."

The embeddedness of the Holocaust in the culture of the non-Jewish segment of the population cannot, however, be explained simply in terms of a good-faith gesture toward the Jewish minority. The Holocaust has assumed a permanent place in the historical consciousness of most Americans. On the national level, much of the discussion about the Holocaust on the part of educators, philosophers, theologians, and museum designers has emphasized the universal significance of the event (even as many of them have simultaneously argued for the centrality of the Jewish dimension).[3] Michael Berenbaum's oft-cited comment about the need to make the Holocaust meaningful to, among other American archetypes, "the Midwestern farmer," as well as Alvin Rosenfeld's observation about an "American ethos" comprising "goodness, innocence, optimism, liberty, diversity, and equality," carries special significance in the present context.[4] Especially in the "Heartland," where the dominant ethos and rhetoric place a high value on decency, civic virtue, fair play, and traditional "family values," the lessons to be derived from the Holocaust about human nature, tolerance, morality, and civil courage tend to resonate very strongly. What is problematic is that individuals and groups prefer to decide for themselves what it means to be decent, virtuous, and tolerant, and so there is no single "universally applicable" significance of the Holocaust. In the process of finding meaning in the Holocaust, Nebraskans, like all Americans, superimpose their own religious, ethnic, and ideological perspectives onto the subject. Although it should be emphasized that no monolithic

Nebraska or Heartland perspective exists, it would be fair to say that views on the Holocaust do often reflect characteristics and self-perceptions that are more common in this place than they are in others.

Of primary importance among these factors is religion—or, at least, religiosity. The profession of Christian faith, regular attendance at church, and adherence to the values that are believed to be rooted in the (Judeo-) Christian tradition are salient features of this culture. Although individuals who do not sincerely subscribe to this hegemonic point of view have sufficient space to dissent from it privately, the public discourse has a distinctly religious flavor. Newspapers and other media devote a good deal of space to stories dealing with religion (usually Christian) and church activities. Membership in Christian organizations is common among high school and college students. Not long ago the Association of Students at the University of Nebraska (the official student government) clashed with the faculty and administration over the issue of prayer at the commencement ceremony. The students, who are in general far more traditional and conservative than the people who teach them, favored prayer. One might even plausibly argue that the deference accorded to Jews may be in part attributable to the majority's perception of them as a community of faith, unlike the perception in the major Jewish population centers, where Jews are often seen by non-Jews in ethnic terms.

The centrality of religion to virtuous living has been recently articulated in a book by the single most revered person in the state of Nebraska: Tom Osborne, the former head coach of the University of Nebraska Cornhuskers football team. A frequent speaker at prayer breakfasts and similar functions, Osborne, who holds a Ph.D. in educational psychology, in 1996 published a book about his coaching experiences. In a chapter titled "Where Faith Comes In," Osborne related how the strength of his religious beliefs helped him to overcome several crises in his football program. He also used the chapter as an opportunity to posit a theory about the ultimate cause of Nazism and the Holocaust. Citing Viktor Frankl, Osborne constructs a chain of causality starting with Nietzsche's declaration that "God is dead," advancing through the secular godlessness of the twentieth century, and culminating in Hitler, Nazism, and genocide. Notwithstanding the merits of Frankl's argument, or of Osborne's representation of it, the reader is presented with an interpretation of the origins of the Holocaust in which Christian anti-Judaism does not warrant mention. Not religion, but rather the absence of it, was the culprit.[5]

The idea that the Holocaust represents the very antithesis of Christian values forms the core of Holocaust consciousness among a great many non-Jews in the American Heartland. Sometimes—but by no means always—this position leads to critical self-reflection about the centrality of anti-Judaism in the Christian tradition. Students who enroll in my course on the history of the Holocaust at the University of Nebraska have often characterized themselves to me as devout Christians whose main motive for taking the course is to learn more about the injustices inflicted by Christians upon Jews. One student, who described herself as a traditional, conservative Catholic, told me that her interest in the Holocaust was stimulated by the Catholic-Jewish dialogue that has been promoted by Pope John Paul II. She praised the pope for recognizing and attempting to rectify a historic wrong and sees it as her responsibility as a Catholic to participate in the process of reconciliation.

Whether such sentiments reflect an acceptance of Judaism as theologically legitimate is hard to say, considering that open discussion of this extremely sensitive dimension of the issue is assiduously avoided by just about everyone. This has been as true in Nebraska as elsewhere in the United States, both for Jews, who desire to remain integrated into the Christian majority, and for Christian believers, who might be torn between their tolerant impulses on the one hand and their faith in Jesus as the savior on the other. When my student told me about her admiration for John Paul's outreach to Jews, it occurred to me to broach the question of the pope's beatification of Edith Stein, but in the end I held back, concluding that such a comment, under the circumstances, would have been counterproductive.[6]

Most American Christians, like most American Jews, have an aversion to theological absolutes, but the number of exceptions seems to be growing. Post-Holocaust Christian theology, and the post-Holocaust American Christian sensibility, have facilitated the Christian majority's acceptance of Jews, but one must wonder about the permanence and generational specificity of this phenomenon. No doubt there has been a great amount of Christian guilt at work over the past half-century, but this condition might well wear off as time passes. The controversy that has erupted in the wake of the Southern Baptist Convention's announcement that it intends to step up its efforts to convert Jews has provided a demonstration of the potential for distress that can ensue when an issue is made of Christian supersessionism. In Nebraska, where Baptists are a minority among Protestants, there is little prospect that such missionary efforts will become a major issue, although it is worth pointing out that several Protestant churches in Lincoln have refused to join the local Interfaith Council on the grounds that the council encompasses non-Christian groups.

In Nebraska, as elsewhere, Christian groups have appropriated the Holocaust and instrumentalized it in the pursuit of a cause that has no connection to Jew-hatred whatsoever: the "pro-life" movement.[7] The use of the term *Holocaust* with respect to abortion and the analogizing of aborted fetuses to Jews killed at Auschwitz have become commonplace in the pro-life discourse. While much of this rhetoric is the product of conscious, arguably cynical, exploitation of a "usable past," there is every reason to believe that the analogy is sincerely subscribed to by many adherents to the pro-life movement. (I have been personally assured of this in conversations with neighbors and associates, not least important of whom is my attorney, who is a leading Catholic pro-life activist in the community.) Such heartfelt sentiments testify to the extent to which the Holocaust has been absorbed into the American consciousness as a paradigmatic evil. Having been encouraged by, among others, Jewish leaders to contemplate the universal significance of the Holocaust, a large segment of American society has chosen to view the "unborn" as the victims of a genocidal campaign much like the one that wiped out millions of defenseless Jews in Europe. The analogy to the Holocaust, however, has been extended well beyond the characterization of the victim group. By likening physicians who perform abortions to SS doctors during the Holocaust, harassment of those physicians is mandated as a moral imperative. The campaign to delegitimize Planned Parenthood has focused on the connections between that organization's founder, Margaret Sanger, and the eugenics movement of the early twentieth century (a movement that, as several historians have recently emphasized, was intimately connected with the Nazi racial anti-Semitism that produced the Holocaust). In mobilizing their forces, pro-life activists cite the historical precedent of the moral failure of the German population to prevent the crimes of the Nazi regime.

Members of the small Jewish minority in Nebraska often take umbrage at such invocations of the Holocaust by Christian groups. They regard them not merely as an appropriation of Jewish history but even more problematically as an appropriation of the very component of Jewish identity that in recent years has done the most to elicit Christian sympathy for the Jewish predicament. For the majority of Jews this appropriation is all the more exasperating because they tend to be politically liberal and pro-choice.

Of equal importance to Christian religiosity as a factor in shaping Holocaust consciousness among non-Jews in Nebraska is the ethnic composition of the state, particularly the preponderance of German Americans. German Americans constitute the single largest group in the United States when national origins are considered. For the most part, German Americans are thoroughly assimilated and display few or no signs of German identity. There are, however, regional pockets of German Americans who have retained a German component of their identity, and Nebraska is one of these pockets. After Wisconsin and the Dakotas, Nebraska has the largest concentration of Americans with German ancestry.[8] German identity has been preserved in small-town agrarian communities, into which few newcomers have migrated since their founding by German settlers in the second half of the nineteenth century. The two world wars of the twentieth century, in which American soldiers were sent overseas to fight against Germans, drastically diminished the public, organized dimension of German American culture in Nebraska, but consciousness of origins has remained strong within families. (In Nebraska communities that were founded by Czech or Danish settlers, overtly expressed pride in Old World ethnic origins was not diminished as the result of international political alignments.)

Nebraska has also been a locus of settlement for two further groups of German immigrants. The first of these were ethnic Germans who left Russia in the late nineteenth and early twentieth centuries. As a distinctive, albeit fairly small, group within a group, the "Germans from Russia" in Nebraska have endeavored especially hard, and with a good deal of success, to nurture a special identity. The national headquarters of the American Association of Germans from Russia is located in Lincoln. The most recent group of German immigrants arrived during or soon after World War II. German prisoners of war were incarcerated in several locations in the state, and several decided to remain upon their release. Moreover, Nebraska, like other sections of the Midwest, attracted ethnic German "displaced persons" who had fled Communist regimes in Eastern Europe. Evidence of this small migration materializes from time to time in my classroom, when a student informs me that his or her grandfather had fought in the Wehrmacht.

Media and scholarly attention to the ethnic-identity movement in contemporary America has tended to focus primarily on "people of color," and sometimes on Jews, but rarely on Christian whites of north and central European origin. The multicultural movement, both in its political and academic incarnations, steadfastly rejects the notion that there is a neutral, generic American ethnicity but ironically has shown little interest in studying the processes and consequences of identity construction among some of the largest American ethnic groups. In the case of German Americans in Nebraska, the legacy of the Holocaust both impacts, and is impacted by, ethnic identity. That ethnically conscious German Americans can have an active interest in the Holocaust, despite not possessing any personal connection to that event, is hardly surprising. Even though the vast majority of German Americans are the descendants of immigrants who arrived in the United States generations ago, the attitudes of American Jews, most of whose ancestors also arrived in the United States before the Holocaust, demonstrate that collective identity can often be more important than personal experience.

If self-identification as a victim group has proved a basic feature of contemporary ethnic consciousness in America—as has been the case among Jews—German Americans in Nebraska have not been immune from this trend. During World War I, Nebraskans of German descent were subjected to considerable harassment, and the German language was banished from several school systems within the state.[9] Although the overall impact of such persecution was to diminish the German component of the identity of German American Nebraskans in the wake of the war, this episode of cultural oppression has attracted the attention of young Nebraskans of German descent who are attempting to rediscover their roots. This subject has been raised by students on several occasions in my classes and in conversation. A more extreme manifestation of the yearning for victim status has been the small movement to achieve recognition of Stalin's "genocide" of Germans in Russia. In 1996 an official ceremony commemorating Stalin's ethnic German victims was held in the very same chamber of the state capitol in which the annual Holocaust Days of Remembrance ceremony takes place. The event received little attention, however, and was probably more a reflection of the legislature's reluctance to say no to a group of middle-class citizens who requested use of the building than it was of any widespread recognition of German suffering.

But among German Americans in Nebraska, the tendency to express embarrassment and contrition for the crimes of Germany under Hitler has been at least as strong as, and often much stronger than, the tendency to seek victim status. When I ask students in my course on the Holocaust to explain why they are interested in the subject, there are always several who claim that they are working to come to terms with their German heritage. One student, who served as a summer intern in the Survivors Registry of the United States

Holocaust Memorial Museum, contemplated the possibility that a "distant relative" of hers might have been a perpetrator, perhaps even contributed to the suffering of some of the very survivors she was meeting. Another, whose grandfather had served in the Wehrmacht, had been thrown into a state of personal confusion in 1993 when as a senior in high school she was taken on a field trip to see *Schindler's List*.

This last case is exceptional in that the student had a direct family connection with the Nazi regime. In most cases it is evident that the German American identity of students has little or no basis in actual knowledge of or contact with German history or culture. They do not seem to realize that German immigrants played an important role in the development of democracy and the promotion of progressive government in nineteenth-century America; they had heard of Heinrich Himmler, but not of Carl Schurz. It is quite plausible in some instances that students have transformed a vague sense of family origins into an ethnic identity in response to the emphasis that contemporary American culture and education place on ethnicity. Groping for identity, but having little real access to the stuff of German culture (e.g., language and literature), they seize upon as a point of reference the Holocaust, the most shameful episode in German history, and one that has been omnipresent in American popular culture over the past several years. Bearing the burden of guilt for the Holocaust thus becomes the price of achieving German American identity, a phenomenon that mirrors the natural tendency of young Jewish Americans to identify with the Jewish victims of the Nazis.

Accepting and working through the moral implications of the Holocaust as a means for developing German American identity has also been observable among some older Nebraskans. A recent incident involving a local neo-Nazi provides a compelling illustration. For about two decades the city of Lincoln had been the base of operations for Gary ("Gerhard") Lauck, a Nebraskan of German American background who was one of the leading suppliers of printed neo-Nazi propaganda to Germany and other countries. Lauck's literature was saturated with anti-Semitic vitriol, and it also promoted denial of the Holocaust. To avoid hassles, Lauck, who was sometimes referred to in the media as the "Farmbelt Fuehrer," actually maintained a very low profile in his own community and region. In the early 1990s, however, the increase of neo-Nazi and antiforeigner violence in Germany brought the existence of Lauck's propaganda pipeline to the fore. The situation was an embarrassing one for the city of Lincoln. Although Lauck's publishing operation was protected by the Constitution, in 1994 a coalition of community organizations in Lincoln brought before the city council a request that the city formally disassociate itself from Lauck and his positions, a resolution that passed unanimously. Notably, the main proponent of this action was the local German American association, which acted in cooperation with the local Jewish community as well as with other local minorities.[10]

The next chapter of the Lauck story was also instructive about the state of ethnic relations in Nebraska. After the city of Lincoln had formally disassociated itself from Lauck, several members of the state legislature introduced a bill that would do the same for Nebraska as a whole. As had been the case with the resolution in Lincoln, the phraseology carefully avoided infringement of First Amendment rights. The resolution, if passed, would have been tantamount to a formal repudiation by the state legislature of the neo-Nazi message. One senator, however, actively opposed the resolution and, employing parliamentary tactics, succeeded in having it tabled. The senator in question was the single African American in the Nebraska legislature. His argument was that it would have been hypocritical for the state to disassociate itself from neo-Nazism while continuing to tolerate racism in other forms. Although this argument was not without some merit, Jews in the state interpreted such opposition as a gratuitous slap in the face. The senator, it should be noted, had in the past been quoted in the press as making remarks that many Jews had considered anti-Semitic.

In a state with very few African Americans and Jews, the affair reflected in microcosm the major fissures that have opened in the relationship between the two groups. Both the Jewish and the African American minorities in the state are concentrated in Omaha. Social and economic relations between the two groups have developed historically along lines essentially similar to those in the major cities of the Northeast. When Jews constituted an important segment of the shopkeeping and small-business class, African Americans were either in their debt or in their employ. As time passed, Jewish success in commerce and the professions coincided with a frustrating lack of progress in the condition of the African American community. Originally located downtown, the Jewish community gradually migrated to newer, more comfortable residential areas on the outskirts of the city, whereas the African American population remained concentrated in lower-income neighborhoods in the inner city. African American Omahans observed the ascent of Jewish Omahans into the city's white elite. As ritualized Holocaust observance emerged as a symbol of Jewish success, it was inevitable that the resentment harbored in some quarters of the African American community would come to focus on such observance. On the national level, African American resentment of the attention that has been focused on the history of Jewish suffering in Europe, especially the Holocaust, has both reflected and reinforced the tension between the two groups. "From a Black perspective," Julius Lester has written, "there is something jarring in hearing white-skinned Jews talk about suffering."[11] It would be understandable for African Americans to interpret the ubiquity of ritualized Holocaust observance among non-Jews as evidence of Jewish attainment of the American dream, the very ideal that has been closed off to African Americans. When this occurs, it does so in spite of encouragement to comprehend the Holocaust in terms that affirm the goodness and righteousness of America, terms that appeal to broad segments of the American population (including, it should be emphasized, many African Americans).

Raul Hilberg has keenly observed that the Holocaust has become "a marker of an absolute evil against which all other transgressions in the conduct of nations could be measured and assessed."[12] A focus on the monstrosities of Nazi Germany brings the virtues of America into sharp relief. Tributes to the role of the United States in the defeat of Nazi Germany and the "liberation" of the concentration camps are built into many Days of Remembrance ceremonies. Indeed, they are built into the exhibition as well as the very structure of the United States Holocaust Memorial Museum in Washington, D.C. American veterans who served in units that stumbled across German concentration camps during their advance into Germany in 1945 have been invited to conceptualize their wartime role as that of "liberators." Historical evidence that contravenes, or at least complicates, this view—concerning, for example, American immigration barriers in the 1930s, or the failure seriously to consider direct use of American air power against Auschwitz—receives far less emphasis.[13] Not only does this representation of history facilitate the integration of the Holocaust into the historical consciousness of Americans, it also promotes a sense of patriotism by juxtaposing the goodness of the United States with the evil of Nazi Germany.

Inasmuch as Nebraskans take pride in their country's contribution to the defeat of Nazi Germany, they are typical of most Americans. Evidence is strong that they have integrated the Holocaust into their comprehension of what was at stake in World War II, even if this comprehension is not accompanied by concrete knowledge about the Holocaust. When public lectures about the Holocaust are held at my university, there are usually some (non-

Jewish) veterans in the audience. In several cases they have entered the auditorium wearing their American Legion or Veterans of Foreign Wars caps. During the question period subsequent to the lectures they have asked questions or made comments that, while not especially germane to the substance of the lecture, evidenced a desire to associate their own wartime experiences with the rescue of European Jews. Even those who did not directly encounter concentration camps have come to view themselves as "liberators." Among many of my students, interest in the Holocaust seems to be an outgrowth of an interest in World War II, which they, like most Americans, consider to have been one of this country's better moments.

As the Holocaust recedes into the past, its place in the American consciousness will inevitably evolve. The course of that evolution is hard to predict. It will depend on a number of variables. The multicultural impulse in American society will likely continue to have its ebbs and flows, with consequences for relations between Jews and African Americans, for German American identity, and for the significance attached to "victim" status in American culture. Representations of the Holocaust in popular culture will continue to be influenced by the creative whims of Hollywood producers. The manner in which the Holocaust is handled in the education system, at all levels, will change in response to cultural climate, budgetary circumstances, and pedagogical fashion. Hypotheses about race as a genetic determinant of intelligence, which have recently been revived, will invite comparisons with Nazi racial theories. If the state of Israel were to be threatened with extinction, attention to the Holocaust would increase. If, on the other hand, Israel were to succeed in attaining peaceful coexistence with its neighbors, the impact on Holocaust "memory" could be quite different. Similarly, in the American Jewish community, concerns about intermarriage and "continuity" might well reduce the Jewish preoccupation with the threat of anti-Semitism. Alternatively, a flare-up of anti-Semitism in Russia might have the opposite effect. Jewish attitudes toward anti-Semitism and the Holocaust will unavoidably influence, and be influenced by, perceptions of these same issues by American Christians.

However things might change, the homogenizing tendencies of American popular culture and mainstream intellectual life will continue to produce a fairly high degree of commonality in the way that Americans think about the Holocaust into the twenty-first century. But ethnic, ideological, and cultural factors, many of which are regionally correlated, will also continue to generate differences in the way that discrete groups within American society will interpret the Holocaust. The case of Nebraska, a state in which slightly more than one-half of 1 percent of the population of the United States resides, exemplifies how even a small patch of middle America, a region seen by Americans elsewhere as a relatively uncomplicated place, can embody an enormous complexity in the way that the Holocaust has become "Americanized."

10 "YOU WHO NEVER WAS THERE"

Slavery and the New Historicism—
Deconstruction and the Holocaust

Walter Benn Michaels

DO THE AMERICANS BELIEVE THEIR MYTHS? OR, BELOVED

The title of this section is derived from Paul Veyne's *Did the Greeks Believe in Their Myths?*—a book that I read several years ago, first with great eagerness and then with a certain disappointment. The eagerness stemmed from my curiosity about whether the Greeks really thought, to take one of Veyne's examples, that events like "the amorous adventures of Aphrodite and Ares caught in bed by her husband" had actually happened;[1] the disappointment stemmed from Veyne's commitment to regarding such curiosity as naive. The book's subtitle is *An Essay on the Constitutive Imagination;* Veyne thinks that "it is we who fabricate our truths, and it is not 'reality' that makes us believe" (113); hence, truth is "plural" and myth, like "history," "literature," and "physics," is "true in its way" (20). So, "of course," the Greeks "believed in their myths," and "what is true of 'them' is also true of ourselves" (129). The answer to the question, Do the Americans believe their myths? is yes.

At the same time, however, from Veyne's perspective, the answer to the question, Do the Americans believe their myths? must be no. Once we recognize that, as he puts it, "'reality' is the child of the constitutive imagination of our tribe" (113), we must also recognize that "truth," as we ordinarily conceive it—in the sense, say, that we might think our myths true and the Greek myths false—"does not exist" (115). Indeed, "as long as we speak of the truth, we will understand nothing of culture and will never manage to attain the same perspective on our culture as we have on past centuries, when people spoke of gods and myths" (113). So if, on the one hand, we must believe our myths, on the other hand, we must not believe that they are true. That is the whole point of "culture" as Veyne understands it: "Culture, without being false, is not true either" (127). And while the Greeks, "of course," believed their myths, insofar as in believing their myths they believed them to be *true*, they were, of course, mistaken. We, who know that our culture is neither true nor false, also believe our myths, but we believe them in the right way; in fact, insofar as "our perspective" on our own culture is "the same" as our perspective on the cultures of "past centuries, when people spoke of gods and myths," we must not only believe our own myths, we must also believe the myths of the past. So not only must the Greeks have believed their myths and must the Americans believe theirs, the Americans must believe the Greek myths, too.

And, in fact, at least some Americans do. In his 1987 bestseller, *Communion*, Whitley Strieber argues that the alien "visitors" who on several occasions have made their presence known to him and who look, he thinks, like the ancient goddess Ishtar, are probably the originals for "the whole Greek pantheon." His theory is that humans, unable to deal with "the stark reality of the visitor experience"—"the bad smells, the dreadful food, and the general sense of helplessness"—dress it up in what he calls "a very human mythology," one that preserves the essential truth of "the visitor experience" while at the same time making it more palatable. But *Communion* is subtitled *A True Story* rather than *An Essay on the Constitutive Imagination;* whether or not the Greeks, in believing their myths, believed them to be true, Whitley Strieber does. His memories of his own experience count as testimony to their truth not only because they provide modern analogies for ancient myths but also because they may be understood to provide more direct evidence: "Do my memories come from my own life," he wonders, "or from other lives lived long ago, in the shadowy temples where the grey goddess reigned?"[2] If they come from his own life, they provide evidence that godlike creatures are currently interacting with humans, and they provoke the reflection that such interactions may have taken place also in the past; if they come from lives lived long ago, they provide evidence that godlike creatures have always interacted with humans and so that the old mythologies are not only compatible with recent experience but true.

But how does the fact that some Americans believe the Greek myths shed any light on the question of whether Americans believe their own myths? It might, of course, be argued that the belief in "visitors" is an American myth and so that, for people like Whitley Strieber, believing in the Greek myths is a way of believing American myths. In my view, however, the fact that Whitley Strieber believes in the Greek pantheon is less relevant to American mythology than the question he raises in the course of stating that belief: "Do my memories come from my own life or from other lives lived long ago?" For it is this question, I want to suggest, that lies at the heart of the myths Americans believe insofar as it is in attempting to answer this question—Do our memories come from our own lives or from other lives lived long ago?—that Americans can come to think of themselves as distinctively American.

"History is to the nation," Arthur Schlesinger Jr. has recently written in *The Disuniting of America,* "rather as memory is to the individual. As an individual deprived of memory becomes disoriented and lost . . . so a nation denied a conception of its past will be disabled in dealing with its present . . . As the means of defining national identity, history becomes a means of shaping history."[3] Memory is here said to constitute the core of individual identity; national memory is understood to constitute the core of national identity. Insofar, then, as individuals have a national as well as an individual identity, they must have access not only to their own memories but to the national memory; they must be able to remember not only the things that happened to them as individuals but the things that happened to them as Americans. The way they can do this, Schlesinger says, is through history. History, in other words, can give us memories not only of what Strieber calls our "own" lives but of "other lives lived long ago." And it is in giving us these memories that history gives us our "identity." Indeed, it is because our relation to things that happened to and were done by Americans long ago is the relation of memory that we know we are Americans. We learn about other people's history; we remember our own.

So American mythology has less (although, as we shall see, not nothing) to do with the belief in aliens (*space* aliens, anyway) than with the belief that we can remember "other lives lived long ago"—or perhaps, to put the point more neutrally, than with our ways of talking as if we remembered "other lives lived long ago." For whether or not the belief that we can remember such lives is widespread, talk about remembering such lives is extremely widespread. To stick for another moment to texts that may, to an academic audience, seem marginal, Greg Bear's science fiction novel *Blood Music* (1985) imagines the restructuring of blood cells so as to enable them to perform a kind of memory transfer, first from father to son ("The memory was there and he hadn't even been born, and he was seeing it, and then seeing their wedding night") and then more generally ("And his father went off to war . . . and his son watched what he could not possibly have seen. And then he watched what his father could not possibly have seen"). "Where did they come from?" he asks about these memories, and when he is told, "*Not all memory comes from an individual's life,*" he realizes that what he is encountering is "the transfer of racial memory" and that now, in "his blood, his flesh, he carried . . . part of his father and mother, parts of people he had never known, people perhaps thousands of years dead."[4] *Blood Music* imagines as science what *Communion*—identifying its "visitors" with the "Greek pantheon" and speculating that they are the "gods" who created us—imagines as religion.

But both *Blood Music* and *Communion* should probably, as I suggested above, be considered marginal texts, not because they haven't been read by many—*Communion,* at least, has been read by hundreds of thousands—but because their account of what *Blood Music* calls "racial memory" is, in a certain sense, significantly anachronistic. By "racial," Greg Bear means "human"; it's the human race, not the white or the black or the red race, that his transfusions of blood unite. And while it is true that, in an amazing moment, Whitley Strieber speaks of "visitor culture" and imagines our encounter with it along vaguely multicultural lines—it may be only "apparently superior"; we will come to understand "its truth" by understanding its "weaknesses" as well as its "strengths"—it is essential to remember that the "visitors" he has in mind are not merely foreigners.[5] Strieber does produce the familiar nativist gesture of imagining himself a Native American, the "flower" of his "culture" crushed by "Cortez"-like invaders, but the vanishing race for which he is proleptically nostalgic is, like Greg Bear's, human rather than American. It would only make sense to understand *Communion*'s aliens as relevant to the question of American identity if we were to understand them as allegories of the aliens threatening American identity. Insofar, however, as the apparatus of the allegory requires the redescription of differences between humans as differences between humans and others, it has the effect of establishing the human as an internally undifferentiated category and thus of making the designation of some humans as American irrelevant. In *Communion* and *Blood Music,* the emergence of "racial memory," of a history made almost literally universal, unites us all.

So the technologies of memory imagined in *Blood Music* and *Communion* provide an image, but only a partial image, of what is required by Schlesinger's invocation of history as memory. If the obvious objection to thinking of history as a kind of memory is that things we are said to remember are things that we did or experienced, whereas things that are said to belong to our history tend to be things that were neither done nor experienced by us, then *Blood Music* and *Communion* imagine ways in which history can be turned into memory. But they don't meet Schlesinger's requirement that this history be national, which is to say that they don't deploy the transformation of history into memory on behalf of the constitution of identity; in *Communion,* the remembered past is merely a testament to the visitors' persistence; in *Blood Music,* the moment in which the past can be remembered actually marks the disappearance of nationality. It is instead in a much more important and influential text of 1987, Toni Morrison's *Beloved,* that Schlesinger's identification of memory, history, and national identity is given a definitive articulation.

And this is true even though *Beloved,* according to Morrison, is a story about something no one wants to remember: "The characters don't want to remember, I don't want to remember, black people don't want to remember, white people don't want to remember."[6] What no one wants to remember, she thinks, is slavery, and whether or not this characterization is accurate, it succeeds in establishing remembering or forgetting as the relevant alternatives. It establishes, in other words, that although no white people or black people now living ever experienced it, slavery can be and must be either remembered or forgotten. Thus, although Sethe's daughter Denver thinks early on that "only those who lived in Sweet Home [where Sethe was a slave] could remember it," it quickly turns out that memories of "places" like Sweet Home can in fact be made available to people who never lived there.[7] A "house can burn down," Sethe tells Denver, "but the place—the picture of it—stays, and not just in my rememory, but out there, in the world" (36). Thus, people always run the risk of bumping into "a rememory that belongs to somebody else," and thus, especially, Denver runs the risk of a return to slavery: "The picture is still there and what's more, if you go there—you who never was there—if you go there and stand in the place where it was, it will happen again; it will be there for you, waiting for you." Because Denver might bump into Sethe's rememory, Sethe's memory can become Denver's; because what once happened is still happening—because, as Denver says, "nothing ever dies"—slavery needn't be part of your memory in order to be remembered by you.

From Sethe's standpoint this is, of course, a kind of threat; she and her contemporaries are, as one critic has put it, "haunted by memories of slavery that they seek to avoid."[8] But if *Beloved*'s characters want to forget something that happened to them, its readers—"black people," "white people," Morrison herself—are supposed to remember something that didn't happen to them. And in insisting on slavery as the thing they are supposed to remember, Morrison not only gives *Blood Music*'s "racial memory" what counts in the late twentieth century as its proper meaning, but she also establishes what we might call, in contrast to the marginality of *Blood Music,* the centrality of *Beloved*—or at least its discursive distance from the genres of science fiction and New Age space invasion. This distance involves, as we have already noted, the political difference between a certain universalism and a certain nationalism, but in fact it's much greater than that. Morrison's race, like Schlesinger's nation, provides the mechanism for as well as the meaning of the conversion of history into memory. *Blood Music* requires weird science to explain how people can "remember stuff" they haven't "even lived through";[9] *The Disuniting of America* needs only the nation, *Beloved* needs only race. And while probably almost no Americans now believe that blood transfusions can make us remember things that did not happen to us, and probably only some Americans now believe that "visitors" can help us remember the lives we lived long ago, probably a great many Americans believe that nationality—understood by Schlesinger as citizenship in a state, transformed by Morrison and by multiculturalism more generally into membership in a race or culture—can do what blood transfusions and visitors cannot. It is racial identity that makes the experience of enslavement part of the history of African Americans today.[10]

So if some Americans believe the Greek myths—believe, that is, in the nonhuman creatures who used to be called "gods" and are now called "visitors"— most Americans need only believe in our own myths: race and nation. The supernatural presence that haunts 124 Bluestone Road outside of Cincinnati, Ohio, should not be understood as a version of the supernatural presence that haunts Whitley Strieber's cabin in upstate New York. At the same time, however, it is a striking fact about *Beloved* that it presents itself as a ghost story, that its account of the past takes the form of an encounter with a ghost, a ghost who is, as Valerie Smith has said, "the story of the past embodied."[11] And if one way to regard this ghost is (along the lines I've just suggested) as a figure for the way in which race can make the past present, another way to regard the ghost is as the figure for a certain anxiety about the very idea of race that is being called upon to perform this function. For while races are, no doubt, more real than "visitors," it isn't quite clear how much more or in what ways they are more real. To what extent, for example, are the races we believe in biological entities? Nothing is more common in American intellectual life today than the denial that racial identity is a biological phenomenon and the denunciation of such a biologism as racial essentialism. The race that antiessentialists believe in is a historical entity, not a biological one. In racial antiessentialism, the effort to imagine an identity that will connect people through history is replaced by the effort to imagine a history that will give people an identity.

If, then, we must not see the ghost in *Beloved* as a real (albeit biologically exotic) entity (like a visitor), we should not see her either as a figure for a real (and also biologically exotic) entity (like a race). She is a figure instead for a process, for history itself; *Beloved* is, in this respect, not only a historical but a historicist novel. It is historical in that it's about the historical past; it is historicist in that—setting out to remember "the disremembered"—it re-describes something we have never known as something we have forgotten and thus makes the historical past a part of our own experience. It's no accident that the year in which *Communion* and *Beloved* were published (1987) is also the year in which the University of California Press New Historicism series was inaugurated, or that the year in which *Beloved* won the Pulitzer Prize (1988) was the year in which *Shakespearean Negotiations*—written by the editor of the New Historicism series, Stephen Greenblatt, and beginning with the author's announcement of his "desire to speak with the dead"—was also published. The ghost story, the story in which the dead speak, either like Beloved in a voice that's "low and rough" (52) or like Shakespeare through "textual traces," is the privileged form of the New Historicism.[12]

If, in other words, the minimal condition of the historian's activity is an interest in the past as an object of study, Greenblatt's account of the origins of his vocation ("I began with the desire to speak with the dead") and his account of the nature of that vocation ("literature professors are salaried, middle-class shamans") both insist on a relation to the past (he calls it a "link") that goes beyond that minimal condition, and beyond also (it's this going beyond that the model of the shaman is meant to indicate) various standard accounts of the continuity between past and present. Greenblatt is not, that is, interested in the kind of continuity offered by the claim that events in the past have *caused* conditions in the present, or in the kind of continuity imagined in the idea that the past is enough like the present that we might learn from the past things that are useful in the present.[13] Indeed, the interest proclaimed here has almost nothing to do with taking the past as an object of knowledge; what he wants is to *speak* with the dead, "to re-create a conversation with them," not to find out or explain what they did. And although he himself proclaims this ambition a failed one, from the standpoint of the heightened continuity that the New Historicism requires, the terms of failure are even more satisfying than success would be: "Even when I came to understand that in my most intense moments of straining to listen all I could hear was my own voice, even then I did not abandon my desire. It was true that I could hear only my own voice, but my own voice was the voice of the dead."[14] If what you want is a "link" with the dead that is better achieved by speaking with them than by studying them—that is achieved, that is to say, by understanding studying them as a way of speaking with them—then it can't really count as a disappointment to discover that what one hears when one hears the dead speak is actually the sound of one's "own voice." "My own voice was the voice of the dead": the link envisioned in conversation is only made stronger by the discovery that the conversation is with oneself. Continuity is turned into identity.

For both Morrison and Greenblatt, then, history involves the effort to make the past present, and the ghosts of *Beloved* and *Shakespearean Negotiations* are the figures for this effort, the transformation of history into memory, the deployment of history in the constitution of identity. If, then, we ask a slightly revised version of the question whether the Americans believe their myths—Which myths do the Americans believe?—the answer turns out to be not visitors, not blood transfusions, not biological races, not even exactly history as such, but history as memory. To put the point in this way is no longer to say with Veyne that the difference between myth and history is erased insofar as the truths of both myth and history are revealed as truths constituted by the imagination. For although this idealism is, as we all know, widespread today, and although it does succeed in establishing, at least by the back door—we don't get our identity from history, history gets its identity from us—the desired link between past and present, the fact that that link must be imposed on the past before it can be derived from it makes it less promising as a ground of identity; if we create our history, then any history might be made ours. So what makes our commitment to history a commitment to myth is not our sense that the history we learn is true in (and only in) the same way that the Greeks thought their myths were true; what makes our history mythological is not our sense that it is constituted but our sense that it is *remembered* and, when it is not remembered, *forgotten*.[15]

Without the idea of a history that is remembered or forgotten—not merely learned or unlearned—the events of the past can have only a limited relevance to the present, providing us at most with causal accounts of how things have come to be the way they are, at least with objects of antiquarian interest. It is only when it's reimagined as the fabric of our own experience that the past can become the key to our own identity. A history that is learned can be learned by anyone, and it can belong to anyone who learns it; a history that is remembered can only be remembered by those who first experienced it, and it must belong to them. So if history were learned, not remembered, then no history could be more truly ours than any other. Indeed, no history, except the things that had actually happened to us, would be truly ours at all.

This is why the ghosts of the New Historicism are not simply figures for history, they are figures for a remembered history. But this is also why there is a problem in thinking about these ghosts as *figures*. For without the ghosts to function as partners in conversation rather than as objects of study, without rememories that allow "you who never was there" access to experiences otherwise available to "only those who" *were* there, history can no more be remembered than it can be forgotten. The ghosts cannot, in other words, be explained as metaphoric representations of the importance to us of our history because the history cannot count as ours and thus can have no particular importance to us without the ghosts. It is only when the events of the past can be imagined not only to have consequences for the present but to *live on* in the present that they can become part of our experience and can testify to who we are. So the ghosts are not merely the figures for history as memory, they are the technology for history as memory: to have the history, we have to have the ghosts. Remembered history is not merely described or represented by the ghosts who make the past ours, it is *made possible* by them. *Beloved*'s ghosts are thus as essential to its historicism as *Communion*'s visitors are to its New Age mysticism; indeed, *Beloved*'s historicism is nothing but the racialized and, hence, authorized version of *Communion*'s mysticism. Without the visitors, the remains of UFOs are just fragments of old weather balloons; without the ghosts, history is just a subject we study.[16] It is only accounts like Sethe's of how other people's memories can become our own that provide the apparatus through which our history can, as Arthur Schlesinger puts it, define our identity.

HOLOCAUST REMEMBRANCE; OR, MARION

"As the eyewitnesses pass from the scene and even the most faithful memories fade," Geoffrey Hartman has recently written, "the question of what sustains Jewish identity is raised with a new urgency."[17] What the eyewitnesses witnessed, and what they have begun to forget, is, of course, the Holocaust; and although the dependence of Jewish identity on the Holocaust is a topic that will require further discussion, the dependence of identity on memory is, as we have already seen, undeniable. So if the idea here is that memories of the Holocaust have sustained Jewish identity, and thus that the imminent disappearance of those memories as even the survivors die poses a threat to Jewish identity, then the task becomes to keep those memories alive if only in order to keep Jewish identity alive. Because some survivors are still alive, the issue here is not yet the transformation of history into memory that we saw at work in *Beloved*'s representation of American slavery; it is instead an effort to forestall what Pierre Vidal-Nacquet has called the "transformation of memory into history."[18] Once memory is transformed into history, it can no longer be relevant to the project of sustaining Jewish identity. Hence, the outbreak, over the last fifteen years, of interest in the Holocaust must be understood less as a response to the idea that people will cease to know about the Holocaust than as a response to the idea that they will cease to remember it.

Indeed, there is, precisely from this perspective, a certain hostility to the idea that the Holocaust is the sort of thing that can be known. Claude Lanzmann, the maker of *Shoah*, has insisted that "the purpose of *Shoah* is not to transmit knowledge" and has instead characterized the film as "an *incarnation, a resurrection*,"[19] thus identifying the ambitions of *Shoah* in terms that we may understand as characteristically New Historicist: the incarnated dead are the ones with whom Stephen Greenblatt wishes to speak. But whereas in the New Historicism understanding the past is at worst an irrelevance and at best an aid to remembering it, understanding the Holocaust seems to Lanzmann an "absolute obscenity," and to try to "learn the Holocaust" is in fact to "forget" it.[20] The representations and explanations of historians, he thinks, are "a way of escaping," "a way not to face the horror";[21] what the Holocaust requires is a way of transmitting not the normalizing knowledge of the horror but the horror itself. And it is this "transmission"—what Shoshana Felman calls "testimony"—that the film *Shoah* strives for and that, according to Felman, is the project of the major literary and theoretical texts of the post–World War II period.

But how can texts *transmit* rather than merely represent "horror"? How, as Felman puts it, can "the act of *reading* literary texts" be "related to the act of *facing horror?*" (2). If it could, then, of course, reading would become a form of witnessing. But it is one thing, it seems, to experience horror and another thing to read about it; the person who reads about it is dealing not with the experience of horror but with a representation of that experience. And Felman has no wish to deny this difference; on the contrary, she wishes to insist upon it, and it is out of her insistence that she produces her contribution to the theory of testimony. For when testimony is "simply relayed, repeated or reported," she argues, it "loses its function as a testimony" (3). So in order for testimony to avoid losing its proper function, it must be "performative" (5); it must "accomplish a speech act" rather than simply "formulate a statement." Its subject matter must be "enacted" rather than reported or represented. The problem of testimony is thus fundamentally a problem about "the relation between language and events" (16). Language that represents or reports events will fail as testimony—will fail, that is, to be properly "performative" or "literary." Language that is itself an "act" and that therefore can be said to "enact" rather than report events will succeed. The reader of the "performative" text will be in the position not of someone who reads about the "horror" and understands it; he or she will be in the position of "facing horror."

But how can a text achieve the performative? How can a text cease merely to represent an act and instead become the act it no longer represents? The idea of the performative is, of course, drawn from Austin's speech-act theory, where it is famously instantiated in the marriage ceremony: "When I say, before the registrar or altar, etc., 'I do,' I am not reporting on a marriage: I am indulging in it."[22] Austin's opposition between reporting and indulging anticipates (in a different key) Felman's opposition between reporting and enacting. But in Felman's *Testimony*, the first exemplar of the performative will not exactly be, as it is in Austin, the act of "saying certain words" (13); it will instead be what Felman calls the "breakdown" or "breakage of the words" (39). Citing these lines from Celan,

> Your question—your answer.
> Your song, what does it know?
>
> Deepinsnow,
>   Eepinow,
>   Ee-i-o.

she argues that it is "by disrupting" "conscious meaning" that these "sounds testify" (37). It is, in other words, at the moment when the words as words begin to "break down" that they become performative, that they begin to enact rather than report. And it is at this moment that the readers of those words are "ready to be solicited" not by the "meaning" those words convey (since, as they break down, it is precisely their meaning that is put in question) but by what Felman calls the "experience" of their author, Celan.

The genealogy of this version of the performative is, of course, as much de Manian as Austinian, and is articulated most explicitly in de Man's well-known reading of a passage from Rousseau's *Confessions* that describes Rousseau's effort to escape being blamed for stealing a ribbon from his employer by blaming the theft instead on a young servant-girl, Marion. Recognizing, with Rousseau, that the crime of having named Marion as the thief is a good deal more serious than the theft itself, de Man works through a series of accounts of what Rousseau might have meant when he said "Marion"—moving from his desire to blame Marion to his desire to possess Marion to his desire for a public scene in which these previous desires are shamefully displayed—but concluding that none of these interpretations is adequate. For ultimately, de Man argues, Rousseau never meant to and did not in fact name Marion. He "was making whatever noise happened to come into his head; he was saying nothing at all, least of all someone's name." So no attempt to understand what "Marion" means can succeed because, properly understood, "'Marion' is meaningless." And de Man goes on to assert that the "essential non-signification" of this text is exemplary of textuality as such: "It seems to be impossible to isolate the moment in which the fiction stands free of any signification. . . . Yet without this moment, never allowed to exist as such, no such thing as a text is conceivable." On the one hand, it is the "arbitrariness" of the sign that makes meaning possible; on the other hand, it is the revelation of that same "arbitrariness"—"the complete disjunction between Rousseau's desires . . . and the selection of this particular name . . . any other name, any other word, any other sound or noise could have done just as well"—that "disrupts the meaning." For de Man, the speech act becomes performative only in the moment that it becomes illegible.[23]

In the wake of the discovery of de Man's wartime journalism, some critics have read "The Purloined Ribbon" and the theory it articulates as a kind of alibi for de Man's own disinclination to acknowledge whatever involvement he may have had in the apparatus that produced the Holocaust. According to Felman, however, the refusal to confess is a sign not of indifference to one's own morally scandalous behavior but of a heightened sensitivity to exactly what is scandalous about it. The "trouble" with confessions, she writes, "is that they are all too *readable:* partaking of the continuity of conscious meaning and of the illusion of the restoration of coherence, what de Man calls 'the readability of . . . apologetic discourse' . . . pretends to reduce historical scandals to mere sense and to eliminate the unassimilable shock of history, by leaving 'the [very] assumption of intelligibility . . . unquestioned'" (151).

What is scandalous in "historical scandals" is what, in Felman's view, marks the Holocaust above all: its resistance to intelligibility. Insofar as confession produces a "referential narrative," it necessarily diminishes the crime it confesses to. Thus, following Lanzmann, who identifies the Holocaust as a "pure event" and who characterizes the effort to make sense of it as a "perverse form of revisionism" (*YFS*, 482), Felman insists on the "refusal of understanding" (*YFS*, 477) as (quoting Lanzmann) "the only possible ethical . . . attitude" (*YFS*, 478). The attempt to explain it can only be an attempt to reduce it.

Felman thus regards what some have thought of as de Man's worst sin— his failure to confess—as his greatest virtue, for confession, diminishing the crime, would excuse the criminal. But whatever we may think of de Man's personal morality, his real contribution here is not his (from Felman's standpoint, admirable) refusal to confess; it is his discovery of the linguistic form that, unlike the "referential narrative," *is* adequate to the Holocaust, the "performative." The essence of the performative is, as we have seen, its irreducibility to "mere sense," and it is precisely this irreducibility that makes it appropriate as a technology for what Lanzmann calls the "transmission" (*YFS*, 486), rather than the representation, of the Holocaust. Felman thus focuses intensely on the moment in *Shoah* when Lanzmann, listening to some Polish peasants describe the efforts of a Ukrainian guard to keep his Jewish prisoners quiet, hears sounds that he recognizes right away are "no longer simply Polish" (230). The Poles are saying, "So the Jews shut up and the guard moved off. Then the Jews started talking again in their language . . . : *ra-ra-ra* and so on" (230). The "*ra-ra-ra*" here is the aural equivalent of "eepinow, / ee-i-o," and both "ee-i-o" and "*ra-ra-ra*" are occurrences of the performativity theorized in "The Purloined Ribbon" and embodied in Rousseau's "Marion." Rousseau "was making whatever noise happened to come into his head," de Man writes; testimony from "inside" the "horror" can only be heard as "pure noise," according to Felman (232). If to understand is, inevitably, to misunderstand, to bear false witness, it is only the "mere noise" one "does not understand" (231) that makes it possible to bear true witness.

The point of the performative, then, is that, itself an event, it "transmits" rather than represents the events to which it testifies. This is what Felman means when she says that *Shoah* "makes the testimony *happen*" (267), and even that it happens "as a second Holocaust." So the Holocaust, like slavery, is never over—it is "an event that . . . *does not end*" (67). And just as the transformation of history into memory made it possible for people who did not live through slavery to remember it, so the transformation of texts that "make sense" of the Holocaust into events that "enact" it makes it possible for people who did not live through the Holocaust to survive it. "The listener to the narrative of extreme human pain, of massive psychic trauma," says Felman's collaborator, the analyst Dori Laub, "comes to be a participant and a co-owner of the traumatic event: through his very listening, he comes to partially experience trauma in himself" (57). "Is the act of *reading* literary texts itself inherently related to the act of *facing* horror?" asks Felman (2). De Man's account of the performative, of the replacement of "meaning" by "event," makes the answer yes.

But what de Man characterized as the failure of reference—in order for a text "to come into being as text," he says, its "referential function" has to be "radically suspended"[24]—Felman cannily characterizes as the return of reference, "like a ghost" (267). Reference has returned because the text, insofar as it ceases to refer to things, has become a thing that can be referred to; it has returned "like a ghost" because the thing it is is a kind of absence, "the very object—and the very content—of historical erasure" (267). When he said "Marion," Rousseau "was making whatever noise happened to come into his head; he was saying nothing at all, least of all someone's name." Both erased and embodied by performativity itself, Marion, like Beloved, walks. But this turn to the ghost makes clear not only an important point of resemblance between deconstruction and the New Historicism but also an important point of difference. The ghosts of New Historicism are, as we have seen, essential to its functioning, but as the simile—reference returns "like a ghost"—suggests, in deconstruction they are essentially supererogatory. In deconstruction the texts do what in New Historicism the ghosts must do. Indeed, if we take the ghosts of New Historicism as a figure for its ambition to turn history into memory, we can understand the "mere noise" of Felman's deployment of de Man as an effort to provide the thematics of historicism with its formal ground. Deconstruction requires no ghosts because the emergence of a meaningless and untranslatable signifier in the poem of Celan or in the film of Lanzmann can actually produce what Lanzmann calls the "resurrection" that a text like *Beloved* only narrates. Understood in these terms, deconstruction is the theory of, rather than the alternative to, the New Historicism; deconstruction explains how texts can not only thematize the transformation of the historical past into the remembered past but, by way of the performative, can actually produce that transformation.

So if the passing of eyewitnesses and the fading of memories do indeed give the question of what sustains Jewish identity a new urgency, this new deployment of deconstruction helps make the Holocaust available as a continuing source of identitarian sustenance. But in seeking to ensure that the Holocaust is not forgotten, deconstruction contributes not only to the maintenance of but also to a change in Jewish identity. For insofar as Jewish identity is understood to depend on what Michael Krausz has recently called "identification" with the "narrative" of the Holocaust as "the most salient episode in contemporary Jewish history," it is significantly detached from the racial base that was definitive for the perpetrators of the Holocaust.[25] The primacy of the Holocaust as a guarantor of Jewish identity marks, in other words, the emergence of an explicitly antiessentialist Jewishness.

This antiessentialist Jewishness is disarticulated from the idea of a Jewish race and also, albeit less sharply, from the idea of a Jewish religion. Many of those who think of themselves as Jews do not think that they are Jews because they have Jewish blood and are in fact skeptical of the very idea of Jewish blood. For them, as for many members of other races (so-called), cultural inheritance takes the place of biological inheritance. And many of those who think of themselves as Jews do not think that they are Jews because they believe in Judaism. But by redescribing certain practices that might be called religious—circumcision, for example—as cultural, Jewishness can sever their connection to Judaism. Thus, Jews can give up the belief in Jewish blood and give up the belief in a Jewish God; what they can't give up is Jewish culture. Hence the significance of the Holocaust and of the widespread insistence that Jews remember it, and hence the importance of the idea that "understanding" the Holocaust is a kind of "obscenity." The prohibition against understanding the Holocaust is at the same time formulated as the requirement that it be *experienced* instead of understood, and this requirement—fulfillable through technologies like the deconstructive performative—makes it possible to define the Jew not as someone who has Jewish blood or who believes in Judaism but as someone who, having experienced the Holocaust, can, even if he or she was never there, acknowledge it as part of his or her history.

And just as remembering the Holocaust is now understood as the key to preserving Jewish cultural identity, the Holocaust itself is now retrospectively reconfigured as an assault on Jewish cultural identity. "The commanding voice at Auschwitz," Lionel Rubinoff writes, "decrees that Jews may not respond to Hitler's attempt to destroy totally Judaism by themselves co-operating in that destruction. In ancient times, the unthinkable Jewish sin was idolatry. Today, it is to respond to Hitler by doing his work." Jews who might today be understood to be doing Hitler's work are not, of course, murdering other Jews, which is to say that Hitler's work, the destruction of Judaism, is understood here as only incidentally the murder of Jews. Rather, the Jews who today do Hitler's work are Jews who "survive" as people but not "*as Jews.*" They stop thinking of themselves as Jews; they refuse the "stubborn persistence" in their "Jewishness" that is required by Rubinoff as the mark of resistance to Hitler.[26] What this means is that the concept of "cultural genocide," introduced in analogy to the genocide of the Holocaust, now begins to replace that genocide and to become the Holocaust. "A culture is the most valuable thing we have," says the philosopher Eddy M. Zemach, and this commitment to the value of culture requires that the Holocaust be rewritten as an attack on culture.[27] Thus, the "Judaism" that Hitler wanted to destroy ceases to be a group of people who had what he thought of as "Jewish blood" and becomes instead a set of beliefs and practices; and the Hitler who in fact "opened almost every discussion on Jewish matters with the assertion that the Jews are not primarily a religious community but a race" is now reimagined as a Hitler who wished above all to destroy Jewish religion and culture.[28] From this standpoint Hitler becomes an opponent of cultural diversity, and those Jews who have, as Zemach puts it, "lost the will to retain their culture" become not only his victims but his collaborators. They do his work by assimilating, and insofar as, according to Zemach, American Jews in particular are abandoning their culture, what Jews now confront is the threat of a second Holocaust: if American Jews give up their Jewishness, Jews "will have lost the greatest and most advanced part of their people" "for the second time this century."[29]

This revaluation of assimilation as Holocaust marks the complete triumph of the notion of culture, which now emerges not merely as the defining characteristic of persons ("the most important thing we have") but as itself a kind of person, whose death has a pathos entirely independent of the death of those persons whose culture it was. The Jew is here subsumed by his Jewishness.[30] The person is transformed into an identity, and the identity is treated as a person.[31] And if we return to the revised version of the question with which we began—Which myths do Americans believe?—we can see that culture, not visitors, races, or even history, is the correct answer. Americans, especially American academics, believe in the myth of culture. Indeed, with respect to American academics, the point could be put more strongly: we do not simply believe in the myth of culture; many of us have accepted as our primary professional responsibility the elaboration and promulgation of the myth, and our theoretical disputes (between, say, deconstruction and the New Historicism) have become only local disagreements about how best to defend it (which are more real, ghosts or performatives?). In American academic life today, the resolution of these disagreements doesn't matter; it doesn't matter whether we say "Beloved" or "Marion." What matters is only that we say one or the other, and that in saying whichever we say, we testify to our belief in entities—that is to say, in cultural identities—exactly as real as Ares and Aphrodite.

11 SUFFERING AS A MORAL BEACON

Blacks and Jews

Laurence Mordekhai Thomas

Soyez Beni, mon Dieu, qui donnez la souffrance
Comme un divin remède à nos impuretés
—Baudelaire

Jews and blacks are two peoples with entirely different histories of suffering. In the former case, there was an explicit aim to exterminate a people; in the latter, an explicit aim to render one people utterly subordinate to the will of another. These facts are undeniable. Unfortunately, there is another undeniable fact, namely, that there is enormous tension between blacks and Jews—a competition, if you will, over who has suffered the most, blacks or Jews.

A great many Jews hold the Shoah to be the worst manifestation of evil known to humankind. Many blacks insist that this dubious distinction holds instead of American slavery. Painfully, both peoples often speak as if the sole measure of an evil event or period were the number of lives that evil has claimed. Jews point to the loss of six million lives during the Shoah, and blacks insist that at least twice that many lives were lost to American slavery. It has been estimated that Native Americans lost as many as eighty million lives to the brutality of those seeking to conquer soil in the Americas. Yet I doubt that any black would suppose that the evil of American slavery is thereby diminished. Similarly, I doubt that any Jew would suppose that the evil of the Shoah is thereby diminished. So we know that the magnitude of evil is not to be understood in terms of body count alone.

In many ways the rivalry between blacks and Jews over which was worse, American slavery or the Shoah, is astonishing, because the suffering characteristic of each form of evil was so radically different. What is more, there is no Jew or black who would prefer the suffering of the other group to the suffering his own people had endured. But more than any of these considerations, what I find most telling is that when one reads the writings of those who actually endured either the Shoah or American slavery—no person having endured both—one is not in the least inclined to make invidious comparisons. Among those who endured and survived the Shoah, Elie Wiesel is one of the most eloquent and poignant writers concerning the experience. Among those who endured and survived American slavery, Frederick Douglass is one of the most eloquent and poignant writers concerning the experience.

In the *Narrative of the Life of Frederick Douglass, an American Slave,* we find the following searing words:

> If any one thing in my experience, more than another, served to deepen my conviction of the infernal character of slavery, and to fill me with unutterable loathing of slaveholders, it was their base ingratitude to my poor old grandmother. She had served my old master faithfully from youth to old age. . . . She had rocked him in infancy, attended him in childhood, served him through life, and at his death wiped from his icy brow the cold death-sweat and closed his eyes forever. She was nevertheless left a slave—a slave for life.[1]

In Wiesel's autobiographical essay *Night,* we find the following searing words:

> Never shall I forget that night, the first night in camp, which has turned my life into one long night, seven times cursed and seven times sealed. Never shall I forget that smoke. Never shall I forget the little faces of the children, whose bodies I saw turned into wreaths of smoke beneath a silent blue sky.
>
> Never shall I forget those flames which consumed my faith forever.
>
> Never shall I forget that nocturnal silence which deprived me, for all eternity, of the desire to live. Never shall I forget those moments which murdered my God and my soul and turned my dreams to dust. Never shall I forget these things, even if I am condemned to live as long as God Himself. Never.[2]

No one reading either of these two passages would be tempted to make an invidious comparison between American slavery and the Shoah. The pain that Douglass and Wiesel expressed is not in any way tied to the belief that no other form of suffering could be worse.

What is more, Douglass's talk of base ingratitude would have been out of place among survivors of the Shoah, for in general Jews did not play the kind of role in the lives of Nazis that blacks played in the lives of slaveholders. The aim of the Shoah was not to produce a body of servile persons, for Jews were deemed too inherently evil for that. Likewise, Wiesel's talk of faith in God being destroyed would have been out of place among black slaves. Putting aside the fact that slavery did not begin with American slavery, African slaves did not conceive of themselves as having special standing with the God of Judaism and Christianity. Accordingly, a sense of having been abandoned by that power was not, and indeed could not have been, a part of their suffering. By contrast, at the very center of Wiesel's pain is not just that Jews died but that to all appearances they had been forsaken by God. Most poignantly, slaves in America never saw slavery as a reason to call into question the soundness of the claims made on behalf of Christianity. And one reason for this, no doubt, is that while slaves could hold out hope for deliverance, there was no way for them to interpret Christian texts as implying that they had special standing with God. In this context, the best they could do, and what many slaves in fact did, was to regard their plight as somewhat, but only somewhat, parallel to the plight of the children of Israel in Egypt.

In the foregoing remarks I have essentially gone over considerations that are obvious, or become obvious upon reflection. But having done so, I would say that the question raised at the outset cries out for an answer even more loudly: Why the rivalry of suffering between Jews and blacks? What is gained if one accepts the judgment that the Shoah was the worst form of suffering, or that American slavery was? Are there other facts that become clearer, more readily grasped? Or do blacks and Jews suppose that whoever has suffered the most is in some way more morally innocent? Thus far it seems that these two possibilities are equally rejected by both groups. Or is it that each group wishes nothing more than to affirm before all the world, and especially before its supposed rival in suffering, that its own suffering was the worst? Raise this question to any Jew or to any black, and the person would recoil in outrage at being considered so petty. No one seems to be interested in simply having suffered more than someone else.

So what gives rise to the rivalry of suffering between Jews and blacks? I doubt that there is just one consideration that will entirely explain this extraordinary conflict. However, I would like to suggest a view that should be a part of any complete explanation. This is the view that the one who has suffered the most thereby has a greater moral understanding of all other forms of suffering. Suffering is thus thought to bring in its wake an otherwise unattainable level of moral sensibility. For better or worse, suffering is seen as the key to a form of moral knowledge.

What has given rise to this idea? Without doubt the Old and New Testaments are two of the most influential sources for this theme. In the former, the life of Job, who is neither Jewish nor Christian, most powerfully exemplifies the theme; in the latter, the life of Jesus does. The just suffer because they are instruments of God. Their suffering represents a way in which the good may manifest itself. And profound wisdom is presented as the greatest reward that can be bestowed upon the just who have suffered. By contrast, the suffering of the unjust represents true punishment.

It is not necessary, I trust, to review the story of Job at length. Appearing before the counsel of God, Satan argues that Job serves God for no other reason than that God has abundantly blessed him. God claims otherwise and invites Satan to test Job's faith. And Satan does precisely that, causing Job to lose his family, his wealth, and his health. Things became so bad that Job's wife counsels him to "curse God, and die" (Job 2:9). The assumption on everyone's part is that Job has sinned, and sinned mightily. But Job maintains his innocence against the onslaught of charges. Finally God appears and engages Job in conversation. This is not the place to rehearse the beautiful poetry of that dialogue, and so I shall not. For our purposes it suffices to say that although God rebukes Job, God also affirms Job's righteousness before the three friends who had systematically accused him of having sinned mightily. And while we all know that at the end of the story Job is rendered far wealthier than he was before, we should not forget that he has also acquired an appreciation of God that he never had before: "I have heard of thee by the hearing of the ear: but now mine eye seeth thee. Wherefore I abhor myself, and repent in dust and ashes" (Job 42:5–6). In both Jewish and Christian texts nothing is deemed more profound than a direct rapprochement with God; recall the story of Moses and the burning bush or the story of Paul's conversion to Christianity. In the end, Job is not only richer than he was before, but he has also achieved a direct rapprochement with God.

As to the Christ story, all the great masters who have accepted this way of faith have insisted on the following: it is because Christ suffered so intensely as a human being, though always without fault, that he could serve as a scapegoat for the sins of man. I am no position to offer an interpretation of the life of Christ. However, it is next to impossible to escape the conclusion that Christ's suffering as a human being is presumed to have deepened his moral grasp of the human condition. If nothing else, it is because he lived and suffered as a human being that he had credibility with other human beings when he spoke of overcoming the desires of the flesh, a credibility he could not otherwise have had.

We are now in a position to shed some light on the tension between blacks and Jews, applying some of the foregoing considerations to American slavery and the Shoah. To begin with, it goes without saying that no group of people could ever be sufficiently guilty as to merit the suffering that was visited upon Jews and blacks during their respective watershed tragedies—indeed, not even if the punishment were divine, at least not without supposing that God is less benevolent than has been supposed. And we know, as the case of Job teaches, that God himself sometimes uses suffering to enrich the life of the just. So putting these considerations together we have something of an Aristotelian syllogism:

—(P1) For the just (or at least for the nonguilty), great suffering carries in its wake deep moral knowledge (let us call this the Principle of Job).
—(P2) Blacks and Jews have both endured an extraordinary form of suffering (historical fact).
—(P3) Neither blacks nor Jews could have been sufficiently guilty to merit their suffering; yet suffering is not in vain (moral hypothesis).
—(C4) Therefore, the suffering that blacks and Jews have endured has served to enhance their moral sensibilities.

Thus, I want to suggest that in the final analysis neither Jews nor blacks have wanted simply to affirm that their particular watershed suffering is the worst. Rather, the people of each group would like to affirm that they possess a profound level of moral knowledge, fashioned by the extraordinary evil they have endured. Perhaps with just this much said, one can see how there might be some tension between the two groups. Which group of people, Jews or blacks, has been elected by divine justice, if you will, to be moral beacons unto the world, or at least unto Americans, concerning the understanding of suffering? Considered in this way, the tension between blacks and Jews becomes more comprehensible. At the very least the tension seems to be over something meritorious: being a moral beacon as opposed to merely having suffered the most.

While these considerations have some explanatory power, they still do not go the distance in making sense of the tension between Jews and blacks. For one thing, surely the world can never have too many moral beacons, even if, to continue the metaphor, they are equally bright. What is more, there is something despicable and petty about two groups of people, both of whom have suffered mightily, quibbling bitterly over who serves as a better moral exemplar to others. And if the focus is upon being a moral beacon, then the preoccupation with having suffered the most seems somewhat out of place, even with the premise that suffering carries moral knowledge in its wake. Let us not forget that the truth of this premise does not make suffering a good thing in and of itself. Yet the way some blacks and Jews talk, one would think that suffering was viewed as a good in itself. Clearly, more needs to be said if we are to make sense of the tension between blacks and Jews over who has suffered the most.

Two considerations are relevant here. One pertains to moral modesty, the other to the fact that the tension between blacks and Jews plays itself out on American soil. I shall say a word about both in turn.

As I noted earlier, Job insisted upon his righteousness before all of his accusers, and for that reason it has seemed to some that he was guilty of self-righteousness. To be righteous is one thing; to insist upon it before others is quite another. Modesty counsels and requires that we forgo the latter. Accordingly, even if Jews and blacks believed that they possessed profound moral knowledge on account of the evil they had each endured, it would be inappropriate for them to insist that this was so; it would be a fulsome display of arrogance. Thus, as a matter of public moral relations, if you will, Jews and blacks could not have privileged the moral insights owing to their respective sufferings. On the other hand, since the tragedy that each group suffered was public, it has always been possible for each to play the role of public historian, concerned to get right the facts of the atrocity it had suffered: What happened to how many, when, and where? Thus, both groups have drawn upon the Principle of Job enunciated in P1 and focused upon the subject of suffering.

Before turning to the second consideration, I want to draw attention to a fallacy in the way people think about suffering. The mistaken view—call it the "transitivity of understanding suffering" principle—seems to be that if group X has suffered more than group Y, then group X understands the suffering of group Y. And, of course, if group X already understands group Y, then group X has no reason to listen to group Y concerning its suffering. But this principle is false. Suppose that John has lost both legs and an arm, whereas Mary has lost an eye. There is a very straightforward sense in which we might think that John has suffered more than Mary. Arguably, he has been rendered more disabled than Mary. Yet it is simply not true that he thereby understands what it is like to have lost an eye. Although he has been rendered more disabled than Mary, John does not understand the kinds of adjustments that have been required of her on account of having lost an eye. His suffering, as great and tragic as it is, does not give him insight into the character of Mary's suffering. Thus, the "transitivity of understanding suffering" principle is false. Accordingly, even if one group can establish that it has suffered more than others, it does not follow that this group thereby understands the suffering of all others and so has no need to listen to others speak about their suffering. Blacks and Jews need to heed this consideration, for both groups have used their own suffering to excuse themselves from hearing about the suffering of the other, each having wrongly supposed that their own suffering gives them insight into the suffering of the other.

The second consideration that I mentioned is that the tension between Jews and blacks plays itself out on American soil. Notwithstanding the official separation of state and religious institutions called for by the Constitution, Christianity has very much been the national religion of this country. Indeed, the careful reader will notice that I departed from the usual expression, "separation of church and state." That wording is revealing in and of itself, for neither a synagogue nor a mosque constitutes a church, nor conversely. It is not likely that the Founding Fathers had in mind either Jews or Muslims when they wrote, "Congress shall make no law respecting an establishment of religion" (Amendment 1). But that is another topic.

The fact that the United States is very much a Christian society is highly significant for our purposes. First of all, there is the view held by Christians that Christianity superseded Judaism and therefore that all the Scriptures of the Old Testament are properly read in the light of the New. Second, one of the central tenets of Christianity is that long-suffering is a virtue—one of the fruits of the Spirit of God, to use the language of the New Testament (Gal. 5:22). Indeed, long-suffering may be the most celebrated Christian virtue after charity (love). Suffering that is owing neither to punishment nor to wrongdoing is a sign that one merits entry into the kingdom of God. Recall the New Testament saying according to which "it is easier for a camel to go through the eye of a needle, than for a rich man to enter into the kingdom of God" (Matt. 19:24). This distinctively Christian view of material wealth is compatible with what I have called the Principle of Job, namely, that great suffering carries in its wake deep moral knowledge. Christianity explicitly eschews the material for the spiritual. And moral knowledge is properly considered a part of the spiritual rather than the material. Indeed, for Christianity, the moral is inextricably a part of the spiritual.

Third, and finally, in the Christian society of the United States, embodying the virtues of Christianity has always been synonymous with good citizenship. In this regard Jews and blacks were at a disadvantage from the start. Jews were at a disadvantage because as a matter of principle they rejected the story of Christ as savior of humanity and thus were often seen as morally reprehensible. (In this respect the Jew who regards herself as secular is no different from the one who practices. The secular Jew is not a Christian-in-waiting, hoping to be moved from her stance on the Christ story; rather, she, like the Jew who practices, rejects the Christ story as a matter of principle.) Blacks, meanwhile, were at a disadvantage because they were seen as intellectually inferior and so unable to exhibit the virtues of moral excellence. Consequently, in times past neither blacks nor Jews were in a favorable position to serve as a moral beacon unto the citizens of America. They were not seen as representative of humanity in the first place, and thus their suffering was not regarded as making them moral beacons unto others, certainly not unto others who were white. In fact, there is a prior problem: because neither Jews nor blacks were seen as suitable moral agents, both groups had to convince others that their suffering even counted in the first place.

Herein, I believe, lies the perversion of the very laudable concern on the part of each group to show that its suffering had given it a profound level of moral knowledge. In a racist and anti-Semitic society, this concern had to take a back seat to getting the society at large to view the suffering of blacks and Jews as counting. Indeed, getting their suffering to count was a way of having their very humanity both acknowledged and affirmed. Thus, blacks and Jews had a reason to focus upon their suffering to the exclusion of the moral insights that might be deemed to follow in its wake. For if their humanity did not count, then their suffering would most certainly not be viewed as a basis for moral insight. Accordingly, the concern with suffering became an end in itself, owing to the significance that Jews and blacks rightly attached to having their suffering be taken seriously by the society at large.

So far so good, perhaps. But I now come to the part that blacks and Jews do not like to hear. To hear either blacks or Jews tell it, their own group has an immunity to X-ism (any form of prejudice) when it comes to others. In fact, in some circles it is fashionable to hold that X-ist attitudes can flow only from those who are socially privileged. This view is so absurd that I find it mindboggling that it has been embraced by otherwise intelligent people. Astonishingly, this view overlooks the social reality that the constituency of the Ku Klux Klan has often been poor whites who could not in any serious way be viewed as socially privileged. Indeed, even in the hallowed halls of political correctness, poor white folk—"rednecks," to use the common vernacular—are still fair game for jokes. Neither being destitute nor having suffered profoundly is any barrier to being deeply prejudiced. Neither blacks nor Jews are the exception here.

In a Christian society the fact that Jews rejected the Christ story has stood as a significant fact—a significant fact not only for Christian whites but for Christian blacks as well. And if for Christian whites this fact could be a reason to call into question the humanity of Jews and thus to discount their suffering, so it could be for Christian blacks. If for Christian whites being a Jew could suffice to make one unfit to be a moral beacon in American society, so it could be for Christian blacks. And if by virtue of these views we have anti-Semitism among Christian whites, then likewise we have anti-Semitism among Christian blacks who have embraced the same views. But to ask the question rhetorically: Was it not whites who brought Christianity to blacks? If, in times past, interpretations of Christianity carried anti-Semitism in their wake, then blacks were imbued with anti-Semitism even as they were converted to Christianity. It is disingenuous on the part of blacks to deny that anti-Semitism has been a significant factor in the black Christian community.

Regarding Jews and the phenomenon of racism, I hold, as I have argued in *Vessels of Evil*, that Jews played a pivotal role in the success of the civil rights movement.[3] During the civil rights movement and since then, Jews have displayed a goodwill toward blacks that far surpasses the goodwill displayed by other nonblack groups toward blacks. Jews rightly point to this fact. But goodwill can be poisoned. In this regard I am reminded of Christian philo-Semites who believe that they know what is good for Jews. Christian philo-Semites hold a view concerning the end of times in which Jews have a central role. For instance, some hold that what is called the Second Coming of Christ will occur when (nearly) all Jews have returned to Israel, and so these Christians want Jews to make *aliyah* (to immigrate to Israel). That Jews do not share this view of the importance of making *aliyah* is quite irrelevant to these Christians. Quite simply, what we have here is an instance of goodwill that is poisoned.

The belief that blacks are intellectually inferior is one of the deep and abiding views of American racism. There is nothing about being Jewish that gives Jews any immunity to this view. One of the ways in which this view plays itself out in the American Jewish community is with the following question: Why have not blacks succeeded despite American slavery as we have succeeded despite the Shoah? The question is not innocent. If the Shoah is one of the most extraordinary evils known to humanity and Jews have flourished in its aftermath, then the observation that blacks have not flourished in the aftermath of slavery is haunting to blacks. It is disingenuous on the part of Jews to deny that racism has been a significant factor in the Jewish community.

In various ways and to varying degrees, then, Jews and blacks have each embraced America's conception of the other. Historically, blacks were not a part of European communities where Jews lived, and Jews were not a part of the many African societies. It was on American soil that these two groups first met in great numbers, that they became conscious of one another. And the reigning ideology in America was that neither Jews nor blacks were fit to be moral beacons unto white America, and that the suffering of neither group counted. Blacks and Jews embraced this American ideology of the other; blacks and Jews looked at one another and discounted each other's suffering. This brings us to the very heart of the rivalry of suffering between the two groups. If I am right, the basis for this mentality is twofold; it developed as each group sought to prove first of all to white America and then to the other that its suffering counted.

Understandably, the first aim was enough to generate fierce competition between Jews and blacks concerning the enormity of their respective sufferings. The stakes were high, namely, acceptance by white America and a hallowing of the group's suffering in the American mind. Which experience would be representative of the suffering that institutions can shamelessly inflict upon innocent human beings—American slavery, or the Shoah? Which experience would serve as an icon for the kind of society that America must at all costs avoid becoming? Which experience would be enshrined in the American mind as representing human beings behaving in their most craven and sullied manner—the Shoah, or American slavery? Yet as each group sought through its suffering to validate its humanity in the eyes of America, each also embraced America's view of the other, albeit in various mutated forms. Consequently, each group saw in the other a representation of America's conception of itself. Now, it is one thing to have to prove one's humanity to those whom one acknowledges to be full moral creatures; it is quite another to find oneself having to prove it to those whom one does not regard in this way but who share society's image of one. In this respect, Jews and blacks have truly been pawns of American society.

I want to end this part of the discussion by making explicit a very poignant consideration. As I have said, in American society at large, neither Jews nor blacks were embraced as full moral creatures; and to varying degrees each group accepted America's view of the other. This means not only that each had deep reservations about whether the other could serve as a moral beacon unto anyone, but also that each had deep reservations about whether it was appropriate to be concerned with being a moral beacon unto the other. In a stern rebuke of some religious groups, Christ is reported as saying, "Give not that which is holy unto the dogs, neither cast ye your pearls before swine" (Matt. 7:6). Blacks and Jews were America's swine and as such were deemed unfit for certain forms of moral enlightenment. It would be disingenuous on the part of both blacks and Jews to deny that, to varying degrees, they each embraced this American conception of the other. Because each did embrace America's conception of the other, it was not only moral modesty that counseled each against presenting itself to the other as a moral beacon but also the belief that the other was not an appropriate object of moral concern.

At this juncture let me return to the point that America has been essentially a Christian nation. As I said earlier, this means that good citizenship has been taken to be synonymous with the embodiment of Christian values. Now, it is a characteristic feature of Christianity that it valorizes the poor. Remember that Christ was of humble origins, the son of a carpenter, although royalty— King David in particular—is said to be a part of his lineage. And of course the very power of the story of Job is that he lived a morally upright life not only when he was rich but when he was utterly destitute and without either health or friends. While the story shows that it is possible both to be rich and to live a morally upright life, it also points to how surprising this combination is. After all, Satan himself was proved wrong, although he is portrayed throughout biblical texts as having considerable wisdom. What is more, he is portrayed as having sufficient access to God that, in the story of Job, we are told that he made an appearance "when the sons of God came to present themselves before the Lord" (Job 1:6). Hence, it is hardly trivial that even Satan mistakenly thought that Job served God only because of the wealth and good fortune God had bestowed upon him.

Strikingly, it would seem to be one of the deep convictions of American society that it is the ordinary person who is best able to exemplify good Christian values and so the values of good citizenship. Americans fantasize about the wealthy and create myths about them; however, they identify with the wealthy only in the context of tragedy. Jacqueline Kennedy Onassis was deeply admired by Americans because although she knew tragedy in many ways, she carried herself with dignity and integrity. This harks back to the importance Americans have attached to suffering: it has been regarded as a test of one's moral mettle. To the American mind, suffering is the crucible that makes one a moral exemplar. These considerations suggest just how much the Christian virtue of long-suffering has been incorporated into the American value system. In many ways, then, America was especially fertile soil for blacks and Jews to be moral exemplars, as both had suffered enormously. Unfortunately, the American soil was also rife with the weeds of anti-Semitism and racism.

I believe that both groups have an important role to play in society as moral beacons. Let me be more precise.

1. It is necessary to distinguish between an incomparable evil and an evil that is worse than all other evils. Whereas the worst of all evils is truly incomparable, an incomparable evil is not thereby the worst of all evils. I do not know if the Shoah is the worst evil that humanity has known. Nor do I know if American slavery is. And I certainly do not know how one would determine such a thing. On the other hand, it seems to me clear that American slavery and the Shoah are, each in its own fashion, incomparable horrors and that the life of each group of people has been shaped by this horror. As moral beacons, we—we who are black and we who are Jews—can both remind American society that evil is not impoverished. Neither the Shoah nor American slavery exhausts the nature of evil.

2. Although neither Jews nor blacks have any moral superiority on account of the watershed evils each has suffered, each has a profound comprehension of some aspect of the nature of evil. This comprehension is based upon experiences of pain, fear, abuse of confidence, and the understandable loss of faith. It is based upon the struggle of each individual to find his way in a world that has made him a target of profound injustice. It is based upon the manner in which each individual is to some extent haunted by the suffering of his past (and if perchance there is anyone who has entirely escaped the evil shadow of his past, one would wish to know how he managed to do so in order to learn from him). As moral beacons, we can bring these lessons and concerns to the forefront in our discussions.

3. To be sure, we have a duty to remember the suffering and the pain that we have endured. But this does not mean recalling our suffering for no other

reason than to blame others and to present ourselves as victims. We can instead recall our suffering in order to nourish the moral character of humanity, to give support to the weak and to fortify those who are already strong. Nothing can properly compensate those who have been the victims of a profound evil. But if on account of the Shoah and American slavery humanity better understands the risks that it takes when it permits acts and the kinds of behavior that are readily coopted by evil, then those who have died will not have died in vain. As moral beacons, we can prevent evil from ever having a posthumous victory.

The Shoah and American slavery have given Jews and blacks, respectively, an extraordinary and incomparable occasion to cast some light on the ways of human beings. And I should like to think that if we fasten upon this task with all our might and soul, then we would no longer concern ourselves with the question of who has suffered the most, blacks or Jews. And when we who are black and we who are Jews have arrived at this point, then we shall become moral beacons, not only unto others but unto ourselves as well.

12   PLAY WILL MAKE YOU FREE

Reprising *The Triumph of the Will*
in Chicago's Nike Town

Andrew Levy

As you walk down Chicago's Michigan Avenue, the upscale North Side shopping district known as the "Magnificent Mile," it can be astonishingly easy to
miss "Nike Town," and many pedestrians make two or three passes before
they locate it. Nike Town's front window displays are sparse, and neither as
dramatic as those of the nearby Cartier jewelry store nor as inviting as the
three-story-tall glass windowfronts that transform the Crate and Barrel
across Michigan into the architectural equivalent of a mail-order catalogue;
even Tiffany's locked and opaque doors, fifty yards south of Nike Town's entrance, are more compelling. In theory, the four burnished-silver sculptures
of athletes that protrude onto the sidewalk airspace from the Nike Town
storefront should clearly mark the site for pedestrians, but they have been
placed just above eye level, where they can be overlooked by anyone who does
not train his or her gaze upward. Even the sign that spells out the store's name
seems to exemplify some form of counterintuitive advertising: plain brown
letters placed flat against a cream-colored building well above eye level, unlit,
essentially invisible to any pedestrian walking on that side of the avenue.

That Nike Town was designed and built by Nike, Inc.—the athletic-
clothing multinational whose marketing staff has made a near-monopoly of
national advertising awards for the better part of a decade—should suggest
that the store's unassuming facade is neither accident nor afterthought. In
fact, pedestrians do find their way through Nike Town's front doors, one hundred thousand a week in the months after its July 1992 opening, five to six
thousand daily ever since, as many as visit any of Chicago's museums or other
tourist sites. And according to *Forbes* magazine, they spend money there,

roughly $2.5 million weekly. In this context, Nike Town's bland face begins to look like a barometer of how far ahead of the game Nike's collective marketing acumen sometimes works: pedestrians may miss those too-high sculptures, but they won't miss the accumulation of other pedestrians stalled on the sidewalk, heads tilted upward gazing at the store's facade. The front of Nike Town may not look like much from the east side of the avenue, but from across the street it appears to be the only storefront on the Erie block of Michigan Avenue that has been composed as an artistic whole, that has been designed to be viewed from a distance, then up close, the way art patrons at the nearby Art Institute shift their perspective to get a clearer sense of what Seurat or Chagall intended. As residents of the 1990s, we have grown to understand that certain stores are stores, and other stores are events. But even by those standards, this is no ordinary store.

It has been over six years since Nike Town opened in Chicago, almost as long since the last feature piece in the *New York Times,* the *Washington Post,* or *Fortune* magazine appeared that hailed it as the "store of the future," and longer still since the last column in the *Chicago Tribune* appeared that wondered whether Nike Town was an "[art] gallery or a museum," or simply the most seditious machine for separating men and women from their money that was ever devised. And while those years have been turbulent ones financially for the American retail industry, they have been remarkable ones from a creative standpoint, ones in which increasingly ingenious (and sometimes desperate) efforts by mall and store designers to fashion memorable "retail environments" have been matched by the increasing sophistication of critics assessing those spaces from both aesthetic and political perspectives. The opening of an "important" new shopping mall (like the Mall of America in Bloomington, Minnesota, for instance), is now reviewed as deeply and as frequently as a new novel by Toni Morrison or Philip Roth, and from more vantage points. Any reader interested in tracing the development of American retail architecture and design in the past six years can read about it in *Newsweek* or in the scholarly presses and choose from the popular architectural criticism of authors like Witold Rybczynski, the new-fashioned visionary socialism of journalists like Mike Davis, the avant-garde geographical work of scholars like Edward Soja, or the local reviews issued by newspapers, city magazines, and the retail outlets themselves. While the past half decade has witnessed a continuation of the decline of traditional literacy in America, it has also witnessed an almost revolutionary uptick in a different kind of literacy: we are learning to read retail, with a degree of critical inquiry that previous generations reserved for art, music, and literature.

Within this context, Nike Town has achieved the status of a classic, a seminal influence in the development of hard sell, 1990s style. It remains one of the best locations nationwide to consider what (or whether) we should be thinking as we linger (as we are meant to) within the likes of the Media Play (a combined book-music-video-software retailer), Walt Disney's mall outlets, Sony's single-brand electronics boutiques, or United Artists' new virtual "Starports." If stores can be viewed as aesthetic achievements, and if corporations can be viewed as their authors, then is it also possible to subject the carefully planned retail spaces of the 1990s to the kind of close reading to which the New Critics of the 1950s submitted Modernist poetry? And what is it one looks for amid the radiant mess of visual and tactile images of a contemporary "retail theater" like Nike Town? Evidence of artistic inspiration, of conscientiously wrought creative decisions plotted by a well-paid, historically astute, iconoclastic design team? Evidence of hidden systems of persuasion, an opportunity to examine how a marketing giant like Nike can (as it has) convince 77 percent of all American males between the ages of eighteen and twenty-five that Nike's athletic shoe is the footwear of first choice? Or, perhaps, evidence of the intent of the author, the opportunity to read the heart and soul of a multinational corporation in the images and design features from which it chooses to construct the store it calls its flagship?

First, Chicago Nike Town is no small Town: five stories high, comprising sixty-eight thousand square feet of floor space, built on the scale of a modest department store or art museum. It was not the first Nike Town; the prototype in Portland, Oregon, was hosting fifty guided tours a week and being named *Money* magazine's "Store of the Year" for 1991 while a close-knit, insular design team of eight was still carving the Chicago store out of an old Saks Fifth Avenue building. Rather, Chicago Nike Town was considered the "concept's real test" (in the words of a *New York Times* reporter), due to its size (three times as large as the Portland store), its financing ($34 million), and its location in a large media market. The "concept" of Nike Town, in turn, had been emerging within Nike's corporate structure for a decade, evolving in part from the tour de force exhibitions Nike offered to institutional buyers at the athletic-gear trade shows of the late 1980s, and in part from the stage set for a sporting-goods store of the future that Nike's chief designer and vice-president, Gordon Thompson, produced for the movie *Back to the Future II*. The name, Nike Town, also bore cinematic roots, adapted from "Toon Town," the mythical Los Angeles ghetto where cartoon characters lived side by side with human beings in Robert Zemeckis's 1988 film *Who Framed Roger Rabbit?*

The "concept" of Nike Town is in fact an amalgamation of concepts. Foremost, the store is an exemplar of the term *controlled retail environment*. Just as companies like Nike expand the size of their overall market by creating and nurturing independent submarkets, Nike Town is divided into eighteen "pavilions," each themed to the sport or product featured there: white lines underfoot in the tennis pavilion, an authentic (if nonregulation) hardwood basketball court alongside the basketball gear. Scattered across the eighteen pavilions are eight "pools" of sound, again themed to the products for sale within each pool: the sound of sneakers squeaking on hardwood in the basketball pavilion, the sound of tennis balls being struck in the tennis pavilion (in the Portland store, hidden fans create a light wind in the bicycle pavilion, and warmer temperatures are programmed for the aqua gear). Last, the buying of goods invokes a sequence of events and images that makes the purchase itself playful, familiar, and essentially invisible: items move swiftly from the fourth-floor storeroom to the cashier stations through clear plastic tubes rimmed with green neon that suggest (as they are meant to) the cartoon future of *The Jetsons*, and they are rung up on cash registers concealed in black rolling carts that (in the words of Mary Schmich of the *Chicago Tribune*) "look more like R2-D2 than a nasty box that gobbles up our money."

As one enters into Nike Town, however, it becomes immediately evident that the direct purchase of goods is, or is designed to appear to be, an afterthought. The retail pavilions themselves are cramped and accessible only through the open atriums designed for the display of art and statuary. There are whimsical, anarchic features everywhere in Nike Town, and they suggest no overriding visual theme aside from Thompson's claim that "people love stimulation." Tropical fish swim in a twenty-two-foot thousand-gallon tank behind the hiking-shoe display; a bank of nine television screens embedded beneath the floor nearby flashes images of glimmering swimming pools and waterfalls. And while most of these video design features suggest a kind of postliterate wit at work, other aesthetic references embedded within Nike Town take on a high-culture sheen, and the quality of architectural drama more often associated with the work of superstar architects. The store's central atrium is three stories tall and produces a dizzying verticality; three sculptures of bicyclists, realistically proportioned and detailed but covered in white plaster in the style of George Segal, have been hung tilted downward from the rafters and appear to be riding swiftly downhill through the atrium space. The escalator from the first to the second floor faces open space on one side and a mural suggestive of Marcel Duchamp's *Nude Descending a Staircase* on the other; as the customer ascends, slender vertical slats placed diagonally to the mural compose themselves into an enormous portrait of an intent female athlete and efface from view the Duchamp-like abstraction. On the second floor, a twenty-foot-tall photograph of Michael Jordan rises against a brick wall behind the small glass-encased basketball court where the sound of squeaking sneakers never stops. A quotation from William Blake, who never made a jump shot in his life, ornaments the photograph and insists upon the poetic grandeur of its subject.

Amidst this clamor, the idea of "purchase" begins to diffuse and bifurcate. Buying a pair of socks, one begins to feel, will signify participation in a system of conduct and belief. Thompson, in a booster moment, suggests that individuals identify with Nike's "creativity and innovation," but he also observes that Nike Town is about "mythology": Michael Jordan larger than life, aloft against a clouded sky; Charles Barkley above eye level, backlit by spotlights, glowering downward; museum-style glass cases everywhere, enshrining Nike athletic gear (Michael Jordan's University of North Carolina jersey, Batman's boot), Nike marketing (a video "theater" that plays a montage of Nike commercials on a continuous reel), and Nike Town itself as though they were athletic events themselves, or at least events of moment in American cultural history. Inspirational slogans can be found everywhere in Nike Town: paragraphs etched on Plexiglas panels extol customers to "Play to Win" or achieve "Total Body Conditioning"; long vertical banners spell out "Test Your Faith Daily"; and rising above everything else, the words "Just Do It," white on white at the top of the atrium. When combined with the evocations of the "street" that mark Nike Town's design—manhole covers with "Nike Town" insignias embedded in floors that mimic concrete sidewalks, iron railings and gratings, and that gorgeous fragment of a basketball court—what emerges is a truly startling and complete vision of what an American mythology of athletic achievement and force might look like, of what you might get if you could read the cacophonous but vivid thoughts of a video-literate seventeen-year-old boy convinced that sports were his sole path to transcendence.

In a store this conscientiously crowded with the image detritus of the late twentieth century, it is hard to believe that nothing is happening, that this disarray cannot somehow be read as an astute if accidental funhouse refraction of the crazed and overflowing aggregation of historical and artistic referents in which our daily lives are intertwined. Spend hours in Nike Town, and look at anything but merchandise, and patterns begin to emerge, or seem to emerge. Thompson has described Nike Town (in several different interviews) as "1939 World's Fair meets theater": one can see this in the art deco details of the lighting fixtures and lettering, in the WPA-meets-Stalinist-poster-art athletes that grace the Nike Town bags and boxes, and mostly in the globes that hang from the ceiling or lie wrapped within the words "Nike Town" on the manhole covers. One can even sense a measure of historical consciousness in Thompson's comparison between Nike Town and that World's Fair, the first where corporations ran impressive themed pavilions side by side with those offered by entire countries, and where companies like AT&T and GM sold their product by selling their image, and sold their image by yoking it to the fair's stated ideal of "Building the World of Tomorrow."

As years go, however, 1939 is no playhouse waiting for our eager and loping postmodern ransack work: the long banners illuminated by winged black spotlights on the facade of Nike Town might look less like Albert Speer–inspired designs if it were not for the nonsense words of German ("Nde-strukt") painted across the front windows or the cogged-wheel design in which Nike places its famous "swoosh" the way swastikas were imprinted within cogged-wheel designs on the covers of many National Socialist Party official documents.[1] If it were not for all these features of Nike Town's entrance, it might be easier to ignore the notion that the Hellenic-style sculptures of idealized athletic figures found at the store would have been much more consonant at the promenade of statuary inside the Olympic Stadium in Berlin in 1936 than among the more avant-garde renderings of George Washington and the Four Freedoms that American sculptors displayed in Queens, New York, three years later; or that Nike commercials bear more resemblance to Leni Riefenstahl's fast-cut athletic propaganda masterpiece *Olympia—Feast of Nations* than to anything Frank Capra ever dreamed up.

Observing that Nike Town's designers show every evidence of historical and artistic astuteness, but that they seem most comfortable harvesting the comparatively short cultural history built to fit on a television screen, it seems reasonable to wonder whether these resonances of the wrong 1939 are the kind of accident that happens more often than we can recognize. Are they the inevitable result of a generation of artists, writers, and architects treating world history like a supermarket of reverberant images without the requisite historical knowledge? (The 1939 World's Fair, for instance, borrowed hugely from the German- and Italian-inflected Parisian Exposition of 1937.) Or perhaps they are no accident at all but the result of some darker spirit of play and self-awareness on the part of the designers, the same kind of irony that inspires franchise names that deconstruct themselves, like "Banana Republic" or "Victoria's Secret." Or perhaps they reflect the conditions of our new, information-age culture. Could the best explanation for the pervasive paranoia that is embraced (albeit in different ways) by individuals from the right, left, and center of American politics be the fact that our public life is Nike Towned, and that where there lies a surfeit of image and information there are bound to emerge patterns that are neither entirely accident nor entirely intention? Behind a glass case on the third floor of Nike Town celebrating and explaining the construction of the store itself sits a well-folded T-shirt upon which are written the words "Building Niketown." Below those words can be found two human figures whose limbs are rendered as slender rectangles in the forms of twisted crosses—not exactly swastikas, but too much like swastikas to ignore. They are painted in purple and black, two colors that playfully approximate, while maintaining a plausible distance from, the red and the black shared by the uniforms of the Chicago Bulls (Nike Town's symbolic home team) and the Nazi flag.

Corporations exist on a deep plain of our cultural life. The thirteen founding states were private corporations before they were "colonies," a small wrinkle in our early history that reminds us that the declaration of a public stock offering has an older claim on the American soul than the Declaration of Independence, if not a truer one. The nature of that claim, however, remains essentially elusive. Whether corporations tell history or write it, whether they exist as the manifestations of our desires or as their manipulators, remain crux questions that shape our responses to the most ordinary of American landscapes and electronic frontiers, to every golden arch and every Nike swoosh. What we test, what we remain constantly testing, is whether or not we believe that what men and women do when they "incorporate"—that is, when they act jointly but privately—can be trusted, and whether the personality of corporate power merely reflects the aggregated personality of its constituent individuals or reflects a strange new force that can be neither measured nor understood.

It is impossible to ignore these swastikas that might not be swastikas. That no one shopping at Nike Town had noticed them or recognized them as swastikas was as plain as the fact that few individuals seeing a photograph of the T-shirt, isolated from the image bombardment that constitutes the Nike environs, could avoid seeing at least a murky rendition of the Nazi icon. That the T-shirt was visible only through glass engraved with a tribute to Nike "teamwork" only complicated the act of vision, forcing the viewer to consider a paean to corporate unity as the central twentieth-century symbol of the dangers of national unity floats dimly but clearly behind the words. It does not seem possible that the "design team" at Nike (as the paragraph engraved onto the glass case calls them) would miss this feature. Gordon Thompson is famed for his attention to detail, and it seems unlikely that an individual who would insist upon color-coordinating the tropical fish that swim behind the shoe displays to the shoes themselves would allow the public display of the central icon of the Third Reich two floors above. It seems equally unlikely that Nike was celebrating some veiled Nazi sympathies. Nothing in Nike's corporate history—which begins in Oregon in the late 1960s among a group of dedicated and decidedly countercultural long-distance runners—would suggest any hidden political agenda aside from that of controlling the world's athletic-footwear market.

To understand why swastikas might be displayed in Nike Town requires a different kind of intellectual expedition, one that does not seek individual agency or concrete motive but rather accepts the logic of American business as it is conducted by multinational corporations like Nike in this decade. While their presence might represent an object lesson concerning the proliferation of images itself, the mistakes that might be made when history is used too cursorily, their presence might also represent a different kind of lesson, configured by a twist of the epistemological kaleidoscope to the left or right. When one sees how the icons of Nazism have been defused of their original meaning in the context of the Nike Town store, one wonders if something very powerful has not taken place: a conscious subversion of those icons (but for the loophole of two conscientiously waving hands on each human figure, the symbols on the T-shirt would be true swastikas); an accidental illustration of the speed with which multinational corporations sweep away the vestiges of old and pernicious forms of nationalism (or the extent to which the men and women who work at multinational corporations stop recognizing the symbols of national identity); or an accidental tribute to the shedding of old national identities in the ecumenical culture chaos of the United States and the global marketplace. What is lost, and what is gained, when the swastika is swept from the moorings that hold it fast to the National Socialist Party and is reconstructed as nothing more than one art deco symbol awash among other art deco symbols in a glorified athletic-clothing store?

Nike, one begins to think, has gone too far, too fast. More than selling shoes, however, that often seems to be the true purpose of the company's existence. Nike's corporate biography for the last decade is laced with activities that defy the unofficial culture canons that have defined loyalty and identity in America for the better part of this century, our sense of what is more important than what else: Michael Jordan denying the National Basketball Association the legal use of his image in 1991 so that Nike could possess sole control of his face; Jordan and Charles Barkley refusing (then relenting) during the 1992 Olympics to wear the United States warmup gear because they bore Reebok emblems, and not Nike swooshes; the 1993 agreement with CAA, the Los Angeles talent agency, that made it possible for Nike to sign athletes to celebrity contracts before they signed contracts with their teams (famously, Alonzo Mourning responded "Nike" in 1992 when asked whether he was signing with the NBA Charlotte Hornets or with the footwear company, a variation on Charles Barkley's observation that Nike gave him "two million reasons" not to wear the USA-Reebok warmup gear at Barcelona). While other athletic corporations offered free clothing to football coaches, Nike made deals with entire universities (the University of Illinois, the University of Georgia), even countries (Kenya); while other corporations dealt directly with entire professional leagues, Nike made deals with rogue owners, like Jerry Jones of the NFL Dallas Cowboys, and challenged league commissioners to respond. And throughout this period Nike continued to produce dynastic advertising campaigns, raising its marketing budget from $20 million in 1985 to $150 million in 1993, the same year in which it won separate awards (the Mercury, Kelly, and Video Storyboard prizes, respectively) for the best radio, magazine, and video advertising campaigns in the country.

It is not hard to calculate the costs of Nike's hyperactivity to Nike. The company was boycotted twice in 1992 (once by Made In The USA for its manufacturing plants in third-world nations, once by Operation PUSH for its overwhelmingly white executive structure), and it has been the subject of repeated jeremiads by editorial writers and of repeated ridicule by competitors (who refer to Nike workers as "The Cult"). It seems almost futile to observe that these are small sacrifices when weighed against a 33 percent market share, annual profits nearing $1 billion, and retail sales in over a hundred countries. One thinks of those long-distance runners who founded Nike, and what an intense, introverted, paranoid thing it means to be running first in any race, especially when (as the in-house Nike slogan describes) "there is no finish line." Much has been made of the extent to which Nike's corporate culture has been adapted from the culture of athletics; but while Nike's athletic competitiveness often plays itself out in cheerful ways, it seems worth noting that when a retail corporation measures victory in terms of market share, the consuming public becomes an ambiguous competitor as long as its actions remain unquantifiable. As Donald Katz reports in *Just Do It*, the buzz-phrase among employees at "Nike World Campus" is that "market share" is "borrowed," never earned. It is small wonder, then, that Nike seems so peeved at us sometimes, telling us to "just do it"—a phrase that might be intended as challenge, or as command, but either way expresses impatience with our indecision. It is even less wonder that almost every major marketing initiative executed by Nike during the last decade has represented an opportunity to take control of images by buying them before they cease being (in CEO Phillip Knight's phrase) "clean"; or that new Nike Towns are in the works, virtual-reality palaces (courtesy of yet another one of Nike's whirling lateral mergers, this with George Lucas's Industrial Light and Magic film factory) that will let shoppers fly like Michael Jordan or serve like Pete Sampras. A company that tells us that "total body conditioning" is attainable has no limits to its aspirations of control, any more than a company that tells us to "Test Our Faith Daily" could be blamed for slowing down in a race with no finish line.

What can be found in a swastika that might not be a swastika? We might find two meanings that might not be meanings at all. We might have found the end of history (again), a place where the passionate nationalisms of the last seven hundred years are rendered irrelevant by the twinned forces of the global marketplace (and the economic payoff perpetually promised therein) and the serene dumbness and short memory of the video-age American educational system. In this context, the swastika—as well as the various other traces of Nazi iconography that appear to have wandered into Nike Town uninvited—is obsolete, defeated, held prisoner behind Plexiglas to a new social consensus so powerful as to make fascism look like a Quaker meeting. Or perhaps we have found this: Hitler, it is well known, believed that buildings had persuasive power. He instructed his architects to pursue (in the phrase of Alexander Von Senger) the "mythic-symbolic-magic" potential of architecture. Eventually those architects created what historian Robert Stone describes as the "Nazi" style, erecting public structures that combined neoclassical references with freestanding sculptures (often athletic Nordic figures), exhorting axioms carved into walls or hung on panels over doorways, and a rich dose of the *Volksch,* a nostalgic design format that incorporated the colors and materials of German folk life into official buildings. It was believed that individuals would pass through these buildings and emerge in "spiritual communion" with other German citizens. We do not need a swastika to know how much this sounds like Nike Town, or how much Nike's efforts to govern a population (on its own small terms) bear uncomfortable resemblances to the strategies for propaganda and control practiced by particularly creative totalitarian states. An uncertain swastika for an uncertain future: Do we want to make generalizations about the will to power, about whether (in some cosmic calculus) it dissipates as humankind progresses? Or will it suffice to wonder aloud about whether or not the mammoth corporations of the late twentieth century are simply muted and fragmented variations on the bad old governments we thought we had defeated?

In retrospect, many of the issues raised in this essay have been clarified, more or less, by accident, more or less. In April 1996, *Harper's* published a truncated version of this essay.[2] Nike allowed *Harper's* to photograph the T-shirt with the pseudo-swastika and briefly allowed other media sources—*Sports Illustrated* (April 1, 1996) and the *Chicago Sun-Times* (March 27, 1996)—to reproduce the photograph or publish their own versions. After a request from Fox Television, however, Nike refused all future press access to the T-shirt and removed it from the museum-style case in which it had resided. In response to press queries, Lee Bernstein, a public relations representative for Nike, argued that I was "intellectualizing to make an extreme point" (which seems obvious), and that the T-shirt and other design features of Nike Town were attempts to replicate "the type of strong graphics used by the Germans and Swiss in the early and middle part of the century"—"not exactly a contradiction," in the words of Richard Roeper of the *Chicago Sun-Times,* "of Levy's larger theories."

From Nike's actions during this brief interlude of media play, it seems possible to make some small inferences about the values that were brought to the design of Nike Town. Nike's openness regarding the *Harper's* and follow-up media requests certainly suggests the company's conviction that photographs of the T-shirt would show nothing even remotely resembling a pair of swastikas. The subsequent refusal of future media requests and the withdrawal of the T-shirt from public display indicate the eventual recognition that some significant share of potential viewers—not as many as I had imagined, but far more than Nike dreamed—would recognize swastika-like designs. In arguing that the design work reflected "the type of strong graphics used by the Germans and Swiss in the early and middle part of the century," however, but not Nazi aesthetics, Nike also offered a concrete theoretical position wrapped inside a denial, arguing that it is possible to appropriate the aesthetic sensibility of a particular time and place without also borrowing its ideology.

In this context, what seems most striking is that the evidence even exists to make this disagreement possible. We might remind ourselves that 58 percent of all athletic-shoe revenues are generated by sales to children under eighteen years old, that expensive sneakers remain a crucial marker of status in the inner city, and that ample anecdotal evidence exists that inner-city minority teenagers are a primary target group of sporting-goods manufacturers. Given these facts, we can then begin to understand who, exactly, Nike might be trying to reach with those "strong" German and Swiss graphics. By offering the poorest, youngest, most helpless citizens (as well as that part of every individual that feels insecure within a troubled yet dynamic culture) visions of superhuman transcendence (a man who can fly) and a philosophy of achievement that shames its possessor out of feeling doubt, or empathizing with failure, Nike seems to sell sneakers very like the way an extremist political party seeks power. In the history of republics, however, there has been no shortage of fascist regimes; and in the shorter but no less expressive history of multinational corporations, there has been correspondingly no shortage of advertising strategies that have adopted the patriotic ideologies of their target audience, or have leaned toward tyrannical methodology. What distinguishes Nike in this instance is the unlikely fact that, employing marketing strategies utilized in lesser or greater amounts by other corporations, it chose to employ the one set of graphic styles and symbols that any other modern multinational would have avoided, and instead invited consumers to potentially link Nike's product and image with the iconic fascists of the twentieth century.

What makes Nike's work in this instance memorable, even insightful, and certainly worthy of critical comment, however, is the fact that almost nobody noticed. We live during a period in which Americans answer "The Holocaust" as often as "Pearl Harbor" or "Hiroshima" when asked to name a single event from World War II. One of the great transformations (if not the greatest transformation) of the American collective memory of its past has been the extent to which World War II has become a story of Germans and Jews, of pornographic power and equally pornographic powerlessness. If Nike periodically appropriates the aesthetic images of the single most unalloyed icon of power that the twentieth century has produced, what seems even more remarkable is how effortlessly it grafted those images onto the All-American symbols that otherwise grace the Nike cosmos. More ambitious, more artistic, even more naive, but certainly more disdainful of the idea of national identity than most corporations—this is, after all, the same firm that prepared an American flag with a Nike swoosh instead of stars for display at the 1996 Olympics—Nike discovered that an American audience in the 1990s could conceivably find a seamless mosaic, not a dissonant clash of world views, in the commingling of Nazi iconography and American culture.

In so doing, Nike argues, the company divests those icons from their association with the ideology that produced them. To a certain extent that statement cannot be denied: if Nike draws upon the symbols of past power, its marketing strategies offer no explicit symbols of victimization, no evident scapegoat, no *loser*—a kind of radical pop retelling of World War II in which Holocaust denial manifests itself as the expression of relentless power with the complete absence of a victim (although it is worth noting that many of Nike's public relations ordeals in the 1990s consist of the efforts of journalists to identify the victim that seems to loom invisibly in the Nike system, whether it be the exploited Asian worker who assembles the shoes or the inner-city child who pays $170 per pair). At the same time, the symbols Nike borrows from the Swiss and German graphics of the early and middle part of this century would be utterly meaningless if they did not produce at least (or at most) the hazy impression of historical resonance. To put it another way, the fact that Nike sells shoes to inner-city African American teens sometimes employing variations of Nazi persuasive strategies, and the fact that anti-Semitism among African Americans is strongest among those same inner-city teens, does not mean that Nike is anti-Semitic, or that Nike is using (even subtly, or accidentally) anti-Semitic gestures to sell shoes to one of its target audiences. It does, however, say a great deal about how the official historical distinction between the winners and losers of World War II fails to account for the fact that the Nazis continue to be useful in unchartable ways. We hear something of this in Cornel West's voice when he explains that Louis Farrakhan sometimes defends Hitler because he "wanted to talk about somebody who created a people out of nothing"—a scholarly statement that means no more and no less than the display in Nike Town that places Charles Barkley in a red and black uniform that he does not wear on the basketball court but that belongs to the team of the ideological unconscious that history and "two million reasons" make him play for every day. It was opportunistic of Nike to create its own all-star team of successful, mostly African American, athletes. But it was an odd alertness to the conditions of our culture that allowed Nike to dress that team in whatever raiments would make it clear that they were men who would never lose.

NOTES

INTRODUCTION

1. These statistics are taken from Katherine Bischoping, "Interpreting Social Influences on Holocaust Knowledge," *Contemporary Jewry* 17 (1996): 106–35.

2. The phrase "unfailingly optimistic" paraphrases Lawrence Graver in *An Obsession with Anne Frank: Meyer Levin and the Diary* (Berkeley: University of California Press, 1995).

3. Ibid., 57.

4. Doubleday has published all editions of *The Diary of Anne Frank.*

5. Lawrence Langer, "The Americanization of the Holocaust on Stage and Screen," in *Admitting the Holocaust* (New York: Oxford University Press, 1995). I am also paraphrasing Alvin Rosenfeld here but will soon directly quote his "The Americanization of the Holocaust," *Commentary*, June 1995.

6. Graver, *Obsession with Anne Frank,* 79.

7. John Simon, "Yours, Anne," *New York,* Oct. 28, 1995.

8. Rosenfeld, "Americanization of the Holocaust," 37; Enid Futterman in *New York Times,* Oct. 28, 1996, 18.

9. Graver, *Obsession with Anne Frank,* 238.

10. Yosefa Loshitsky, ed., *Spielberg's Holocaust: Critical Perspectives on Schindler's List* (Bloomington: Indiana University Press, 1997).

11. Rosenfeld, "Americanization of the Holocaust," 35.

12. Berenbaum's statement of the museum's mission is much quoted. Rosenfeld refers to it in his article. See also Michael Berenbaum, *After Tragedy and Triumph: Essays on Modern Jewish Thought and the American Experience* (Cambridge: Cambridge University Press, 1990).

13. Tara DeSilva, ed., *In Memory's Kitchen: A Legacy from the Women of Terezin* (Northvale, N.J.: Aronson, 1996).

14. See Jack Nusan-Porter, "Toward a Sociology of the Holocaust," *Contemporary Jewry* 17 (1996).

15. See Seth Mydans, "Not Guilty: The Lawyers—In the Joy of Victory, Defense Team Is in Discord," *New York Times*, Oct. 4, 1995, 11.

16. Kathleen Jamieson quoted in *New York Times*, Oct. 23, 1995, 12.

17. Rosenfeld, "Americanization of the Holocaust," 37.

18. James Brooke, "Elie Wiesel Says $70 Million Ought to Go to Nazi-Era Survivors," *New York Times*, May 9, 1997, 13.

19. Information and quotations about Spielberg's life were taken from a biography about him in the Pop Culture Legends series: Elizabeth Ferber, *Steven Spielberg* (Philadelphia: Chelsea House, 1997).

20. See Bernard Reisman, "Baby-Boomers Come of Age," *Contemporary Jewry* 17 (1996).

21. Michael Goldberg, *Why Should Jews Survive? Looking Past the Holocaust toward a Jewish Future* (New York: Oxford University Press, 1995), 49, 63.

22. Philip Roth, *Portnoy's Complaint* (New York: Bantam Books, 1969), 68.

23. See Edward S. Shapiro, *A Time for Healing: American Jewry since World War II* (Baltimore: Johns Hopkins University Press, 1992), 117.

24. See Raymond Hernandez, "New Curriculum from Albany," *New York Times*, Dec. 1, 1996, 52.

25. Arthur Hertzberg, *The Jews in America: Four Centuries of an Uneasy Encounter: A History* (New York: Simon and Schuster, 1989), 382.

26. Michael Marrus, *The Holocaust in History* (New York: New American Library, 1989), 202.

CHAPTER 1. HILENE FLANZBAUM / THE IMAGINARY JEW
AND THE AMERICAN POET

For the intellectual support, guidance, and stimulation necessary to write this essay, I owe a great deal to Walter Benn Michaels and the participants of his 1995 NEH summer seminar, "Modernism and the Emergence of Cultural Identity," especially Ingrid Walker-Fields, Sean McCann, and Christopher Zinn.

1. John Berryman, "The Imaginary Jew," *Kenyon Review* 7, no. 4 (1945): 532–39. Hereafter cited parenthetically.

2. Karl Shapiro, *V-Letter* (New York: Random House, 1945). Hereafter cited parenthetically.

3. For an overview of the controversy surrounding Plath's Holocaust poems, see Alvin Rosenfeld, *A Double Dying* (Bloomington: Indiana University Press, 1980), and James Young, "The Holocaust Confessions of Sylvia Plath," in *Writing and Rewriting the Holocaust* (Bloomington: Indiana University Press, 1988).

4. Charles Stember, *Jews in the Mind of America* (New York: Basic Books, 1966), 268.

5. Charles Silberman, *A Certain People: American Jews* (New York: Summit Books, 1985), 51.

6. Charles Silberman writes that he still felt Jewish even though "the operative

principle on which my generation of American Jews was raised was 'Shah! Don't speak of it.' When I was growing up it was not just a question of avoiding the embarrassment that arose from being conspicuous; the message Jews received was that to be accepted they had to stop being Jewish—or at least *visibly* Jewish." Ibid., 59.

7. Lucy Dawidowicz, *What Is the Use of Jewish History?* (New York: Schocken Books, 1992), 217.

8. This confusion is well illustrated in Philip Roth's story of 1959, "Defender of the Faith," included in the 1959 collection of stories *Goodbye, Columbus.* The protagonist, Nathan Marx, an assimilated American Jew who loves hot dogs and egg rolls, baseball and beer, cannot remember when Passover is. After being decorated for his bravery in Europe during World War II, he now commands a basic-training unit where three markedly ethnic Jews tease and haunt him, demanding that he show them fraternity and favoritism. Marx, who has seen great atrocities in Europe, presumably even the death camps, struggles with the debt he owes these three Jewish soldiers in the wake of what he has witnessed in Europe. Roth presents his character's ambivalence clearly: as a soldier in the United States Army, he occupies a position of responsibility and honor; he sees himself as an American through and through; he can associate little with being Jewish except the memory of his grandmother calling him "lieben" (the Yiddish word for love). What connection does he have with these three pushy, cowardly, and conniving trainees, even if they are Jewish? And how, if at all, has the Holocaust strengthened that attachment?

9. The editor's note to *V-Letter* (vii) tells us that "the author for the last twenty-six months has been on active duty in the southwest Pacific area, where all these poems [except one] were written."

10. Richard Polenberg, *One Nation Divisible* (New York: Viking, 1980), 50.

11. David Daiches, "Review of *V-Letter,*" *Poetry* 66, no. 5 (1945): 270–75, at 273.

12. Karl Shapiro, "A Poet Dissects the Modern Poets," *New York Times Sunday Magazine,* Sept. 23, 1945, 20.

13. Karl Shapiro, "Essay on Rime." *Poetry* 66, no. 14 (1945): 199.

14. Paradoxically, the phrase "international Jew" has long been used to denounce Jews as greedy, treacherous, and traitorous to nation. The literary and political climate of the 1940s transformed the term to suggest virtue: among other things, it implied cultivation, worldliness, and world-weariness. Moreover, treason to a nation so obviously debauched was increasingly viewed as heroic among a certain sector of the literary community.

15. Delmore Schwartz, "The Isolation of the Poet," in *Collected Essays,* ed. Donald Dike and David H. Zucker (Chicago: University of Chicago Press, 1970), 9.

16. Allen Tate, "To Whom Is the Poet Responsible," in *Essays of Four Decades* (Chicago: Swallow, 1966), 27.

17. Randall Jarrell, "Obscurity of the Poet," in *The Poet and the Age* (New York: Vintage Books, 1953), 17. The high drama of Jarrell's sentiments may owe something to his relationship with Hannah Arendt, the Jewish social philosopher and refugee from Germany. After reading Jarrell's poetry she asked him to translate some German poems, and an impassioned, though platonic, relationship began between them. In

1947 he sent her one of his poems about the camps. In 1950 Arendt sent Jarrell an early copy of her masterpiece, *The Origins of Totalitarianism,* a book that attempted to explain why the Holocaust had happened when and where it did. Jarrell was wildly enthusiastic; soon after, he replied with the essay quoted here. Arendt replied "that she was intoxicated with agreement" and that they stood together "against a world of enemies." Arendt's sympathy for Jarrell's plight is remarkable, considering that she fled Nazi Germany in 1940. Yet her words intimate the meaning of Jewish ethnicity at this time. Jarrell and Arendt held the common notion that the intellectual in post-Holocaust America occupied the marginal position that the Jew had held in Europe during the previous decade.

18. Mary Randall, ed., *Complete Letters of Randall Jarrell* (Boston: Houghton Mifflin, 1985), 251.

19. Some would even say it disappears. Indeed, the anti-Semite "makes" the Jew. See Jean-Paul Sartre's discussion of this in *Anti-Semite and Jew* (New York: Schocken Books, 1948), 65–75.

20. My own essay on this topic is forthcoming.

21. Karl Shapiro, "The Conscientious Objector," *Partisan Review* 13, no. 3 (1946): 348.

22. Stephen Gould Axelrod apparently agrees. In *Robert Lowell: Life and Art* (Princeton: Princeton University Press, 1978) he begins his section on Lowell's conscientious-objector status with a quotation from Shapiro's poem.

23. Lowell to Pound, Oct. 24, 1956, Lowell Archives, Houghton Library, Harvard University.

24. This is Paul Breslin's term, from *The Psycho-Political Muse* (Chicago: University of Chicago Press, 1987), 42.

25. I am of course quoting Sylvia Plath's well-known "Daddy," published in her 1960 collection *Ariel.*

26. Karl Shapiro, *Poems of a Jew* (New York: Random House, 1958).

CHAPTER 2. JEFFREY SHANDLER /
ALIENS IN THE WASTELAND

1. Peter Novick, "Holocaust Memory in America," in *The Art of Memory: Holocaust Memorials in History,* ed. James E. Young (New York: Jewish Museum; Munich: Prestel, 1994), 159.

2. For a more extensive discussion, see Jeffrey Shandler, *While America Watches: Televising the Holocaust* (New York: Oxford University Press, 1998).

3. Jeffrey Shandler, "'This Is Your Life': Telling a Holocaust Survivor's Life Story on Early American Television," *Journal of Narrative and Life History* 4, nos. 1–2 (1994): 41–68.

4. See Newton Minow, *Equal Time* (New York: Atheneum, 1964), chap. 1, "The Vast Wasteland," 45–69; the speech is reproduced on 48–64.

5. J. Fred MacDonald, *Blacks and White TV: Afro-Americans in Television since 1948* (Chicago: Nelson-Hall, 1983), 102.

6. *The Defenders:* "The Avenger" (CBS, aired Nov. 17, 1961); *Sam Benedict:* "Season of Vengeance" (NBC, aired Mar. 30, 1963); *Dragnet:* "The Big Explosion" (NBC, aired Jan. 19, 1967); *The FBI:* "The Butcher" (ABC, aired Dec. 8, 1968).

7. This and all following quotations from *The Twilight Zone,* "Death's Head Revisited," were transcribed by the author from a videotape copy of the broadcast housed in the National Jewish Archive of Broadcasting of the Jewish Museum of New York, item no. T380.

8. Serling wrote a second script for *The Twilight Zone* that deals with the Holocaust. Entitled "He's Alive!" the drama first aired on Jan. 24, 1963.

9. Joel Engel, *Rod Serling: The Dreams and Nightmare of Life in the Twilight Zone* (Chicago: Contemporary Books, 1989), 189.

10. Hannah Arendt, *Eichmann in Jerusalem: A Report on the Banality of Evil* (New York: Viking, 1963).

11. See, e.g., Homer Bigart, "Eichmann to Stay in Glass Cage If He Testifies at Israeli Trial," *New York Times,* June 5, 1961, 5.

12. This and all following quotations from *Star Trek,* "Patterns of Force," were transcribed by the author from a videotape copy of the broadcast housed in the National Jewish Archive of Broadcasting of the Jewish Museum of New York, item no. T1309.

13. See Jeffrey Shandler, "Is There a Jewish Way to Watch Television? Notes from a Tuned-in Ethnographer," *Jewish Folklore and Ethnology Review* 16, no. 1 (1994): 19–22.

14. Alasdair Spark, "Vietnam: The War in Science Fiction," in *Science Fiction, Social Conflict, and War,* ed. Philip John Davies (Manchester, U.K.: Manchester University Press, 1990), 124.

15. John Hellmann, *American Myth and the Legacy of Vietnam* (New York: Columbia University Press, 1986), 220.

16. The phrase originally appears in George Santayana, *The Life of Reason,* vol. 1, *Reason in Common Sense* (New York: C. Scribner's Sons), 1905–6. Santayana's words are often cited in Holocaust memory culture (e.g., in promotional material for the Simon Wiesenthal Center of Los Angeles).

17. *Cannon:* "The Man Who Couldn't Forget" (CBS, aired Nov. 20, 1974); *Columbo:* "Now You See Him" (NBC, aired Feb. 29, 1976); *Quincy, M.E.:* "Stolen Tears" (NBC, aired Mar. 17, 1982); *Kojak:* "The Belarus File" (CBS, aired Feb. 16, 1985); *L.A. Law* (NBC, aired Mar. 19, 1992); *Bodies of Evidence* (CBS, aired Aug. 27, 1992); *Law and Order* (NBC, aired Feb. 3, 1993); *Lou Grant:* "Nazis" (CBS, aired Oct. 18, 1977); *All in the Family:* "Archie Is Branded" (CBS, aired Feb. 24, 1973); *The Adventures of Superboy* (Universal): "Back to Oblivion" (1988) and "Golem" (1990).

18. Owen S. Rachleff, "Assessing *Holocaust,*" *Midstream* 24, no. 6 (1978): 51.

CHAPTER 3. HENRY GREENSPAN / IMAGINING SURVIVORS

1. Edward T. Linenthal, *Preserving Memory: The Struggle to Create America's Holocaust Museum* (New York: Viking, 1995), 11.

2. David Wyman, "The United States," in *The World Reacts to the Holocaust,* ed. David Wyman and Charles Rozenzveig (Baltimore: Johns Hopkins University Press,

1996), 721. The earlier date refers to the appearance of the film *Judgment at Nuremberg*, which premiered in 1961, the same year as the Eichmann trial.

3. Raul Hilberg, "Opening Remarks," in *Lessons and Legacies: The Meaning of the Holocaust in a Changing World*, ed. Peter Hayes (Evanston, Ill.: Northwestern University Press, 1991), 18.

4. Cf. Alvin H. Rosenfeld, "The Americanization of the Holocaust," *Commentary*, June 1995. As Rosenfeld also notes, one must not underestimate the importance of survivors' own efforts in all these developments. But such efforts were not new. Only in the late 1970s did survivors begin to find a much wider interested audience.

5. Joan Ringelheim, *A Catalogue of Audio and Video Collections of Holocaust Testimony*, 2d ed. (Westport, Conn.: Greenwood, 1992). A preliminary survey by Alain Goldschlager of some two thousand published survivor memoirs suggests the same trend worldwide: a dramatic increase in published memoirs beginning in 1978. Goldschlager, personal communication and fax, Feb. 14, 1997.

6. This initial study became "Who Can Retell? On the Recounting of Life History by Holocaust Survivors" (Ph.D. diss., Brandeis University, 1985). In recent writing I have placed a good deal of emphasis on a distinction between survivors' *recounting* and their *testimony*. Here, however, the terms are used interchangeably. See my *On Listening to Holocaust Survivors: Recounting and Life History* (Westport, Conn.: Praeger, 1998).

7. Primo Levi, *Survival in Auschwitz*, trans. S. Wolff (New York: Summit Books, 1986), 123.

8. Elie Wiesel, *The Accident*, trans. A. Borchardt (New York: Bantam Books, 1982), 54.

9. Charlotte Delbo, *Days and Memory*, trans. Rosette Lamont (Marlboro, Vt.: Marlboro, 1990), 1–4. See the discussion in Lawrence Langer, *Holocaust Testimonies: The Ruins of Memory* (New Haven: Yale University Press, 1991), 1–38. The phrase "twofold being" comes from Rosette Lamont's translation of Delbo. Later on I will also draw on Langer's translation of the passage, which differs slightly.

10. Isabella Leitner, *Saving the Fragments* (New York: Plume, 1985), 94; and in Langer, *Holocaust Testimonies*, 53–54.

11. Delbo, *Days and Memory*, 3–4.

12. Jean Amery, *At the Mind's Limits*, trans. S. Rosenfeld and S. P. Rosenfeld (Bloomington: Indiana University Press, 1980), 34.

13. Elie Wiesel, *The Town beyond the Wall*, trans. S. Becker (New York: Schocken Books, 1982), 91.

14. Delbo, *Days and Memory*, as translated in Langer, *Holocaust Testimonies*, 7.

15. See, e.g., Greenspan, "Who Can Retell?" 26–31; Sidney Bolkosky, "Listening for the Silences," *Witness* 1 (Spring 1987): 66–75; and Lawrence Langer, *Admitting the Holocaust* (New York: Oxford University Press, 1995), 3–12.

16. Dori Laub and Nanette Auerhahn, "Failed Empathy: A Central Theme in the Survivor's Holocaust Experience," *Psychoanalytic Psychology* 6 (1989). In particular, Laub and Auerhahn write, "The character structures of many survivors show a sur-

prising mosaic of high level psychological functioning coexisting with the potential for severe regression. It is as though we see 'black holes' in an otherwise throbbing, pulsating, and alive galaxy. . . . The traumatic state operates like a black hole in the person's mind" (391).

17. See, e.g., Paul Chodoff, "Psychotherapy of the Survivor," in *Survivors, Victims, and Perpetrators: Essays on the Nazi Holocaust,* ed. J. Dimsdale (Washington, D.C.: Hemisphere, 1980), 205–18; Hillel Klein, "Problems in the Psychotherapeutic Treatment of Israeli Survivors of the Holocaust," in *Massive Psychic Trauma,* ed. H. Krystal (New York: International Universities Press, 1968), 233–44; and Shamai Davidson, *Holding on to Humanity: The Message of Holocaust Survivors—The Shamai Davidson Papers,* ed. Israel Charny (New York: New York University Press, 1992), esp. xxi–xxii.

18. Krystal, *Massive Psychic Trauma,* 95.

19. I have argued that very few survivors can be said to have "integrated" the Holocaust. Yet a good many seem to have integrated this lack of integration itself, finding a way to balance the different worlds within which survival takes form. Such a comment, however, is also purely descriptive and does not provide a theoretical understanding of this capacity. See my "Lives as Texts: Symptoms as Modes of Recounting in the Life Histories of Holocaust Survivors," in *Storied Lives: The Cultural Politics of Self-Understanding,* ed. George Rosenwald and Richard Ochberg (New Haven: Yale University Press, 1992), and "Making a Story from What Is Not a Story: The Oral Narratives of Holocaust Survivors," in *Texts and Identities: Studies on Language and Narrative III,* ed. Joachim Knuf (Lexington: University of Kentucky, Department of Communications, 1994).

20. Cf. the descriptions of early responses to survivors in Robert H. Abzug, *Inside the Vicious Heart: Americans and the Liberation of the Nazi Concentration Camps* (New York: Oxford University Press, 1985); Hilberg, "Opening Remarks"; William Helmreich, *Against All Odds: Holocaust Survivors and the Successful Lives They Made in America* (New York: Simon and Schuster, 1992); and Rosenfeld, "Americanization of the Holocaust." While this paper concerns survivors' experience in the United States, their stigmatization in the very different context of Israel makes for a fascinating comparison. See especially Tom Segev, *The Seventh Million: The Israelis and the Holocaust,* trans. H. Watzman (New York: Hill and Wang, 1993), and Dalia Ofer, "Israel," in *World Reacts to the Holocaust,* ed. Wyman and Rozenzveig.

21. Elie Wiesel, "A Plea for Survivors," in *A Jew Today,* trans. M. Wiesel (New York: Random House, 1978), 193–94.

22. Both of the survivors whose reflections appear in this section—"Manny Petchek" and "Paula Marcus"—are identified by pseudonyms.

23. See Wyman, "United States," esp. 720–21, and Annette Wieviorka, "On Testimony," in *Holocaust Remembrance: The Shapes of Memory,* ed. Geoffrey Hartman (Oxford: Blackwell, 1994), 22–32.

24. Levi, *Survival in Auschwitz,* 9. See also Ferdinando Camon, *Conversations with Primo Levi* (Marlboro, Vt.: Marlboro, 1989), 42.

25. Wiesel, *Jew Today,* 200.

26. Paula Marcus's diary was originally written in Hungarian and translated into English by Marcus herself. This extraordinary document will be included in its entirety in *Reflections,* Marcus's soon-to-be-published memoir.

27. A scene somewhat similar to Paula's memory is described in the testimony of Shmuel Krakowski. Krakowski wrote about a first meeting between women survivors of the death marches and Jewish soldiers in the Polish Armored Corps:

> The officers asked many questions. They were eager to know where the women came from and all the details of their suffering in the ghettos and camps. One after the other, the women told their story of their unbelievable experiences under the Nazis. The stories were interrupted with expressions of great happiness: to be able to sit here, secure, with Jewish officers, to tell them their stories. . . .

In Yehudit Kleinman and Nina Springer-Aharoni, eds., *The Anguish of Liberation: Testimonies from 1945* (Jerusalem: Yad Vashem, 1995), 16.

28. Cf. Greenspan, "Who Can Retell?" 77–78.

29. Quoted in Sylvia Rothchild, ed., *Voices from the Holocaust* (New York: New American Library, 1981), 373.

30. In ibid., 381–82.

31. See Raul Hilberg, both "Opening Remarks" and *The Politics of Memory: The Journey of a Holocaust Historian* (Chicago: Ivan R. Dee, 1996), 123–24; Wyman, "United States," 724–28.

32. Cf. Hank Greenspan, "On Being a 'Real Survivor,' " *Sh'ma,* Mar. 29, 1996, 1–3.

33. Christopher Lasch, *The Culture of Narcissism: American Life in an Age of Diminishing Expectations* (New York: Norton, 1979), 2–7, 52–70; Lasch, *The Minimal Self: Psychic Survival in Troubled Times* (New York: Norton, 1984), 60–129.

34. *New Yorker,* Jan. 8, 1979, drawing by Warren Miller, 40. Cf. Lasch, *Minimal Self,* esp. 60–73. In general, I would suggest that the depth of the late-1970s preoccupation with extremity remains unappreciated, a trend that extended from the core to the periphery of popular imagination. Among the other kinds of survival stories that suddenly surfaced in this period are those of victims of satanic cults, UFO abduction, and the variety of tabloid television programs about them. Likewise, beyond the personal choices of America's most successful filmmaker, there is also much shared preoccupation that connects films like *Close Encounters of the Third Kind* (1977), *Poltergeist* (1982), and *Schindler's List* (1993): a preoccupation with surviving "far out" encounters.

35. Beyond such references to "downsizing," cynicism, and so on, this essay does not address the question of *why* the wider culture of "survivors" and "survivalism" itself developed. That discussion, important as it is, would take us too far beyond the scope of present purposes. But, along with Lasch's two volumes listed above, I would at least mention the following recent analyses, which differ philosophically but are all essential reading on this question: Kai Erikson, *A New Species of Trouble: The Human Experience of Modern Disasters* (New York: Norton, 1994); Donald Kanter and Philip Mirvis, *The Cynical Americans: Living and Working in an Age of Discontent and Disil-*

lusion (San Francisco: Jossey-Bass, 1989); Charles Derber, *The Wilding of America* (New York: St. Martin's, 1996); and Michael Sandel, *Democracy's Discontent: America in Search of a Public Philosophy* (Cambridge: Belknap Press of Harvard University Press, 1996). This essay won't do much to remedy the situation, but it might be said that, in general, the discussion of the "Americanization of the Holocaust" has tended to go on outside systematic analysis of American culture itself.

36. On the surge of general psychological writing on "posttraumatic stress" since the late 1970s, see Dudley David Blake, Anne Marie Albano, and Terence Keane, "Twenty Years of Trauma: *Psychological Abstracts* 1970 through 1989," *Journal of Traumatic Stress* 5 (1992): 477–84. An excellent piece on the association between the general discussion of "PTSD" and Holocaust survivors specifically is Ghislaine Boulanger's review of Judith Herman's *Trauma and Recovery* in *Tikkun*, Mar.–Apr. 1994, 84–85. Both of these articles note that "posttraumatic stress disorder" became a diagnostic entity officially recognized by the American Psychiatric Association in 1980.

37. Gustav Bychowski, "Permanent Character Changes as an Aftereffect of Persecution," in *Massive Psychic Trauma*, ed. Krystal, 86.

38. PBS, "Holocaust: The Survivors Gather—June 15, 1981," June 15, 1981.

39. The following excerpts from an article about Denver-area survivors who attended the World Gathering speak for themselves:

> As international reporters made headlines out of the occasional tearful reunions of relatives of friends, Samuel Silver witnessed the looks of disappointment on the faces of those who found nobody. . . . "All those years, we lived with wounds that stopped bleeding," Silver illustrates. "But the wounds were still there. In Jerusalem the wounds started to bleed again."
>
> Stephanie Gross bristles when told that some observers have said that the World Gathering of Jewish Holocaust Survivors represented a "victory over death."
>
> She points to a collection of old family photographs on the wall, showing the faces of in-laws murdered by the Nazis. "How could this be a victory?" she asks. "Everybody loses. This was no victory. It was survival."

From Chris Leppek, *Intermountain Jewish News* (Denver), July 3, 1981.

40. PBS, "Holocaust: The Survivors Gather—June 17, 1981," June 17, 1981.

41. Ibid., June 18, 1981.

42. It should be noted that the rhetoric of "legacies" and "stories" is also applied to other groups who have suffered massive misfortune. As a single example, a prepublication ad for the book *Polio's Legacy: An Oral History* was written in a language virtually identical to the fliers one receives for new collections of survivor testimony. The copy stated, "This book shows readers the reality of polio and how it alters human lives. Thirty-five polio survivors open their hearts to explain their experiences. . . . The result is this written tribute to the survival of the human spirit. . . . Readers will see how polio's legacy reveals itself through these stories."

43. In light of the contemporary fascination with survivors' testimony and their psychology, it is recurrently surprising to read the eulogies for survivors of an earlier

time. Discussing the benefits of offering survivors psychotherapy, Paul Chodoff wrote this in the late 1970s, on the very edge of the new interest in survivors that would soon follow: "With the passage of time, their melancholy tale is almost told. Even those who were small children during the persecution have now reached middle age, while most of the survivors still left are even older. Thus, although certainly they deserve whatever help we can give them . . . the focus of our attention should be shifting to the problems of the second generation . . . [the] children of the survivors." Chodoff, "Psychotherapy of the Survivor," 216.

44. Louis Uchitelle and N. R. Kleinfeld, "On the Battlefields of Business, Millions of Casualties," *New York Times,* Mar. 3, 1996 ("The Downsizing of America: First of Seven Articles").

45. Ibid.; N. R. Kleinfeld, "The Company as Family, No More," *New York Times,* Mar. 4, 1996.

46. Ibid.

47. Cf. esp. Lasch, "The Survival Mentality," in *Minimal Self,* 60–99, and Kanter and Mirvis, "Cynicism in American Life," in *Cynical Americans,* 1–25.

48. Indeed, given how *untypical* is the sentimentalizing of Holocaust survivors' experience in the wider discourse on "survival" in America today, we might wonder how deep it actually goes. To say it differently: it has been almost a truism in work in this area, including my own, that the prevailing American tendency is to romanticize and sentimentalize the Holocaust. That is certainly accurate descriptively. But perhaps we should keep in mind that relying too much on American sentimentality may itself be sentimental. And the celebratory discourse on Holocaust survivors—particularly as it becomes most mawkish and insistent—may well overlay much darker intuitions. Although there are only hints to this point, we may in fact be witnessing the emergence of a "cynical discourse" about Holocaust survivors as well. It takes the form of idealizing survivors as hyperrealists, quintessentially "savvy" and "street smart." Lasch described an earlier version of this in his discussion of the reception of the film *Seven Beauties.* See his *Minimal Self,* 122–24.

49. "On the Battlefields of Business."

50. Sara Rimer, "A Hometown Feels Less Like Home," *New York Times,* Mar. 6, 1996.

CHAPTER 4. JAMES E. YOUNG / AMERICA'S HOLOCAUST

1. See James E. Young, *The Texture of Memory: Holocaust Memorials and Meaning* (New Haven: Yale University Press, 1993), 1–15. This essay is adapted from part 4 of that book, "America: The Politics of Memory," 283–349.

2. See Peter Burger, *The Theory of the Avant Garde,* trans. Michael Shaw (Minneapolis: University of Minnesota Press, 1984). Burger defines the "functional analysis of art" as an examination of the artwork's "social effect (function), which is the result of the coming together of stimuli emanating from within the work itself and a sociologically definable public" (87).

3. From the Jewish Telegraphic Agency press bulletin, Dec. 2, 1942. I am grateful to Lucia Ruedenberg for alerting me to this reference in her "'Remember 6,000,000':

Civic Commemoration of the Holocaust in New York City" (Ph.D. diss., New York University, 1994).

4. See Atay Citron, "Pageantry and Theatre in the Service of Jewish Nationalism in the United States: 1933–1946" (Ph.D. diss., New York University, 1989).

5. Quoted in "City Rejects Park Memorials to Slain Jews," *New York Times*, Feb. 11, 1965, 1; and in "Two Jewish Monuments Barred from Park," *New York World Telegram and Sun*, Feb. 10, 1965, 1.

6. For more on the political dimension of this memorial museum, see Michael Berenbaum, *After Tragedy and Triumph: Essays on Modern Jewish Thought and the American Experience* (Cambridge: Cambridge University Press, 1991), 3–16. For an explicit record of the museum's conceptualization and development, see Edward T. Linenthal, *Preserving Memory: The Struggle to Create America's Holocaust Museum* (New York: Viking, 1995). For further details on the controversy surrounding the establishment of the U.S. Holocaust Memorial Commission, see Judith Miller, *One by One by One: Facing the Holocaust* (New York: Simon and Schuster, 1990), 255–66.

7. Charles Maier, *The Unmasterable Past: History, Holocaust, and German National Identity* (Cambridge: Harvard University Press, 1988), 165.

8. Undated press release of the U.S. Holocaust Memorial Council.

9. *The Campaign for the United States Holocaust Memorial Museum*, published by the U.S. Holocaust Memorial Council, n.d., 4.

10. Ibid.

11. George Will, "Holocaust Museum: Antidote for Innocence," *Washington Post*, Mar. 10, 1983.

12. Berenbaum, *After Tragedy and Triumph*, 20.

13. Quoted in Cassandra Burrell, "Supporters of African-American Museum Object to Smithsonian Control," Associated Press, Sept. 15, 1992.

14. James Ingo Freed, "The United States Holocaust Memorial Museum," *Assemblage* 9 (1989): 61. Hereafter cited parenthetically.

15. James Ingo Freed, "The United States Holocaust Museum: What Can It Be?" printed by the United States Holocaust Memorial Museum, n.d.

16. For details on the exhibition walkthrough, I rely here on both my own visits and on museum project director Michael Berenbaum's provisional walkthrough, "A Visit to the Permanent Exhibition: The United States Holocaust Memorial Museum," which he generously provided me before the museum's opening.

17. See Jonathan Rosen, "America's Holocaust," *Forward*, Apr. 12, 1991.

18. Berenbaum, *After Tragedy and Triumph*, 7.

CHAPTER 5. ANDREW FURMAN / INHERITING THE HOLOCAUST

Epigraph: Thane Rosenbaum, *Elijah Visible* (New York: St. Martin's, 1996), 58–59. Hereafter cited parenthetically.

1. Lionel Trilling, *The Liberal Imagination* (Garden City, N.Y.: Doubleday, 1953), 256.

2. See S. Lillian Kremer, *Witness through the Imagination: Jewish American Holocaust Literature* (Detroit: Wayne State University Press, 1989), 36–45.

3. Quoted in Granville Hicks, "One Man to Stand for Six Million," *Saturday Review*, Sept. 10, 1966, 37.

4. Robert Alter, "Confronting the Holocaust: Three Israeli Novels," *Commentary*, Mar. 1966, 67.

5. Alan L. Berger, *Crisis and Covenant: The Holocaust in American Jewish Fiction* (Albany: State University of New York Press, 1985), 160.

6. Alan L. Berger, "American Jewish Fiction," *Modern Judaism* 10 (1990): 226.

7. Philip Roth, *The Ghost Writer* (1979; New York: Fawcett Crest, 1980), 209.

8. Ibid., 136, 174.

9. Michael E. Staub, "The Shoah Goes On and On: Remembrance and Representation in Art Spiegelman's *Maus*," *MELUS* 20, no. 3 (1995): 33.

10. Cynthia Ozick, interviewed by Elaine M. Kauvar, "An Interview with Cynthia Ozick," *Contemporary Literature* 34, no. 3 (1993): 381.

11. Ibid., 390, 391.

12. Cynthia Ozick, "The Art of Fiction XCV," *Paris Review* 29 (1987): 184–85.

13. Ted Solotaroff, "The Open Community," introduction to *Writing Our Way Home: Contemporary Stories by American Jewish Writers*, ed. Ted Solotaroff and Nessa Rapoport (New York: Schocken Books, 1992), xxiii.

14. Kremer, *Witness through the Imagination*, 15.

15. Solotaroff, "Open Community," xxiii.

16. Victor Strandberg, *Greek Mind/Jewish Soul: The Conflicted Art of Cynthia Ozick* (Madison: University of Wisconsin Press, 1994), 38.

17. See Alan L. Berger's "Ashes and Hope," in *Reflections of the Holocaust in Art and Literature*, ed. Randolph L. Braham (New York: Columbia University Press, 1990), 97–116; "Bearing Witness," *Modern Judaism* 10 (1990): 43–63; and esp. *Children of Job: American Second-Generation Witnesses to the Holocaust* (Albany: State University of New York Press, 1997).

18. See Philip Roth, "Eli, the Fanatic," in *Goodbye, Columbus, and Five Short Stories* (1959; New York: Modern Library, 1995), 249–98.

19. Leslie Fiedler, *Fiedler on the Roof: Essays on Literature and Jewish Identity* (Boston: David R. Godine, 1991), 160.

20. Julius Lester, "The Lives People Live," in *Blacks and Jews: Alliances and Arguments*, ed. Paul Berman (New York: Delacorte, 1994), 173.

21. Robert Cohen, *The Here and Now* (New York: Scribner, 1996), 257.

22. Philip Roth, *The Counterlife* (1987; New York: Penguin, 1988), 188–89.

23. Arthur Hertzberg, *The Jews in America: Four Centuries of an Uneasy Encounter: A History* (New York: Simon and Schuster, 1989), 332.

24. See Saul Bellow, "The Old System," *Mosby's Memoirs and Other Stories* (1968; New York: Penguin, 1984), 43–83.

1. Art Spiegelman, *Maus, A Survivor's Tale, Part I: My Father Bleeds History* (New York: Pantheon Books, 1986), 159. Hereafter cited parenthetically as *I*.

2. Berel Lang, "The Representation of Limits," in *Probing the Limits of Representation,* ed. Saul Friedlander (Cambridge: Harvard University Press, 1992), 316. Hereafter cited parenthetically as RL.

3. Eddy M. Zemach, "Custodians," in *Jewish Identity,* ed. David Theo Goldberg and Michael Krausz (Philadelphia: Temple University Press, 1993), 123.

4. Barbara Kingsolver, *Pigs in Heaven* (New York: HarperCollins, 1993).

5. Paul Ritterband, "Modern Times and Jewish Assimilation," in *The Americanization of the Jews,* ed. Robert M. Seltzer and Norman J. Cohen (New York: New York University Press, 1995), 378.

6. Charles S. Liebman, "Jewish Survival, Antisemitism, and Negotiation with the Tradition," in *Americanization of the Jews,* ed. Seltzer and Cohen, 436–37. The whole of "Part Seven: Surviving as Jews in Twenty-first-Century America" in that volume is of interest with regard to these issues.

7. See Arthur Hertzberg, "Conclusion: The End of Immigrant Memory," in *The Jews in America: Four Centuries of an Uneasy Encounter: A History* (New York: Simon and Schuster, 1989), 377–88.

8. Zemach, "Custodians," 123.

9. See ibid., 128. It is clear that Zemach is committed not to the intrinsic value of perpetuation but rather to the intrinsic value of diversity, though the rhetoric of cultural death cannot be said to be the same as the interest in diversity. It is the pathos of dying that motivates the effort to avoid cultural death, while it is the value of different kinds of life that motivates the effort to ensure diversity.

10. Michael Goldberg, *Why Should Jews Survive? Looking Past the Holocaust toward a Jewish Future* (New York: Oxford University Press, 1995).

11. See Hertzberg, *Jews in America,* 382–83, for one brief account of how, and why, the Jewish community turned to the Holocaust as the ground for Jewish identity.

12. Lang summarizes his formula as follows:

> The formula thus asserts that the risk or burden of evidence incurred in choosing among alternative historical representations increases—first—in proportion to the distance between the alternative chosen and those rejected; and secondly, with that distance multiplied by a moral weight assigned to the common issue at stake between them. In its mathematical form this would be $R = (A_1 - A_2) \times W$. How the "weight" (of W) is determined is not itself part of the formula, although it emerges as a function of the moral community in which the judgment is made. (RL, 309)

13. To summarize the difference, the functionalist account takes the absence of a "*Führer* order" in the chronicle to mean that Hitler did not intend the entire trajectory of the Final Solution, that the killing of the Jews and others in camps was the result of many individual actions and intentions. The intentionalist account asserts that

Hitler and the top Nazi officials did conceive of and intend the entire shape and trajectory of violence against Jews during the war.

14. It is tempting, because of its title, to assimilate to Lang's point of view Pierre Vidal-Naquet's argument in *Assassins of Memory: Essays on the Denial of the Holocaust* (originally published in France in 1987, subsequently translated by Jeffrey Mehlman and published by Columbia University Press in 1992). But I would suggest that for Vidal-Naquet the rhetoric of murder is a sign of the intensity of his criticism of the revisionist historians rather than the indicator of a theoretical stance with regard to representations. Vidal-Naquet attacks the revisionists—albeit reluctantly—on the grounds of history and on the grounds of their clear anti-Semitic intentions, not on the grounds that the facts they distort are morally present and by right should be treated like persons. It is worth noting, however, that the French have indeed embraced a definition of revisionism that appears to be grounded on the conflation I have described in Lang's philosophy: Holocaust denial—or the denial of genocide—is now a crime in France, which suggests that the Holocaust itself (as it exists in non-revisionist representations of history, that is) merits protection in the same way that persons (in libel laws, for example) merit protection.

15. Lang cites an attempt made by a group of French historians to curb such revisionism in which the historians claim "a moral presence for matters of fact" (RL, 313). Again, only persons have moral *presence;* such presence is not, in our practical experience, attributed to inanimate objects. The extent to which an inanimate object—a chair, for instance—is at issue in moral dilemmas is the extent to which it is attached to human beings: I do not take that chair because it belongs to someone else; if I do take it, I violate the *person's* rights, not the chair's.

16. The relative weight of each part of this dual mission has been the subject of controversy throughout the museum's short history. For an account of the effort to define the museum's mission, see Jeshajahu Weinberg and Rina Elieli, *The Holocaust Museum in Washington* (New York: Rizzoli, 1995).

17. The identity cards are just the first stage of the complete identification the museum design seeks to produce over the course of any individual's visit. Museum designer Ralph Applebaum describes how the entire interior of the museum seeks to replicate the journey of the victims "as they moved from their normal lives into ghettos, out of ghettos into trains, from trains into camps, within the pathways of the camps, until finally to the end. . . . [If] visitors could take that same journey," Applebaum claims, "they would understand the story because they will have experienced the story." Applebaum, "For the Living," WETA-TV (PBS) transcript, roll 128, t-27, 3–4, quoted in Edward T. Linenthal, "The Boundaries of Memory: The United States Holocaust Memorial Museum," *American Quarterly* 46 (1994): 410.

18. *Schindler's List,* dir. Steven Spielberg (Universal Pictures, 1993).

19. See, among other articles about the director and the film, Edward Guthman, "Spielberg's 'List': Director Rediscovers His Jewishness While Filming Nazi Story," *San Francisco Chronicle,* Dec. 12, 1993, reprinted in *Oskar Schindler and His List: The Man, the Book, the Film, the Holocaust, and Its Survivors,* ed. Thomas Fensch (Forest Dale, Vt.: Paul S. Eriksson, 1995), 50–55.

20. Art Spiegelman, *Maus, A Survivor's Tale, Part II: And Here My Troubles Began* (New York: Pantheon Books, 1991), 11. Hereafter cited parenthetically as *II*.

21. Spiegelman has subsequently produced an ironic twist on this use of Nazi discourse to define identities in the present. "Mein Kampf, My Struggle," a two-page cartoon spread appearing in the *New York Times Magazine*'s special issue on confessional writing (May 11, 1996, 36–37), shows the (human-headed) cartoonist walking the underground terrain of his mind, stalked by an enormous mouse. In this version of *Mein Kampf*, Hitler's paranoia about the Jews becomes Art's paranoia about the success of his Jewish mice. He complains that "remembering those who remembered the death camps is a tough act to follow." But it seems that the camps will define Jews forever, even against the discontinuity of generations that Spiegelman points out here ("My parents died," he writes in a box over the frame showing his crying son Dashiell, "before I had any kids"). The cartoon ends as Art begins the story of the next generation: "Dash is four years old, and his sister is almost nine. (Two of their grandparents survived Auschwitz.)" Here Spiegelman appears to recognize the tyranny of *employing* the Nazi definition, casting himself in Hitler's role as he bequeaths that definition to the next generation. When speaking of *Maus*, on the other hand, Spiegelman is clear that employing the Nazi definition was felicitous: he claims that *Maus* "was made in *collaboration* with Hitler" (original emphasis; Art Spiegelman, "Drawing Pens and Politics: Mightier Than the Sore-head," *The Nation*, Jan. 17, 1994, 46, quoted in Thomas Doherty, "Art Spiegelman's *Maus*: Graphic Art and the Holocaust," *American Literature* 68 [1996]: 74). Doherty examines how Spiegelman's cartoon constructs its relation to the history of certain visual media, including that of Third Reich political cartooning and cinema—which is why he is interested in this "collaboration." Doherty's essay, along with Joseph Witek's study, *Comic Books as History: The Narrative Art of Jack Jackson, Art Spiegelman, and Harvey Pekar* (Jackson: University Press of Mississippi, 1989), provides a historical and generic context in which to understand *Maus*, making it distinct both from the main body of existing *Maus* criticism and from the present essay.

22. See Marianne Hirsch, "Family Pictures: *Maus*, Mourning, and Post-memory," *Discourse* 15, no. 2 (1992–93): 3–28. Hirsch writes that "the really shocking and disturbing breaks in the visual narrative—the points that fail to blend in—are the actual photographs and the one moment in which the drawing style and convention changes (in *Prisoner on the Hell Planet*)" (16). I argue just the opposite, that these are precisely not breaks in narrative but rather the endpoint of narrative's work, which is to make the mouse head *real.*

23. The question of why Spiegelman uses mouse-persons is of course taken up—in passing, at least, if not as a central concern—by every critic who writes about these books. Short reviews have tended to read the animal heads as a way of defamiliarizing what has become a commercialized story. Michael Rothberg pushes this thesis to its limit with his claim that the animal heads give the reader a "shock of obscenity" that will be Spiegelman's strategy for representing a particularly American version of Jewish identity (Rothberg, " 'We Were Talking Jewish': Art Spiegelman's *Maus* as 'Holocaust' Production," *Contemporary Literature* 35 [1994]: 661–87). Joshua Brown reads

the heads as an allegory for "the social relations of Eastern Europe"; he argues that Spiegelman's use of Hitler's racist paradigm undermines that paradigm because the animal heads bring it to "its fullest, tense realization" (Brown, "Of Mice and Memory," *Oral History Review* 16 [1988]: 105–8). While the allegory might hold for Vladek's story, it does not explain why Americans like Art still wear the marks of the "social relations of Eastern Europe"; accounting for this fact would require Brown to make a distinction—which he does not in fact make—between the mouse head and the mouse mask. Miles Orvell, on the other hand, recognizes the distinction between the mouse mask and the mouse head and reads in it a distinction between Art (who, Orvell argues, feels "inauthentic" once his father has died) and his father (whose identity is "more authentic"). Art's "inauthenticity" is the sign of what Orvell calls the "sense of living posthistorically" (Orvell, "Writing Posthistorically: *Krazy Kat, Maus,* and the Contemporary Fiction Cartoon," *American Literary History* 4 [1992]: 110–28). While Orvell is undoubtedly correct that the mask indicates inauthenticity, he leaves unexamined the way Art becomes inauthentic and the way he returns to authenticity; these transitions, rather than the fact of the mask itself, reveal the character of the identity Spiegelman creates with the mouse head. Hirsch has explained the change from head to mask as progress from duplication of "the Nazi's racist refusal of the possibility of assimilation or cultural integration" to a moment when "in *Maus II* these dichotomous attitudes blur" (Hirsch, "Family Pictures," 13). For Hirsch, then, the heads extend the divisions of history into the present, but the changes from mask to head and back indicate only that "access to [Spiegelman's] mouse identity [has become] more mediated" (13).

24. Spiegelman has claimed that in fact it is his lack of specific information about his father and mother's experience that makes the "blank" mouse faces appropriate, and that makes them attach more closely with real persons. He explains that "it would be counterfeit to try to pretend that the drawings are representations of something that's actually happening. I don't know what a German looked like who was in a small town doing a specific thing. . . . To use these ciphers, the cats and mice, is actually a way to allow you past the cipher at the people who are experiencing it. So it's really a much more direct way of dealing with the material." Spiegelman and Françoise Mouly, "Jewish Mice, Bubblegum Cards, Comics Art and Raw Possibilities," interview by Joey Cavalieri, *Comics Journal* 65 (1981): 105–6, quoted in Witek, *Comic Books as History,* 102.

25. Art conflates himself with his mother as well in the first volume of *Maus.* In the short comic "Prisoner on the Hell Planet: A Case History" included in *Maus I,* Art accuses his mother of having "*murdered*" (original emphasis) him when in fact she has killed herself. Outside the covers of *Maus,* Spiegelman has described his breakdown at the age of twenty—just before his mother's suicide—in terms of conflation with his parents: in the hospital he apparently actually hoarded string as his father had at Auschwitz (see David Gerber, "Of Mice and Jews: Cartoons, Metaphors, and Children of Holocaust Survivors in Recent Jewish Experience: A Review Essay," *American Jewish History* 77 [1987]: 164). Michael Staub has claimed that both Art's accusation of his mother and his accusation of Vladek at the end of *Maus I* "work to undercut . . . any impulse readers might have to see survivors—or their children—as either saints or he-

roes" (Staub, "The Shoah Goes On and On: Remembrance and Representation in Art Spiegelman's *Maus*," *MELUS* 20, no. 3 [1995]: 41). While it may be the case that the behavior we see in these scenes makes it difficult to categorize characters as "saint" or "hero," what is more important is that the scenes *do* produce other categories—"murderer" and "victim" and by extension "survivor"—that can be occupied in turn by Art, Vladek, and Anja. In contrast, Hirsch's reading of *Maus's* photographs, while both registering and describing the conflation, in fact relies on it. She argues that "these family photographs are documents both of memory (the survivor's) and of what I would like to call post-memory (that of the child of the survivor whose life is dominated by memories of what preceded his/her birth)" (Hirsch, "Family Pictures," 8). Crucially, Hirsch's sentence does not make clear whose memories dominate the child's life; they appear to belong to the child in spite of the fact that the memories are of things that "preceded his/her birth." The analysis, then, not only describes the conflation but replicates it.

26. For a brief description of this debate and of Wardi's place within it, see Dina Wardi, *Memorial Candles: Children of the Holocaust*, trans. Naomi Goldblum (New York: Routledge, 1992), 5–6. For another version of the "second-generation" debate—one that does not share Wardi's assumptions—see Gerber, "Of Mice and Jews," 164–65. Gerber also provides a list of the key texts in this debate.

27. Wardi, *Memorial Candles*, 2, 5.

28. The members of the group frequently share memories and imagined scenarios. Their conversations with one another often focus on comparing dreams and the feelings that go with them, and often seem to produce an agreement that their dreams mean similar things. On some occasions group members take the images of another's dream and play them out in their own imagination of their parents' traumas. It is clear from Wardi's commentary on these conversations that the "work" of therapy is done through the production of emotion; in the effort to produce emotion—or to put it in the language of popular psychology, to *access* emotion that is already there in the unconscious—any kind of imaginative work, including making up stories or focusing on someone else's dream images, is helpful if it produces the desired response. Wardi would not claim that these constructions constitute memory or that their truth is either available or important, and she reminds herself and her reader more than once that these young people did not in fact experience the Holocaust; nevertheless, the identification with the survivor figure that the therapists encourage relies on these images and on the transferability of memory and emotion between persons.

29. Freud admits that he needs a biological transmission of guilt and trauma in order to produce the kinds of behavior he thinks make up the Jewish character; cultural or "face-to-face" transmission alone is not enough to produce the powerful influence of the primal murder that he sees in the history of the Jewish people. Notoriously, Lamarckism provided that biological account, but Freud knew that Lamarck's theories had been discredited by modern genetics. Freud's history is, of course, speculative (he originally called it a "historical novel"); he does not presume to have solved the problem of transmission even if he does think that *Moses and Monotheism* tells the truth about Jewish character.

30. The notion of absorption is the most striking of these because it relies on physical transmission rather than on cultural or psychological transmission while nevertheless avoiding the claim of biological transmission. Wardi suggests that as a baby she "absorbed" some of the "thoughts and anxieties running through her father's head" when he came home and held her in his arms after doing relief work for Jews in prewar Italy. Wardi, *Memorial Candles,* 2.

31. The process of therapy itself aims to produce Jewish identity, or, to use Wardi's terms, the late stages of therapy are often signaled by an interest in seeing oneself as part of the Jewish nation. Wardi describes this as a sign of health, as the marker of "mature" identification with the traumas the parents experienced.

32. In 1997, a year after this analysis was completed, Art Spiegelman came out with a children's book entitled *Open Me . . . I'm a Dog!* (New York: HarperCollins). A black fabric leash dangles from the top of the book's spine, the front and back fly-leaves are cut from fuzzy paper, and the blurb on the back cover reads, "Through the magic of words and pictures leaps a book that's not only playful as a puppy—it is a puppy! Honest." It seems clear that the point I am making here about *Maus* brings to light what we can now see as Spiegelman's continuing interest in imagining representation as if it were the equivalent of a person—or in this case, a talking dog.

33. Art Spiegelman, "A Problem of Taxonomy," *New York Times Book Review,* Dec. 29, 1991, 4.

34. This is not the only time the *Book Review*'s categorizing has given rise to this argument. The editors placed Forrest Carter's *The Education of Little Tree,* a memoir about growing up with Cherokee grandparents, on the nonfiction list, but critics soon revealed that Carter was in fact a Ku Klux Klan member and segregationist speechwriter, a.k.a. Asa Carter, and that despite the claim on the front cover, "A True Story by Forrest Carter," the story of Little Tree was entirely fabricated. The *Book Review* duly moved the title to the fiction list. It is no coincidence that this other case of "taxonomic difficulty" (as Spiegelman puts it in his letter to the editor) also arose with regard to racial or cultural identity. As Henry Louis Gates Jr. has pointed out, fake testimonials and memoirs attributed to minority authors have been used for over a century for purposes ranging from the effort to abolish slavery to the need to sell books. While Gates goes on to reflect about the importance of literal truth value in only the vaguest of ways—reminding the reader, for example, that "a book is a cultural event; authorial identity, mystified or not, can be part of that event," and that "fact and fiction have always exerted a reciprocal effect on each other" (Gates, "'Authenticity,' or the Lesson of Little Tree," *New York Times Book Review,* Nov. 24, 1991, 29)—*Maus* makes it quite clear why literal truth value is powerful, and why it is powerful in works of the 1980s and 1990s in a way that it is not in the slave narratives Gates points to. Narratives of cultural identity—and in particular minority cultural identity—in the twentieth century assume the status of personhood in a way that slave narratives in the nineteenth century did not. Thus, the classification of these representations as fiction or nonfiction has come to imply a classification of people.

CHAPTER 7. JOYCE ANTLER /
"THREE THOUSAND MILES AWAY"

This is a revised version of my essay "The Americanization of the Holocaust," which appeared in American Theatre, Feb. 1995, 16–20, 69. I am grateful to Elinor Fuchs and Daniel Jacobs for comments on an earlier version. See also Joyce Antler, "Historical Resonances," in Broken Glass Playbill, Long Wharf Theater, Mar.–Apr. 1994, 25, 27.

1. Arthur Miller, *Broken Glass* (New York: Penguin, 1994), 20. Hereafter cited parenthetically.

2. Quoted in Lawrence Graver, *An Obsession with Anne Frank: Meyer Levin and the Diary* (Berkeley: University of California Press, 1995), 94. See also Meyer Levin, *The Obsession* (New York: Simon and Schuster, 1973), and Frances Goodrich and Albert Hackett, *The Diary of Anne Frank* (New York: Random House, 1956). Lawrence L. Langer writes about *The Diary of Anne Frank*, Arthur Miller's *Incident at Vichy*, and other early U.S. representations of the Holocaust in "The Americanization of the Holocaust on Stage and Screen," in *From Hester Street to Hollywood: The Jewish-American Stage and Screen*, ed. Sarah Blacher Cohen (Bloomington: Indiana University Press, 1983), 213–30. On film, see also Judith E. Doneson, *The Holocaust in American Film* (Philadelphia: Jewish Publication Society, 1987). More recently, see Cynthia Ozick, "A Critic at Large: Who Owns Anne Frank?" *New Yorker*, Oct. 6, 1997, 76–87.

3. See also the reviews of 2 in *Philadelphia Inquirer*, Jan. 9, 1994, and of *Who Will Carry the Word?* in *New York Times*, Nov. 10, 1993.

4. Arthur Miller, "A Foreword by the Author," *After the Fall*, quoted in Alice Griffin, *Understanding Arthur Miller* (Columbia: University of South Carolina Press, 1996), 114.

5. Quoted in Edward Isser, "Arthur Miller and the Holocaust," *Essays in Theatre* 10, no. 2 (1992): 158.

6. Enoch Brater, "Ethics and Ethnicity in the Plays of Arthur Miller," in *From Hester Street to Hollywood*, ed. Cohen, 130. Brater notes that the play's title refers not only to the biblical Fall, the expulsion from the Garden of Eden, but also, according to Miller, to Camus's *The Fall*, in which a juror, walking home along an embankment, fails to act when he sees a Jew pushed into the canal.

7. Quoted in Richard I. Evans, *Psychology and Arthur Miller* (New York: Praeger, 1981), 74.

8. Barbara Gelb, "Question: 'Am I My Brother's Keeper,'" *New York Times*, Nov. 29, 1964, quoted in Griffin, *Understanding Arthur Miller*, 135.

9. Isser believes that in this script as well as in *After the Fall* and *Incident at Vichy*, Miller exhibits a "fallacious understanding of the historical situation" that is more like propaganda than fact. Isser, "Miller and the Holocaust," 158–59.

10. Ibid., 82–83.

11. "The Jew in me shie[s] from private salvation as something close to sin," Miller noted in *Timebends* (New York: Grove, 1987). "One's truth must add its push to the evolution of public justice and mercy" (82–83).

12. See, e.g., James A. Robinson, "Both His Sons: Arthur Miller's *The Price* and Jewish Assimilation," in *Staging Difference: Cultural Pluralism in American Theatre and Drama,* ed. Mark Maufort (New York: Peter Lang, 1995), 123.

13. In 1939 Miller began a play called *The Golden Years* about the violence of Kristallnacht, which triggers the events of *Broken Glass.* But he put the play aside, and it received its first performance only in 1987. In this regard it is the progenitor of *Broken Glass.* Christopher Bigsby, "Arthur Miller's Journey to *Broken Glass,*" in *Broken Glass* Playbill, Long Wharf Theater, Mar.–Apr. 1994, 20.

14. Miller notes that when he was working in the Brooklyn Navy Yard in the early 1940s, none of his fellow workers, many of them profoundly anti-Semitic, had any idea of the horrors of Nazism. Anti-Semitism remained a taboo topic in fiction and drama. Arthur Miller, "The Face in the Mirror: Anti-Semitism Then and Now," *New York Times,* Oct. 14, 1984.

15. Bigsby, "Miller's Journey to *Broken Glass,*" 21.

16. Douglas Century, "Miller's Tale of 'Tribalism': The Playwright Returns to His Roots," *Forward,* Apr. 22, 1994.

17. Henry L. Feingold, *A Time for Searching: Entering the Mainstream, 1920–1945* (Baltimore: Johns Hopkins University Press, 1992), 250–52. See also Feingold, *Bearing Witness: How America and Its Jews Responded to the Holocaust* (Syracuse: Syracuse University Press, 1995), and Deborah E. Lipstadt, *Beyond Belief: The American Press and the Coming of the Holocaust, 1933–1945* (New York: Free Press, 1986), esp. 98–109. On Kristallnacht, see also Michael Berenbaum, *The World Must Know: The History of the Holocaust as Told in the United States Holocaust Memorial Museum* (Boston: Little, Brown, 1993).

18. Lynne Sharon Schwartz, *Leaving Brooklyn* (Boston: Houghton Mifflin, 1989), 48.

19. See, e.g., Deborah Dash Moore, *At Home in America: Second-Generation New York Jews* (New York: Columbia University Press, 1981), 24–25.

20. On the Goldbergs, see Donald Weber, "The Jewish-American World of Gertrude Berg: The *Goldbergs* on Radio and Television, 1930–1950," in *Talking Back: Images of Jewish Women in American Popular Culture,* ed. Joyce Antler (Hanover, N.H.: University of New England Press, 1997), 85–102.

21. Lucy Dawidowicz, "Jewish Identity: A Matter of Fate, a Matter of Choice," in *The Jewish Presence: Essays on Identity and History* (New York: Holt, Rinehart, and Winston, 1977), 7. On anti-Semitism in the United States, see Leonard Dinnerstein, *Anti-Semitism in America* (New York: Oxford University Press, 1994), and David A. Gerber, ed., *Anti-Semitism in American History* (Urbana: University of Illinois Press, 1987).

22. Miller, *Timebends,* 27. On German Jewish women's responses, see Marion A. Kaplan, "Jewish Women in Nazi Germany: Daily Life, Daily Struggle, 1933–1939," in *Different Voices: Women and the Holocaust,* ed. Carol Rittner and John K. Roth (New York: Paragon House, 1993), 199.

23. See Hélène Cixous and Catherine Clement, *The Newly Born Woman,* trans. Betsy Wing (Minneapolis: University of Minnesota Press, 1986).

24. For contemporary writings about women and hysteria, see Elaine Showalter,

"Hysteria, Feminism, and Gender," in Sander L. Gilman et al., *Hysteria beyond Freud* (Berkeley: University of California Press, 1993), 286–344, and Sander L. Gilman, *Freud, Race, and Gender* (Princeton: Princeton University Press, 1993).

25. Quoted in Elin Diamond, "Realism and Hysteria: Toward a Feminist Mimesis," *Discourse* 13, no. 1 (1990–91): 62.

26. See, e.g., Hélène Cixous, *Portrait de Dora* (Paris: Des femmes, 1976); Joan Schenkar, "Signs of Life," in *Signs of Life: Six Comedies of Menace* (Middletown, Conn.: Wesleyan University Press; Hanover, N.H.: University Press of New England, 1998); and Maria Irene Fornes, "Fefu and Her Friends," *Performing Arts Journal* 2, no. 3 (1978): 112–40.

27. See, e.g., Joyce Antler, *The Journey Home: Jewish Women and the American Century* (New York: Free Press, 1997), 100–129.

27. See, e.g., Rittner and Roth, eds., *Different Voices*.

29. David Thacker, who directed *Broken Glass* at the Royal National Theatre, explains that Miller's appeal to British audiences is strong because "his work brings together the psychological, the intellectual, the philosophical, the political, the emotional, through language. He is a poet who writes plays which are to do with the expression of ideas." Richard Eyre, director of the National Theatre—which has produced five of Miller's plays; the Young Vic has produced eight—goes even further, comparing Miller with Shakespeare because he "connects private morality and public morality and that's what Theatre does terribly well." *Evening Standard,* Aug. 4, 1994.

30. Miller, *Timebends,* 24, 62, 70.

31. Ibid., 62–63, 167.

32. Ibid., 63.

33. Cynthia Ozick, "Roundtable Discussion," in *Writing and the Holocaust,* ed. Berel Lang (New York: Holmes and Meier, 1988), 284; author interview with Cynthia Ozick, July 15, 1994.

34. See Ozick, "Roundtable," 284; Susanne Klingenstein, "Sweet Natalie: Herman Wouk's Messenger to the Gentiles," in *Talking Back,* ed. Antler; and Joyce Antler, ed., *America and I: Short Stories by American Jewish Women Writers* (Boston: Beacon, 1990), 15.

35. Cynthia Ozick, *The Shawl: A Story and a Novella* (New York: Alfred A. Knopf, 1989).

36. Quoted in Roberta Elliott, "Cynthia Ozick's New Scene," *Jewish Week,* Aug. 12–18, 1994; see also Mary Cummings, "Footlights Lure from Past for Lumet," *New York Times,* Aug. 7, 1994, and Alvin Klein, "Lumet Directs 'Blue Light,'" *New York Times,* Aug. 21, 1994.

37. "We learned that the exquisite poetry of the soliloquies fell flat dramatically," producer Kathy Levin admits. Author interview with Levin, July 1994.

38. All quotations from Ozick's *Blue Light* are from dialogue at the play's premiere at the Bay Street Theater in Sag Harbor, Aug. 1994.

39. Author interview with Sybille Pearson, July 1994.

40. Sybille Pearson, "Unfinished Stories," playscript, *American Theatre* 9, no. 9 (1993): 16.

41. Edward T. Linenthal, "The Boundaries of Memory: The United States Holocaust Memorial Museum," *American Quarterly* 46, no. 3 (1994): 407–8. See also Linenthal, *Preserving Memory: The Struggle to Create America's Holocaust Museum* (New York: Viking, 1995).

42. Elinor Fuchs, ed., *Plays of the Holocaust: An International Anthology* (New York: Theatre Communications Group, 1987), xii, xxi–xxii.

43. Author interview with Cynthia Ozick, July 1994. See also Richard Shepard, "Cynthia Ozick Dramatizes the Diabolical Imagination," *Forward*, July 8, 1994, and Elliott, "Cynthia Ozick's New Scene."

44. Author interview with Cynthia Ozick, July 1994. On Holocaust denial, see Deborah Lipstadt, *Denying the Holocaust: The Growing Assault on Truth and Memory* (New York: Free Press, 1993).

CHAPTER 8. SARA R. HOROWITZ / THE CINEMATIC
TRIANGULATION OF JEWISH AMERICAN IDENTITY

1. Robert Rosenberg, *The Cutting Room* (New York: Penguin, 1993). Hereafter cited parenthetically.

2. Twentieth-Century Fox Release Synopsis, quoted in Judith E. Doneson, *The Holocaust in American Film* (Philadelphia: Jewish Publication Society, 1987), 51. See also Ilan Avisar, *Screening the Holocaust* (Bloomington: Indiana University Press, 1988), 106–8.

3. All quotations are from my transcription of the video.

4. Sander Gilman discusses the link between the "other" and disease metaphors in his *Difference and Pathology: Stereotypes of Sexuality, Race, and Madness* (Ithaca: Cornell University Press, 1985).

5. At the same time, the film subtly confirms stereotypical notions of the Jew, as Doneson (*Holocaust in American Film*) and others have pointed out. While both Dave and Phil have dark eyes and hair, the film's "real" Jew is shorter with curlier hair.

6. Azriel Fellner has observed that the character of Irving Weinberg, not in the original Hobson story, was added to represent the protests mounted by Jewish groups against the filming of *Gentleman's Agreement* for fear that it would draw unwanted attention to the Jewish community and fan the flames of anti-Semitism. Fellner, "Jews and American Movies," lecture, University of Delaware, Apr. 1996. According to Ilan Avisar (*Screening the Holocaust,* 108), the American Jewish Committee attempted to halt production of the film.

7. Both Doneson, in *Holocaust in American Film,* and Avisar, in *Screening the Holocaust,* criticize the film's dynamics whereby the Jewish victim of Nazism is recast in the role of perpetrator, or at least facilitator, of injustice. Annette Insdorf, more sympathetically, sees the film as portraying him "caught . . . between heartless exploiters and oppressed neighbors . . . [and] between exterminated Jews and manipulative blacks." Insdorf, *Indelible Shadows: Film and the Holocaust,* 2d ed. (Cambridge: Cambridge University Press, 1989), 34.

8. Another prominent American film to focus on Holocaust memory in which the state of Israel plays no role is Alan Pakula's 1982 film *Sophie's Choice,* based on William Styron's novel of the same name. The film and the novel both explore a decidedly not Jewish version of the Holocaust, featuring a Polish Catholic protagonist as the victim of Nazi atrocity, psychologically tormented years later by an American-born Jew in Brooklyn. In both versions of *Sophie's Choice* the Holocaust provides a concretization of ultimate evil that provides the fulcrum for Southern American writer Stingo's loss of innocence and coming of age.

9. In her discussion of Wallant's 1965 novel *The Pawnbroker,* the basis for Lumet's film, Dorothy Bilik notes the Jewish author's own discomfort with Jewishness and "Jewish material." See her *Immigrant-Survivor: Post Holocaust Consciousness in Recent Jewish-American Fiction* (Middletown, Conn.: Wesleyan University Press, 1981).

10. For further discussion of this aspect of Jewish American literature, see my "Portnoy's Sister—Who's Complaining? Contemporary Jewish American Women's Writing on Judaism," in *Jewish Book Annual,* ed. Jacob Kabakoff (1993–94), 51: 26–41.

11. All quotations are from my transcription of the telecast.

12. Interestingly, the movie eliminates all traces of Morris's past as recounted in the novel. In Uris's book, Morris and his brother go to Palestine early in the century to build the Jewish state, but for reasons of ill health Morris later comes to the United States. During the Holocaust he struggles unsuccessfully to get his remaining family out of Nazi-controlled Europe; afterward, he is haunted by guilt for his failure to do so. Thus, in the novel Abraham Cady grows up with an awareness of the Holocaust, a personal sense of bereavement, and a commitment to the Zionist vision. In the movie, Morris is presented paradoxically as an immigrant from nowhere, with no particular connection articulated with the murdered Jews of Europe. This change in characterization isolates Cady both from the Holocaust and from Israel until his moment of epiphany at his father's burial.

13. The scoring was changed for the Israeli release of the film, eliminating Shemer's song.

14. For further discussion of this aspect of *Schindler's List,* see my "But Is It Good for the Jews? Spielberg's Schindler and the Aesthetics of Atrocity," in *Spielberg's Holocaust: Critical Perspectives on Schindler's List,* ed. Yosefa Loshitsky (Bloomington: Indiana University Press, 1997).

15. See, e.g., Jacob Neusner, *The Way of Torah: An Introduction to Judaism,* 5th rev. ed. (Belmont, Calif.: Wadsworth, 1993).

16. While Joel Brand's earlier film *Kaddish* (1985), about the relationship between Yossi Klein and his father, a Holocaust survivor, contains much of this personal element, *Kaddish* contemplates the competing meanings of the Holocaust for the Boro Park community that Klein's family inhabits and for the radicalized Jewish American youths of the 1960s. Here the conflicts of Jewish American identity are resolved for Yossi by *aliyah* (immigration to Israel).

CHAPTER 9. ALAN E. STEINWEIS / REFLECTIONS
ON THE HOLOCAUST FROM NEBRASKA

1. It should be emphasized that I am not attempting an empirical study of this subject. Other scholars have indeed begun to subject Holocaust-related knowledge and opinions to sociological analysis that takes into account such factors as gender and ethnicity. See, e.g., Katherine Bischoping, "Interpreting Social Influences on Holocaust Knowledge," *Contemporary Jewry* 17 (1996): 106–35. There is also the widely discussed report prepared for the American Jewish Committee by Jennifer Golub and Renae Cohen, *What Do Americans Know about the Holocaust?* (New York: American Jewish Committee, 1993).

2. As Alvin H. Rosenfeld has keenly observed in his influential essay "The Americanization of The Holocaust," such "established instruments of commemoration, education, and ritualized observance" are crucial to the dissemination of knowledge about the Holocaust, and "careful attention to precisely what images of the Holocaust are being conveyed through such agencies and to whom would go far toward telling us how Americans come to possess the kinds of information they have about the Nazi period and the crimes against the Jews." Rosenfeld, "The Americanization of the Holocaust," the David W. Belin Lecture in American Jewish Affairs (Ann Arbor: Frankel Center for Judaic Studies, University of Michigan, 1995), 6 (reprinted in *Commentary*, June 1995). One might add that the substance, scale, and circumstances of such "instruments" can convey messages about the standing of Jewish minorities in their respective communities.

3. The "uniqueness/universality" issue generated an immense literature in the 1980s. A thorough review of the arguments and their implications is provided in Stephen Katz, *The Holocaust in Historical Context*, vol. 1, *The Holocaust and Mass Death before the Modern Age* (New York: Oxford University Press, 1994).

4. Michael Berenbaum, writing in *After Tragedy and Triumph: Essays in Modern Jewish Thought and the American Experience* (Cambridge: Cambridge University Press, 1990), 22, quoted in Rosenfeld, "Americanization of the Holocaust," 16, as well as Rosenfeld's own comment on 8.

5. Tom Osborne, *On Solid Ground* (Lincoln: Nebraska Book Publishing Co., 1966), 123–24.

6. Edith Stein, a Jewish woman who converted to Catholicism, died in Auschwitz, the result of having been classified as Jewish according to Nazi racial laws. For a discussion of this controversy in the context of John Paul II's relationship with Jews, see James Carroll, "The Silence," *New Yorker*, Apr. 7, 1997, 52–68.

7. Note Alvin Rosenfeld's observation that "the language of 'Holocaust' has been used by those who want to draw public attention to the crimes, abuses, and assorted sufferings that mar the quality of social life in today's America." Rosenfeld, "Americanization of the Holocaust," 7–8.

8. James Paul Allen and Eugene James Turner, eds., *We the People: An Atlas of America's Ethnic Diversity* (New York: Macmillan, 1988), 225. Using a formula for weighing single and multiple ancestry, and employing data from the 1980 census, the

Atlas ascribes German ancestry to 37.9 percent of the population of Nebraska. The percentage is 41.2 for Wisconsin, 39.7 for South Dakota, and 39.2 for North Dakota. Just below Nebraska in terms of German ancestry is Iowa, at 37.5 percent.

9. Frederick C. Luebke, *Bonds of Loyalty: German-Americans and World War I* (De Kalb: Northern Illinois University Press, 1974).

10. Since this incident, Lauck was arrested by Danish authorities during a visit to neo-Nazis in Copenhagen and was subsequently extradited to Germany, where he was convicted of breaking German laws against neo-Nazi activity and sentenced to five years in prison.

11. Julius Lester, "The Lives People Live," in *Blacks and Jews: Alliances and Arguments,* ed. Paul Berman (New York: Delacorte, 1994), 173.

12. Raul Hilberg, *The Politics of Memory: The Journey of a Holocaust Historian* (Chicago: Ivan R. Dee, 1996), 123.

13. For an informative history of how the museum exhibition was designed, see Edward T. Linenthal, *Preserving Memory: The Struggle to Create America's Holocaust Museum* (New York: Viking, 1995).

CHAPTER 10. WALTER BENN MICHAELS / "YOU WHO NEVER WAS THERE"

This essay is a revised version of my essay in Narrative, *vol. 4, no. 1 (January 1996). Used by permission of Ohio State University Press.*

1. Paul Veyne, *Did the Greeks Believe in Their Myths? An Essay on the Constitutive Imagination* (Chicago: University of Chicago Press, 1988), 20. Hereafter cited parenthetically.

2. Whitley Strieber, *Communion: A True Story* (New York: Beech Tree Books, 1987), 123.

3. Arthur Schlesinger Jr., *The Disuniting of America* (New York: W. W. Norton, 1991), 20.

4. Greg Bear, *Blood Music* (New York: Arbor House, 1985), 111–12, 217. I am grateful to Joanne Wood for bringing this book to my attention.

5. Strieber, *Communion,* 297.

6. Toni Morrison, "The Pain of Being Black," *Time,* May 22, 1989, quoted in Mae G. Henderson, "Toni Morrison's *Beloved:* Re-membering the Body as Historical Text," in *Comparative American Identities: Race, Sex, and Nationality in the Modern Text,*" ed. Hortense J. Spillers (New York: Routledge, 1991), 83.

7. Toni Morrison, *Beloved* (New York: Knopf, 1987), 13. Hereafter cited parenthetically.

8. Valerie Smith, "'Circling the Subject': History and Narrative in *Beloved,*" in *Toni Morrison: Critical Perspectives Past and Present,* ed. Henry Louis Gates Jr. and K. A. Appiah (New York: Amistad, 1993), 345.

9. Bear, *Blood Music,* 197.

10. Which is not, of course, to say that enslavement is the only or necessarily the

defining racial experience. Indeed, Paul Gilroy follows Morrison in claiming that too often slavery "gets forgotten," and he explicitly opposes Morrison's memory of slavery to the memories of Kemet, the "black civilization anterior to modernity" that Afrocentrists sometimes invoke "in its place" (Gilroy, *The Black Atlantic: Modernity and Double Consciousness* [Cambridge: Harvard University Press, 1993], 190). The difference matters to Gilroy because he associates the appeal to Kemet with the attempt to "recover hermetically sealed and culturally absolute racial traditions," and he thinks of the appeal to slavery "as a means to figure the inescapability and legitimate value of mutation, hybridity and intermixture" (223). Gilroy prefers hybridity to purity, and so for the purposes of "identity construction" he would rather remember slavery than Egypt; but from the standpoint of the argument developed in this essay, the questions of which past you choose to remember and what kind of identity you choose to construct obviously matter less than the commitment to constructing identity by remembering the past in the first place.

11. Smith, "'Circling the Subject,'" 350.

12. Stephen Greenblatt, *Shakespearean Negotiations: The Circulation of Social Energy in Renaissance England* (Berkeley: University of California Press, 1988), 1. Candor requires the acknowledgment that my own book, *The Gold Standard and the Logic of Naturalism,* was published in 1987 as the second volume in the New Historicism series. In a recent essay ("The Ironic Romance of New Historicism," *Arizona Quarterly* 51 [1995]: 33–60), Charles Lewis has also pointed to a relation between *Beloved* and the New Historicism, identifying them both as forms of "historical romance" (54) and arguing that Morrison's "appropriation of the conventions of romance" should be understood to pose a critical challenge to New Historicism's assertion of "a stable connection between those narrative techniques and a particular ideology" (51). Lewis is, in my view, right to see the relation but mistaken in his account of what's being related, missing what is distinctive about both the New Historicism and *Beloved*. What's new about the New Historicism is not that it seeks to establish connections between literary works and social history but that it seeks to reconfigure the relation between the historical past and the present. And what's important about *Beloved* is not that it challenges the connection between "narrative techniques" and "ideology" but that it produces its narrative techniques as the technology for a politics committed to replacing ideology with identity.

13. For a critical discussion of these two forms of interest in the past (Greenblatt calls them the interest in "continuity" and in "analogy") and especially of the effort to imagine the historical past as simultaneously connected to and like the present, see Steven Knapp, *Literary Interest* (Cambridge: Harvard University Press, 1993), 106–36.

14. Greenblatt, *Shakespearean Negotiations*, 1.

15. In an appendix to the revised edition of his influential history of the origins of nationalism, *Imagined Communities* (London: Verso, 1991), Benedict Anderson distinguishes between "real" memory and "mythic" memory and suggests the problematic relation of the "mythic" to the "real" by putting the mythic in scare quotes: "memory." In these terms, the question addressed here is, What does it mean to believe in this myth, in "memory"?

16. Caroline Rody accurately describes the appeal of *Beloved*'s historicism when she observes that "writing that bears witness to an inherited tragedy approaches the past with an interest much more urgent than historical curiosity or even political revisionism" and goes on to contrast what she calls an "objective 'prehistory of the present'" to "the subjective, ethnic possession of history understood as the prehistory of the self" (Rody, "Toni Morrison's *Beloved*: History, 'Rememory,' and a 'Clamor for a Kiss,'" *American Literary History* 7 [1995]: 97). Insofar as to inherit a tragedy involves something more than living with its consequences—as, of course, it must, since everybody is already living with the consequences of past events—it is only through some mechanism of "possession" that any tragedy can count as an inherited one. The sense of urgency, in other words, is entirely dependent on the claim to possession. So one implication of my suggestion in this essay (and elsewhere) that no history can, in the required sense, be possessed by us is that there can be no real urgency to the study of history and no coherent motive beyond curiosity. And one by-product of the replacement of an indefensibly usable past with a defensibly useless one would presumably be a diminished interest in history.

17. Geoffrey Hartman, "Introduction: Darkness Visible," in *Holocaust Remembrance: The Shapes of Memory,* ed. Geoffrey Hartman (Oxford: Blackwell, 1994), 7.

18. Pierre Vidal-Naquet, *Assassins of Memory: Essays on the Denial of the Holocaust,* trans. Jeffrey Mehlman (New York: Columbia University Press, 1992), 57.

19. Claude Lanzmann, "An Evening with Claude Lanzmann," May 4, 1986, quoted in Shoshana Felman and Dori Laub, *Testimony: Crises of Witnessing in Literature, Psychoanalysis, and History* (New York: Routledge, 1992), 213–14. *Testimony* hereafter cited parenthetically.

20. Claude Lanzmann, "Seminar on *Shoah,*" *Yale French Studies* 79 (1991): 85. Hereafter cited parenthetically as *YFS.*

21. Claude Lanzmann, "The Obscenity of Understanding: An Evening with Claude Lanzmann," *American Imago* 48, no. 4 (1991): 481.

22. J. L. Austin, *How to Do Things with Words* (New York: Oxford University Press, 1965), 6.

23. Paul de Man, *Allegories of Reading* (New Haven: Yale University Press, 1979), 39, 40, 36–37.

24. Ibid., 44.

25. Michael Krausz, "On Being Jewish," in *Jewish Identity,* ed. David Theo Goldberg and Michael Krausz (Philadelphia: Temple University Press, 1993), 272.

26. Lionel Rubinoff, "Jewish Identity and the Challenge of Auschwitz," in *Jewish Identity,* ed. Goldberg and Krausz, 150, 136.

27. Eddy M. Zemach, "Custodians," in *Jewish Identity,* ed. Goldberg and Krausz, 122.

28. Yisrael Gutman, "On the Character of Nazi Antisemitism," in *Antisemitism through the Ages,* ed. Shmuel Almog (Oxford: Published for the Vidal Sassoon International Center for the Study of Antisemitism, the Hebrew University of Jerusalem, by Pergamon, 1988), 359.

29. Zemach, "Custodians," 129.

30. This is, of course, different from saying that the *individual* Jew is subsumed by

the *group* of Jews. The issue in cultural (as in racial) identity, despite the assertions of polemicists on both sides, has nothing to do with the relative priority of the group over the individual; it has to do instead with the identification of a certain set of beliefs and practices as appropriate for a person or persons in virtue of the fact that those beliefs and practices are his, hers, or theirs. What's wrong with cultural identity, in other words, is not that it privileges the group over the individual but that it (incoherently) derives what you do from what you are.

31. This is, to some extent, implicit in the very idea of genocide, inasmuch as genocide is understood as the extermination of a people rather than as mass murder. In genocide, it is what makes the people a people that is the ultimate object of destruction, so the murder of persons is in a strict sense only incidental to the elimination of the people. If, of course, the people are understood as a race, then genocide will require that they be killed or sterilized; if the people are understood as a culture, then genocide will require only that they be forced to assimilate. From this standpoint, even writers who have not lost sight of the fact that Hitler's goal was physical extermination rather than cultural assimilation may find themselves subordinating the death of persons to the destruction of a people. Thus, Berel Lang describes Nazi genocide as worse than cultural genocide because "where life remains, as in cultural genocide or ethnocide, the possibility also remains of group revival; but this is not the case where genocide involves physical annihilation" (Lang, *Act and Idea in the Nazi Genocide* [Chicago: University of Chicago Press, 1990], 13). The point here is that physical destruction is the worst kind of genocide because, unlike cultural genocide, it is in principle irreversible. The relevant difference between physical and cultural genocide is not, in other words, the fact that in cultural genocide no persons may be killed, which is to say that what's worse about physical genocide is not, on this account, the fact that so many persons must die. For genocide involves the extermination not of persons but of a people. So cultural genocide is less bad than physical genocide not because no persons have been killed but because the people ("the *genos*") may still be revived. It is not less murderous (in both cases the group dies); it is less irreversibly murderous (in the second case, the group may live again).

CHAPTER 11. LAURENCE MORDEKHAI THOMAS / SUFFERING AS A MORAL BEACON

This essay is a substantially revised version of my essay "La Lumière moral et la rivalité de la souffrance: Juifs et noirs," Portulan *(1997).*

1. *Narrative of the Life of Frederick Douglass, an American Slave,* ed. Houston Baker (New York: Penguin, 1986), 91, 92.

2. Elie Wiesel, *Night* (New York: Bantam Books, 1982), 32.

3. See Laurence Mordekhai Thomas, *Vessels of Evil: American Slavery and the Holocaust* (Philadelphia: Temple University Press, 1993).

1. These mock-German displays were removed from Nike Town by the end of 1995. Other displays mentioned here were altered or subsequently removed.

2. See Levy, "The Swastikas of Niketown," *Harper's* 292 (Apr. 1996): 32–33.

CONTRIBUTORS

JOYCE ANTLER is a professor of American Jewish history and culture at Brandeis University, where she is also the chair of American Studies. Among other works about Jewish history, she is the author of *The Journey Home: Jewish Women and the American Century* (1997) and the editor of *America and I: Short Stories by American Jewish Women Writers* (1990). Her most recent work is *Talking Back: Images of Jewish Women in American Popular Culture* (1997).

HILENE FLANZBAUM is an associate professor of twentieth-century American literature at Butler University. She has published articles about American poetry in *MELUS*, the *New England Quarterly*, and *ELH*. She is also a co-editor of *Jewish-American Literature: A Norton Anthology*, forthcoming in 1999.

ANDREW FURMAN is an assistant professor of English and comparative literature at Florida Atlantic University and associate editor of *Studies in American Jewish Literature*. He has recently published a book in SUNY's Modern Jewish Culture series, *Israel through the Jewish-American Imagination: A Survey of Jewish-American Literature on Israel, 1928–1995* (1997).

HENRY GREENSPAN is a psychologist and playwright who teaches in the Residential College of the University of Michigan. He is the author of *On Listening to Holocaust Survivors: Recounting and Life History* (1998) along with numerous articles about survivor testimony. A number of his plays also concern survivors, most notably *Remnants*, which has been broadcast over National Public Radio and produced throughout the United States and Europe.

SARA R. HOROWITZ is the author of *Voicing the Void: Muteness and Memory in Holocaust Fiction* (1997) and is currently completing a book called *Gender, Genocide, and Jewish Memory*. She is director of the Jewish Studies Program and associate professor of English literature in the Honors Program at the University of Delaware.

AMY HUNGERFORD is a graduate student in the English Department at the John Hopkins University writing a dissertation about postwar American literature.

ANDREW LEVY, an associate professor of English at Butler University, has written *The Culture and Commerce of the American Short Story* (1993). He has also co-authored, with Fred Leebron, *Creating Fiction* (1995) and, with Fred Leebron and Paula Geyh, *Postmodern American Fiction: A Norton Anthology* (1997).

WALTER BENN MICHAELS is a professor of English and the humanities at the Johns Hopkins University. He is the author of *The Gold Standard and the Logic of Naturalism* (1987) and of *Our America: Nativism, Modernism, and Pluralism* (1995).

JEFFREY SHANDLER is a Dorot Junior Teaching Fellow of the Skirball Department of Hebrew and Judaic Studies at New York University. He has been a fellow of the Annenberg School for Communications and the Center for Judaic Studies at the University of Pennsylvania. He is the author of *While America Watches: Televising the Holocaust* (1998).

ALAN E. STEINWEIS is a professor of modern European and Jewish history and director of the Center for Judaic Studies at the University of Nebraska, Lincoln. He is the author of *Art, Ideology, and Economics in Nazi Germany: The Reich Chambers of Music, Theater, and the Visual Arts* (1993).

LAURENCE MORDEKHAI THOMAS is a professor of philosophy and political science at Syracuse University, where he is also a member of the Jewish Studies Department. He has written a book about American slavery and the Holocaust entitled *Vessels of Evil* (1993). His first book, *Living Morally: A Psychology of Moral Character,* appeared in 1989.

JAMES E. YOUNG is a professor of English and Judaic studies at the University of Massachusetts at Amherst. He is the author of *Writing and Rewriting the Holocaust* (1988) and *The Texture of Memory* (1993) and the editor of *The Art of Memory* (1994), a catalogue for an exhibition of the same name he curated at the Jewish Museum in New York.

INDEX